International Social Work and the Radical Tradition

Edited by Michael Lavalette and Iain Ferguson

Series Editors:
Brian Littlechild
Karen Lyons
Henry Parada

VENTURE PRESS

BASW website: http://www.basw.co.uk

Published by
VENTURE PRESS
16 Kent Street
Birmingham
B5 6RD
www.basw.co.uk

British Library Cataloguing-in-Publication Data
A catalogue record for this book is available from the British Library

ISBN-13: 978-1-86178-076-8 (paperback)

Printed by:
Hobbs the Printers Ltd
Brunel Road
Totton
SO40 3WX

Printed in Great Britain

Contents

Acknowledgements

We would like to thank each of the contributors for their patience as we put this collection together. We put considerable pressure on them to submit early – and then had a delay of a couple of months at our end! Nevertheless, putting a collection together with writers from across the globe (in less than a year) is something that would not have been possible without their help and good grace.

Venture Press have been fantastic. They have just let us get on with it. What more could you ask from a publisher?

As we were completing the book we organised a conference on the future of radical social work in Britain. We expected about 100 participants (and then some colleagues thought we were being overly optimistic). As it turned out, we sold out with two weeks to spare. There were 280 social work academics, practitioners, students and service users at Liverpool University in Britain for two days debating how to fight to 'save' the social work project in the face of the neo-liberal assault in Britain. It was an inspiring event and convinced us that the time to fight for a radical and engaged social work is now – and that in the mass movements against war, imperialism and neo-liberalism there exists the 'resources of hope' that can help forge a more humane social work and another, better world.

Michael Lavalette
Iain Ferguson

Notes on the Contributors

Naimeh Baidoun is Director of the Psycho-social Unit of the Centre for Continuing Education, Birzeit University, Ramallah, Occupied Palestinian Territories. Naimeh provides professional development programmes for social workers and counsellors working in Palestine.

Ziad Faraj is Chief of Field Relief and Social Services for the West Bank, Occupied Palestinian Territories. founding member of the Union of Social Workers, Psychologists and Sociologists of Palestine and Head of the Bethlehem Branch. Professional social worker.

Iain Ferguson is Senior Lecturer in Social Work at the University of Stirling, UK. He has published widely on the Mental Health Users Movement, working with asylum seekers and Marxist approaches to social work and social policy.

Jill Hanley is Assistant Professor of Social Work at McGill University, Montreal, Canada. She has been active in community organising around issues of immigration, labour and housing. Her research and writing has focused on these same issues, with organising for access to social rights as a theme.

Chris Jones is Emeritus Professor of Social Work at the University of Liverpool, UK. He has written about radical social work for close to thirty years and has recently undertaken research into social workers' working conditions in the state social work sector in Britain.

Michael Lavalette is Senior Lecturer in Social Policy at the University of Liverpool, UK. He has published widely on child labour and children's rights, social movements and Marxist approaches to social work and social policy.

Jane Lindsay is Principal Lecturer in Social Work at Kingston University, London, UK. She has worked on a pro-bono basis with the Centre for Continuing Education at Birzeit University, Palestine from 1997 to 2006 (and ongoing) contributing to programme development and evaluation of courses offered to professional social workers and counsellors.

Catherine McDonald is Associate Professor in Social Work at the University of Queensland, Australia and Incoming Professor of Social Work at RMIT University in Melbourne. Her interests involve welfare reform, institutional reconfiguration, the impact on vulnerable populations and on social work.

Nalini Nayak is an activist/social researcher based in India. She has worked for over three decades in people's movements with a focus on coastal communities and women in India and coordinated work in other countries. She has also published widely on these subjects.

Josephine Norma Norward is Associate Professor of Social Work at Kean University, New Jersey, USA. She worked as a social worker in Soweto prior to, and after, the 1976 riots. Presently, she is involved in a research project on HIV/AIDS education in the informal settlements of Gauteng, South Africa.

Laura Penketh is Lecturer in Social Work at the University of Manchester, UK. At present she is undertaking research into the experiences of second and third generation Muslim women in Britain.

Iris Prado Hernández is Director of the Department of Social Sciences at the Universidad Centroamericana in Managua, Nicaragua. She has 20 years of experience teaching, researching and writing on a variety of themes related to social work and social development, and is currently coordinator of a collaborative project on social vulnerability and urban development with several Canadian universities.

Cornelia Schweppe is Professor of Social Work at the University of Mainz, Germany. She has published widely on international social work, the professionalisation of work, social movements in Latin American, and social work research.

Eric Shragge teaches community organising and development in the School of Community and Public Affairs, Concordia University, Montreal, Canada. His interests are the role of local organising and progressive social change. He is active at the Immigrant Workers Centre, Montreal.

Maureen G. Wilson is Professor and Associate Dean (Academic) of Social Work at the University of Calgary, Canada. She has taught and worked with development projects in a number of Latin American countries, is interested in popular responses to the human impacts of neo-liberal globalisation, and is currently engaged in collaborative research with activist groups on the effectiveness of their work.

Jelka Zorn is Lecturer in Social Work at the Faculty of Social Work, University of Ljubljana, Slovenia. She has published on asylum and immigration in Slovenia, especially on the Erased people. She is active in campaigns which advocate their rights and NoBorder networks

Towards a Social Work of Resistance: International Social Work and the Radical Tradition

Michael Lavalette and Iain Ferguson

> Indifference is the dead weight of history ... [It] is a powerful force ... It works passively ... Generally events take place not because lots of people desire them, but because many people don't commit themselves, they let things happen ... The apparent random nature of history is nothing but an illusion created by indifference ...
>
> I take sides. I live. In the active consciousness of my side I already feel the future society being built. In this human chain nobody carries a heavy weight, everything which happens is not the result of luck or fate, but is the result of ... conscious work.
>
> I am alive, therefore I take sides. That's why I hate those who don't take sides, those who are indifferent.
>
> (Gramsci, 1917/1977, pp. 17-18)

The beginning of the 21st century has witnessed the expansion of social work internationally. In many West European countries there are increasing numbers of social workers being trained in universities and recruited by states and a range of non-governmental organisation (NGO) and community welfare providers. In other parts of the globe, the spread of neo-liberal globalisation has created a situation in which social work as a profession is beginning to emerge and develop in many countries where previously it did not exist.

Several factors have contributed to this phenomenon. These include the need for governments to respond to the rapid growth of poverty and social inequality arising from the operation of market forces, the social and personal problems caused by rapid urbanisation and alienation, the inability of informal social networks to cope with the demands of market society, and easier access, through improved communications, to Western social work ideas, philosophies and practices.

In this situation, models of social work developed in Western liberal democracies are likely to be extremely influential in shaping the ways in which social work develops in these countries. Yet this poses two issues. First, the growth of social work internationally is taking place at a time when there is widespread acceptance that social work in many of these Western countries is in crisis. In Britain, for example, we have witnessed, since the early 1990s, the increasing domination of many areas of practice and welfare service delivery by market forces and ideologies, whether in the form of institutionalised competition, the dominance of care management approaches, or the growth of the private sector in every area of practice.

Furthermore, social workers increasingly find themselves expected to take part in the regulation and control of clients; to be the bearer of the 'bad news' that there are no resources or services to meet service users' needs; to be the frontline implementer of local or national policy that leaves them feeling uneasy. In Britain there is growing unease at the way social workers are increasingly expected to control and regulate young people as part of the state's drive against 'anti-social behaviour', or to intervene to remove children from asylum-seeking families as part of the political campaign against refugees.

These issues pose questions about the nature of social work, about the kind of profession it should be, about what social workers can and should do when faced with institutional demands which clash with the profession's basic values – values which, as the International Federation of Social Workers asserts, are steeped in social justice, human rights and social development (www.ifsw.org).

Further, in the context of growing social and economic inequality, there is no evidence that such a commodified, neo-liberal and 'controlling' social work is capable of meeting the needs of service users, while the effect of the domination of practice by managerial imperatives and budgetary considerations has been to demoralise large numbers of social workers. It is difficult to see how such a model of social work could be of value to those seeking to develop social work education and practice for the first time.

Moreover, the dissatisfaction with the way in which market forces have transformed social work is just one aspect of a much wider mood of unease and anger concerning the increased insecurity, poverty and environmental destruction accelerated by the spread of neo-liberal globalisation. That anger and unease have fuelled the growth in recent years of international resistance with the emergence of new social movements around issues of war, poverty, genetically modified foods and the destruction of the environment, on a scale not seen since the 1960s. The slogans of these movements, such as 'The world is not a commodity' or 'Another world is possible' express the profound unhappiness felt by millions of people towards the domination of every aspect of our lives by market forces.

This directly leads to the second issue – how should we conceptualise social work practice. The majority of workers join the profession because they want to 'help people' and (in an unspecified way) address the problems that affect their lives. Though service users' problems are normally expressed in individual ways – mental ill-health, stress, addictions, crime, and so on – most workers and service users recognise that these problems are caused or acerbated by the material realities of life – poverty, unemployment, poor housing, abandoned communities and alienation, for example, provide many of the structural conditions, or public causes, behind so many private troubles. Thus, 'helping people' – if we are to provide long-term solutions – involves addressing the material, social and personal needs of those we work with.

Similarly, when students join social work courses they are sometimes taught about, for example, oppression and structural inequalities, and the need to take account of these issues in their practice. The International Federation of Social Workers includes, within its definition of social work, the statement that:

> The social work profession promotes social change, problem solving in human relationships and the empowerment and liberation of people to enhance well-being. (IFSW/IASSW, 2004)

And, of course, the job of social work brings us into daily contact with the poorest, the most victimised and the most marginalised sections of the population. This exposure poses sharp questions about the social conditions service users face and the social impositions on their lives. Thus, as we undertake our work, the question of social justice is never far from the surface.

This paradox – between the structural or institutional constraints of neo-liberal social work practice and the ethical commitment of many practitioners – is not new. The particular forms of controlling social workers may have changed but social work (as an activity) has always been concerned with controlling the poor and separating workers off from clients and service users for fear that social workers may become 'contaminated' by progressive socio-political ideas (Jones, 1983).

The interesting point of note, however, is that despite these efforts to separate social workers and service users there has always been a critical edge running through social work – and within this a 'radical kernel' (Butler and Pritchard, 2002) – which has stressed the need for workers and service users to stand together and address the political and socio-economic conditions that negatively impact on our lives.

That radical kernel has been marginalised within official histories of social work yet there is increasing evidence (some of it in the chapters that follow) that this has been an important tradition (though one that is 'hidden from history') from the very inception of social work.

The radical kernel is located in the combination of two elements. First, as we have noted, the experience of social work practice in societies structured by inequality and oppression means that, more than any other welfare profession, we work closely with people whose lives are blighted by forces beyond their direct control. In these circumstances dominant models of practice offer little in the way of long-term solutions and explanations which attempt to pathologies service users are worthless – they do not offer solutions to the problems individuals face, indeed they make their lives worse.

The second element is the existence of mass social movements which offer the space for social workers (and many, many others, of course) to debate alternative ways of working and living and to consider the possibility of 'another world'.

The history of the 20th century was a history of repeated waves of revolutions and mass protests (Harman, 1988, 1999; Tarrow, 1998). The world, and its leading states, were shaken by significant collective protest movements in 1905, between 1910 and 1914, from 1917 to 1925, between 1933 and 1939, in 1945/46, from 1968 to 1975, and in 1989. These were general periods of upheaval that shook the most powerful states and challenged their legitimacy. We could add to this list: the national liberation struggles of the 1950s and 1960s, for example, or events that were more easily contained within the confines of a particular nation state (like the Iranian Revolution of 1979, for example, or the removal of the Sukharto regime in Indonesia in 1998). These protest waves are an inevitable feature of a world divided by vast inequalities, lack of political accountability, economic competition and the incessant drive to war. John Rees (2006, p. 3), in a seminal account of the modern world, has described the 'three titans of the modern world' as:

> The power of nation-states, of the international economy and the power of working people on whom all states, armies and corporations, ultimately must depend. Many of the most important events in the modern world take place at the intersection where these three forces collide.

As this 'third titan' moves, as ordinary people come together to challenge the power of the powerful, to challenge the economic and political elites whose choices disrupt and disfigure our world, they are faced with some very real, and very difficult, questions: How would you organise things differently? What changes to the world are necessary? How can we ensure greater freedom, equality, solidarity and justice? What shape and form would any new and 'decent society' take?

Answers to these and similar questions are not prescribed. But the broader and the more embracing the movements for change, the greater the resources of hope and inspiration they draw together, because movements become stronger when they listen and learn from each other.

In terms of radical social work this means something quite specific. The impulses for radical challenges to existing forms of practice, the demands for more equitable distributions of resources and support, the confidence and the ideas to assert that 'another social work is possible' originate outside the profession – in the world of social protest and contestation. This was the case in the early part of the 20th century when (in Britain) trade union struggle, the movement for women's suffrage and engagement with various anti-war and anti-imperialist movements generated a small, radical current within social work. It was the case, as Reisch and Andrews (2002) point out, in the US in the early and mid-points of the century. And was more generally the case when the great social movements of the 1960s and early 1970s gave birth to a more visible 'radical' current in social work.

The relevance of all this is that the 21st century has begun by following the pattern of the 20th. As the 20th century drew to a close the World Trade organisation held its Third Ministerial in Seattle in November 1999. The protests that erupted marked the initial action of what was quickly to become a vast international movement for global justice. In the months that followed the movement announced its arrival with massive demonstrations in Prague, Genoa, Quebec and various others towns and cities across the world where the representatives of global capital met to plan how to privatise much of the world and, in particular, the services that ordinary people relied on.

The movement drew people together who felt that they had to challenge the relentless neo-liberal drive to open up economies to multinational interests, to deregulate working conditions, to marginalise trade unions, to privatise state welfare and public utilities, to threaten the environment, and to ruin the lives of small farmers and indigenous peoples across the world by undermining all variety of forms of traditional social practices.

The movement was soon to face a great challenge. In the aftermath of the attack on the Twin Towers on 11 September 2001, George W. Bush announced his 'war on terror'. Innocent people – without the remotest connection to the attack on the Twin Towers – in first Afghanistan, then Iraq faced the prospect of having to try and survive US 'shock and awe' (Callinicos, 2003).

The response was the repositioning and reconceptualisation of the movement as one that was against both neo-liberalism and imperialism (in essence, Rees's first two titans). The reach of this movement is really remarkable. On its most notable day of protest, 15 February 2003, literally millions marched across the world against the imminent attack on Iraq (Murray and German, 2005). The movement has roots in each continent across the globe – but perhaps the most remarkable confrontations to date have taken place in Latin America where

Argentina, Brazil, Bolivia and Venezuela, in particular, have been rocked by a series of confrontations.

But this has not simply been a movement of and on the streets. It has produced a vast outpouring of texts, manuscripts, blogs and other means of communicating and discussing what the problems of the present world are, and what should be done to put them right. At the heart of this dialogue has been the creation of a variety of forums where people come together to listen, to debate, to engage and to think about how we can challenge the deterministic logic of neo-liberalism at both the local and the global level. The World Social Forum (and its various sectoral off-shoots) represents a significant and vibrant resource for those who wish to consider the present direction of social work and the problems service users face.

For those of us who wish to establish a 'partisan social work', with social justice as a core value, which attempts to link structural factors and personal experiences, which relates 'public issues' and 'private troubles', which emphasises the value of collective approaches, and sees the need to make connections between social work practice and wider social movements, then the present offers a great opportunity. It is an opportunity to engage in the fight to establish social work as an ethical career. An opportunity to assert that there is much of value in the social work profession and an opportunity to make a stand against the hollowed-out, controlling activity that the neo-liberal agenda would like to turn social work into, a 'social work [that] might continue as an occupation but perish as a caring and liberal profession' (Jones, C. and Novak, T. 1993).

This may seem dramatic. But this is a critical moment for social work academics, practitioners and service users. To take us back to the quotation from Gramsci at the start of this chapter – this is not the time for indifference. For too long, too many of us (especially in Britain) have hoped that by 'adapting', by compromising over core elements of professional social work training, by adopting what Butler and Pritchard (2002, p. 8) have termed 'the flexible exploitation of ambiguity' the profession will 'survive'. As a result we have allowed the leaders of the social work profession to accommodate to increased marketisation and managerialism. Now is the time to assert that social work is 'a profession worth fighting for'.[1]

The intention of this book is to present radical social work to a new international audience and to explore its relevance to practice in an era of globalisation. It does so through a series of case studies from several different countries that explores the forms which radical social work has taken there. It seeks to show the ways in which social work practice in these countries has been shaped by social movements. Finally, it explores the ways in which a new engaged practice might emerge out of the current dissatisfaction with neo-liberal social work practice on the one hand and the ideas, energy and organisations of social movements – including service user movements, the anti-capitalist or global justice movement, and the anti-war movement – on the other.

The book is broadly divided into four sections. The first part covers Chapters 1, 2, 3 and 4 and looks at our past. In different ways each chapter looks at the 'hidden history of radical social work' and starts broadly to consider what a future radical social work might look like. The chapters covered look at Britain (Ferguson and Lavalette), Australia (McDonald), Canada (Hanley and Shragge) and Nicaragua (Wilson and Hernández).

Chapters 5, 6 and 7 look more closely at radical forms of practice. Schweppe counters many of the themes of neo-liberal social work by developing an analysis which draws on the work of Paulo Freire. She then develops her chapter by applying her analysis to the 'soup kitchen' movement in Peru.

Nayak's chapter tells her story as social worker and activist among the Indian fishing communities. This rich story tells of her own and the communities' struggle for recognition and representation. It offers a fantastic glimpse of what a 'partisan social work' can achieve.

Zorn's chapter provides an account of the involvement of social workers in Slovenia in campaigns to protect the rights of asylum seekers and 'the erased', those who lost their citizenship rights with the creation of Slovenia.

Chapters 8 and 9 are different again. These chapters look at the development of social work as part of the struggle for nationhood. Norward looks at social work and social activism in post-apartheid South Africa. The euphoria we all felt in 1989 when Mandela walked from prison has been replaced in recent years by an awful realisation that while apartheid may have been dismantled, South Africa still remains one of the most unequal societies on the planet. Norwood looks at the role of social work in an increasingly fractious society.

We are particularly pleased to include the chapter by Lindsay, Faraj and Baidoun. As we write these words (July 2006), Israel is, once again, launching ferocious attacks on the Palestinians of the Gaza. The Gaza is one of the most over-crowded spots on earth – the Israelis have targeted sewage systems, electricity supply stations, and roads and bridges. Such attacks are a 'collective punishment' against the Palestinians and as such have been argued to be in contravention of international law. The plight of the Palestinians is desperate across both the Gaza and the West Bank. The grinding poverty – especially in the vast refugee camps – is beyond most of our imaginations. Yet the Palestinians also have an immense resilience. In such a society, what is the role of social work? Faraj and Baidoun are both leading members of the Palestinian Union of Social Workers and it is a great honour to have them writing here.

Chapters 10 and 11 look towards the future. Chapter 10, by Chris Jones, presents a short reflection on the future of social work. For a long time Jones has been identified with the radical social work tradition in Britain. His book *State Social Work and the Working Class* is an early, and very important, statement about the nature and contradictions of state social work. His inclusion here is a very real link between the radical movement of the 1970s and the movement today.

Chapter 11 reprints the 'social work manifesto' that was written by Chris Jones, Laura Penketh and ourselves in 2004. We have decided to reprint it here because it has almost taken on a life of its own. Over 500 people have signed up to the manifesto and it has been the subject of several articles in the national media in Britain. We feel it poses the question of 'what kind of social work do we want?' very sharply – and we hope it will stimulate debate on this topic in the wider international social work community.

Our intention is that all the chapters gathered here will help to re-open debate about radical social work, about its hopes and aspirations and to start the process of thinking through what a radical practice can look like. The international spread of the chapters also emphasises that radical social work is not a 'Western' phenomenon but has much to learn from an active engagement with traditions from across the globe. Taken together we hope the chapters can help to germinate the seed of radicalism, to open the debate and be part of a process of establishing that 'another (better) social work is possible'.

Note

1   This was the title of a conference we organised in Liverpool in April 2006. We expected a small number of 'engaged' academics and practitioners.   As it turned out, 280 people (mainly practitioners) packed into the venue and we had to turn others away. Further details are available on the dedicated website at www.socialworkfuture.org

Chapter 1

'The Social Worker as Agitator': The Radical Kernel of British Social Work

Iain Ferguson and Michael Lavalette

Introduction

In April 2006, 280 social worker practitioners, students and academics, service users and campaigners travelled from all over Britain to Liverpool University in the North West of England to attend a highly unusual conference: *A Profession Worth Fighting For? Social Work in the 21st Century*. The conference attempted to explore the ways in which the neo-liberal agenda, pursued since the early 1980s by Conservative and New Labour governments, has transformed every aspect of social work practice in the UK. Over two days, conference delegates discussed and debated the ways in which criminal justice, mental health and children and families social work has changed during this period, as well as reflecting on broader issues of user and carer involvement, the demonisation of young people, and the role of social work with asylum seekers. What made the conference different, however, was not just its content or its composition (with academics very much in a minority) but the fact that an explicit aim of the conference was to move beyond discussion and analysis to begin building networks of resistance to the dominant neo-liberal agendas: to paraphrase Marx, not simply to interpret social work, but to change it.

As national media commentators have noted (*The Guardian*, 22 March 2006; *Community Care*, 6 April 2006), the conference reflected a renewed interest among social workers in the UK in more radical forms of practice than those which are currently dominant. This chapter will explore some of the factors contributing to that renewed interest in radicalism. 'Radical social work' is, of course, a tradition usually associated in the UK with the struggles of the 1970s. But, we argue, the roots of radicalism in the UK go back much earlier, indeed there was a 'radical kernel' at the very birth of British social work in the late nineteenth and early 20th centuries.

In the first part of the chapter, therefore, we look at the period from 1870 until the outbreak of the First World War in 1914 and at the emergence of radical currents in social work in opposition both to the dominant ideas of the time and in response to the great social struggles of the early 20th century. A central concern of the chapter will be the relationship between social movements and struggles in the wider world and the development of radical currents within social work. The next part of the chapter will discuss the emergence of radical social work in the 1970s and consider the extent to which that tradition is still relevant. Finally, we shall examine the reasons for the renewed interest in radical social work in the first decade of the 21st century and attempt to assess the prospects for the development of new, engaged forms of social work practice rooted in notions of social justice.

The birth of social work

State social work in Britain can trace its roots to the Charity Organisation Society (COS), established in 1869 (Stedman Jones, 1976; Jones, 1983). COS was an organisation tied to what were known as the 'principles of 1834' – of deterrence and 'less eligibility'. In 1834 the Poor Law (Amendment) Act was passed in Britain. It was both a brutal and a brutalising piece of legislation. Its aim was to stigmatise the poorest and ensure that benefits (or 'relief') were only offered on the most parsimonious terms. Reference to 'the principles of 1834' became a by-word for policy harshness and of identifying the problems of poverty and pauperism as essentially problems of moral failing on the part of the poor.

COS saw its role as strictly controlling and rationing charitable giving. The organisation argued that misguided elements among the middle-classes were being too generous in their distribution of alms and this was undermining the rationale of the 1834 legislation. Too often, it was claimed, alms-giving was exploited by the 'undeserving poor': they obtained sufficient donations to allow them to avoid work and spend money luxuriously. COS saw its role, therefore, as co-ordinating and organising charitable giving in line with the 'principles of 1834'.

The dominant ideology within the organisation was a pathologising one, which blamed clients for their alleged character failings, rather than locating individual misery within wider socio-economic structures. Thus, in 1881 The *Charity Organisation Review* stated:

> There can be no doubt that the poverty of the working classes of England is due, not to their circumstances (which are more favourable than those of any other working population in Europe); but to their improvident habits and thriftlessness. If they are ever to be more prosperous it must be through self-denial and forethought.
> (quoted in Jones, 1983, p. 76)

The ethos of the COS can be gathered from a minute of the London Council of the Society, which solemnly opined that 'When an applicant is truly starving he may be given a piece of bread if he eats it in the presence of the giver' (cited in Lewis, 1995, p. 47).

COS was always a highly political organisation. Its leaders consciously saw it as a bulwark against the spread of socialist ideas. Its opposition to almost every progressive measure of the day flowed from an ideology which saw casework as:

> the antithesis of mass or socialistic measures and ... proving that there is still much to be said for what can be described as individualism.
> (Milnes, quoted in Walton, 1975, p. 150)

In its fierce opposition to free school meals for children, old-age pensions and national insurance (introduced by the reforming Liberal government of 1906-1912), the COS richly merited future Labour Prime Minister Clement Attlee's description of it as an organisation 'essentially designed for the defence of the propertied classes' (cited in Lewis, 1995, p. 86).

The harsh brutality of COS principles, however, provoked a reaction from both inside and outside the organisation and sparked a search for more humane and sometimes more radical forms of help-giving. The late nineteenth and early 20th centuries also saw, for example, the spread of the 'Settlement movement'. The first Settlement started at 'Toynbee Hall' in 1884 and by the turn of the century a number of universities sponsored Settlements in inner-city areas across Britain. Young middle-class volunteers were sent to inner-city areas to 'remoralise' the poor. Some social work commentators, notably Mullally (2003), have seen in the Settlement movement the origins of the progressive or critical tradition in social work. This is an exaggeration. Many of the ideas associated with the Settlement movement mirrored those of COS and their mission to improve the 'residuum' (see, for example, Whelan, 2001). Nevertheless, the movement does provide an early example of collective, community development approaches and in the USA in particular, the Settlement movement often became involved in more radical activities, such as supporting striking trade unionists (Reisch and Andrews, 2002).

In addition, inside COS and the Settlements there were numerous examples of 'silent protest' or workers refusing to abide by harsh punitive rules. In her biography of Eleanor Rathbone, for example, Pederson cites the example of Maude Royden, like many volunteers a young woman from a wealthy family, who spent eighteen months working in the Liverpool Settlement:

> She was not judgemental, and some of her encounters would have made the theorists of the Charity Organisation Society turn pale. When one docker's wife confessed that she had squandered every penny of the £300 she had received for her husband's death, Royden thought it was 'grand, that, just for once, she had the chance to do so!' The woman recounted some of the things that she had bought, and she and Maude 'laughed like hyenas'. (Pederson, 2004, p. 86)

Royden was clearly frustrated by the inadequacy of the Settlement's theories and programmes as a means of addressing poverty. She was, she admitted,

> 'an idiot at grasping the difference between the deserving and the un-!'... All of the women looked 'unspeakably poor' to her, and she could understand why they would drink like fiends: 'Poor, poor dears. I should drink if I lived in Lancaster Street'. (Pederson, 2004, p. 86).

To prevent such 'demoralisation' and 'contamination' among its volunteers, COS 'engaged in an active and imaginative educational programme, especially between 1895 and 1912, which it directed primarily at its own workers and recruits.' (Jones, 1983, p. 98). In 1897 a formal training sub-committee was established and in 1902 it set up the School of Sociology in London (Jones, 1983).

The School of Sociology was a direct response to the growing influence of Fabianism and its role in setting up the London School of Economics and Political Science. Established in 1884 the Fabian Society was closely associated with Sydney and Beatrice Webb (Beatrice had previously been a COS visitor). Fabianism was a relatively mild form of reformism but it was utterly opposed to the rabid individualism of COS. It attracted a number of early social workers because it focused on the social conditions in which the poorest lived. It also argued that government action and direction (of economic and social life) was needed to address poverty, poor housing and ill-health. Such ideas started to exert influence over many social work volunteers. As Powell (2001, p. 27) notes:

> There was a growing sense amongst social workers that there needed to be a fundamental reform of the existing political order, and this posed a major challenge to the Social Darwinism advocated by the leadership of emerging Victorian civil society ... Politics was therefore in evidence in social work from its infancy and shaped its historic mission into a concern for the poor and the oppressed.

Contact with, and work beside, the poorest clearly led many volunteers to question some aspects of existing society: to view the issue of poverty as part of a broader question of 'social justice'.

But some early social workers were also deeply affected by the social protest movements of the era and went further than the timid radicalism of the Fabians. From the late 1890s to the outbreak of the First World War British society was shaken by a number of protest movements. These can be grouped together into two broad waves of protest. The first was associated with 'the new unionism' of the1890s (Charlton, 1999), and the second the 'great unrest' of 1910-1914 (Haynes, 1984). But generally this entire period saw agitation over trade union rights and working conditions, over the right to vote (most notably the question of women's suffrage), over questions of independence for Ireland and the other colonies and a range of social issues.

Many of those who described themselves as social workers at this period became highly involved in these movements and saw a direct link between their 'social work' and their wider political agitation. In many histories of social work this tradition has been written out – it is 'hidden from history'. As social work became professionalised, its most radical edge – and those who practised a more radical form of social work practice – has been excised from the record. But there is no doubt that, at the time, people like Clement Attlee, Emmeline Pethick-Lawrence, Mary Hughes, Sylvia Pankhurst and George Lansbury saw what they were doing as both political agitation and social work.

Attlee, future Prime Minister of the great reforming Labour government of 1945, wrote a book in 1920 called *The Social Worker*. The book had a chapter called 'The social worker as agitator' and stressed the need for both individual initiatives and collective action to change society (Pearce, 1997, pp. 24-25).

Similarly, in his autobiography (Attlee, 1954) there is a chapter called 'Social work and politics'. This chapter retells various experiences from 1909-1914 where there is a complete confusion (to the present eye) of politics, social movement activity and social work. He recalls organising soup kitchens for the families of striking dockers, of campaigning against the Poor Law, and involvement in the School Care Committee of Trafalgar Square School. He also discusses his role in supervision of free school meals because, though London County Council had been forced to provide these meals, 'they did the work very grudgingly. As a result, the supervision of meals was left to voluntary workers and I frequently supervised the meals of over 400 children of various ages' (Attlee, 1954, p. 31).

Suffragist and socialist Emmeline Pethick was born in 1867 to a wealthy family. In 1891 she became a voluntary social worker at the West London Methodist Mission. She was shocked by the poverty she encountered and started working with young working-class girls. In 1895 she formed the Esperance Club. This involved helping a group of young women establish a co-operative dressmaking business – itself a direct result of her growing criticism of the exploitation and long hours in the East End tailoring trades. Her particular contribution to youth work was the recognition of a social and political dimension to work with young women. In 1898 she argued that it was necessary to take account of the client-group's

> conditions, not only of the home, but of the factory or
> workshop ... It became our business to study the industrial
> question as it affected the girls' employments, the hours,
> the wages, and the conditions. (Pethick, 1898, p. 104)

She would later become heavily involved in the campaign for working-class women to have access to birth control (Pethick-Lawrence, 1938).

Mary Hughes worked in social work in London's East End. She came from a wealthy background but became convinced that her class was unjustly privileged. She decided that she did not want to 'visit the poor' but, instead, wanted to be with the poor and be poor herself. She chose to live in the East End, living the ideals of Christian Socialism in a direct way. In the period after the First World War she moved into the Dew Drop Inn – a hostel and meeting place for the poor in the East End. People came with all sorts of problems, and help and support was given to all.

But as well as rooms for lodgers and direct social work the Inn contained space for trade union meetings and, on Sundays, Christian Socialist religious services. By the late 1920s Mary had grown disillusioned with the Labour Party and became much closer to the Communist Party – though she was never a member of the organisation. She continued to be involved in a range of campaigns and voluntary social work up until her death in 1941 (Hobhouse, 1949).

Sylvia Pankhurst is best known as a militant suffragette and fighter for women's liberation. Along with her mother and sisters she set up the Women's Political and Social Union in 1903 and got involved in various forms of direct action to demand representation. At the outbreak of the First World War she had broken politically with her mother and sister (who had turned to active support for the war-effort) and set up the East End Federation of Suffragettes. Over the next few years she was involved in intense political and social work. As the privations of war were felt in an already impoverished working-class community, Pankhurst was involved in a series of practical community-based schemes to relieve poverty. She set up a free milk distribution service for children, a communal 'Cost Price' restaurant providing cheap and nourishing food, an infant clinic and even a toy factory bringing toys and jobs to local people (Pankhurst, 1932/1987).

But she also – with her colleagues – took up a vast amount of casework. Mothers with children would daily appear at the Federation offices and Pankhurst and her team would deal with a range of problems and issues. She was also appointed as a caseworker for the Poplar Relief Committee (which was tasked with distributing allowances during the war). As Pankhurst noted:

> The War brought into poor slumdom an ... influx of the leisured and the prosperous, to whom the bedraggled meanness of aching poverty seemed mere sluttish absence of self-respect ... To these remote ones ... the allowance anxious mothers craved for the nourishing of little bodies ... appeared merely 'money to spend in drink'. (1932/1987, p.98)

But Pankhurst was determined to ensure that she would attain full relief for her 'clients' and reject any attempt to reduce or cut their relief due to their perceived 'inappropriate behaviour'.

George Lansbury combined campaigning on social and political issues, representation of working people on public bodies and voluntary work (Shepherd, 2004). He was one of the first working men elected onto his local Board of Guardians – in Poplar in London's East End in 1892. From his position he led an attack on the 'principles of 1834' and came into direct conflict with the local COS. He used his position on the Board (and later in the local council) to argue for more generous relief, for better conditions within workhouses and for the creation of a farm colony to provide work for the unemployed. In 1909 he was one of the signatories of the famous *Minority Report on the Poor Law*, which argued that unemployment and poverty were the responsibility of society, not of individual failing.

In 1910 he was elected to Parliament, though he gave up his seat in 1912 to fight a by-election on the issue of women's suffrage (he lost). In the immediate post-war period he led the struggle of the Poplar councillors for 'rate equalisation' (to force wealthy areas of the city to support the needs of the poorest), which saw Lansbury and 29 of his colleagues imprisoned throughout the summer of 1921 (Lavalette, 2006). In 1922 he became a Member of Parliament and remained so until his death in 1940.

He was an early supporter of the Russian Revolution, an advocate the rights of the unemployed, a trade unionist and an outspoken critic of the British Empire. He was one of the greatest orators the British Left has ever produced.

But Lansbury combined this more overt political representation with more intense work with individuals, families and communities. He represented (and accompanied) individuals when they went to the Poor Law guardians for money and goods. He helped organise his local community to demand better public baths and washing facilities. He sat on school boards and demanded that poor local East Enders be listened to and 'given a voice'. During dock strikes in the East End he organised food kitchens and helped co-ordinate support for families of strikers.

Attlee, Pethick-Lawrence, Hughes, Pankhurst and Lansbury are relatively well-known as political activists from the East End of London. Yet they are not viewed as part of any social work tradition. The demarcation of a 'professional history' has led to their campaigning, social and voluntary work being excised from a broader social work history. But there is no doubt that they (and many of their followers) offer a glimpse of another, more radical, social work past. Their committed advocacy and community action strategies to address the needs of local communities and poor working-class 'clients' prefigures developments often associated with the next period of social work radicalism in the 1970s.

The fire last time: radical social work in the 1970s

The radical social work movement of the 1970s and early 1980s in the UK presents an interesting paradox for contemporary social workers. On the one hand radical social work has never been the dominant tradition within social work, even in its heyday in the mid-1970s. At the same time, as Powell correctly observes, 'radical social work has exercised an influence over social work's epistemology totally out of proportion to its minority status' (Powell, 2001, p. 68). As he notes, one reason for this is that radical social work links a structural analysis of clients' problems to an ethical imperative to act, a combination that has proved attractive since the early 1970s to social workers who feel that a concern for social justice should be a central part of social work.

In explaining why radical social work emerged when it did, three factors are of particular importance. The first was the perceived failure of the welfare state, and of social work within it, to eradicate poverty. Britain in the 1950s and 1960s had been dominated by a consensus politics (sometimes referred to as 'Butskellism', after the Conservative Education Minister of the time, Rab Butler, and the then Labour Party leader Hugh Gaitskell), which assumed that the apparent success of post-war Western capitalism in overcoming its problems on the one hand, coupled with the operation of the welfare state on the other, meant that poverty would soon be a thing of the past. Problems that did remain were seen not as structural but rather as reflecting the defects of individuals, families or communities (hence the centrality of the notion of 'the problem family' within social work during this period). This Panglossian worldview was shattered by the 'rediscovery of poverty' in the 1960s and even more so by the re-emergence of economic crisis on a world scale in the early 1970s. In Britain, that crisis led to the return of mass unemployment on a scale not seen since the 1930s and, from 1976 onwards, severe cuts in public sector spending, carried out by a Labour government at the behest of the International Monetary Fund. In the context of widespread poverty, which clearly could not be blamed on individual failings, a social work practice which persisted in employing concepts drawn from a bowdlerised psychoanalysis, was not relevant to the needs of clients.

A second factor fuelling social work's radical turn was the re-emergence of social revolt and rebellion in the late 1960s and early 1970s. Within this period the key year was 1968. As Kurlansky has noted, there had been other years of revolution – 1848, for example, or 1919.

> What was unique about 1968 was that people were rebelling over disparate issues, and had in common only that desire to rebel, ideas about how to do it, and a profound distaste for authoritarianism in any form. (Kurlansky, 2004, p. xvii)

Fuelling that rebellion, he suggests, were four main factors: the example of the civil rights movement in the USA; a generation that felt completely alienated from consumer society; a universally unpopular war in Vietnam; and the impact of television.

That movement and the feeling that 'everything was possible' sparked off a much more profound questioning of every aspect of human life, including such diverse issues as the place of women in society, the meaning of madness, and our understanding of sexuality. It gave rise to the women's liberation movement on the one hand; on the other, in Britain and France in particular, it linked with economic grievances to give rise to the biggest waves of workers' struggles seen in Europe since the 1920s and 1930s. In terms of social work, it led to a search for new ways of relating to clients based on human solidarity, more critical understandings of the family as an institution, and a recognition of the value of collective approaches.

The crisis, both economic and ideological, of the welfare state on the one hand and the re-emergence of collective protest on the other gave rise to the third factor fuelling the emergence of a new, radical social work: the entry into social work in the late 1960s and early 1970s of young people, often sociology graduates, for whom working in the new, generic social work departments appeared to offer a way of making a living that was to some degree compatible with their social and political ideals, an ethical career.

A study by Pearson in the early 1970s found that:

> The dominant impulse which brought them into the job was a rebellion against a life which they feared, otherwise, would waste their own human selves; they were runaways from commercialism, the 'rat race' and what they would describe as 'boredom'. (Pearson, 1975, p. 139)

Key themes

In common with most social movements, the radical social work movement which developed in Britain during the 1970s did not possess a single coherent ideology but rather was made up of a number of different strands, sometimes overlapping, sometimes contradictory. Three in particular are worth noting. First, there was the revolutionary socialist influence, expressed through the magazine *Case Con*. The emphasis of this current was on rank and file activism, the encouragement of democracy within the workplace and the union, and the development of closer links between workers and clients on the basis of common class interests (Simpkin, 1982; Langan, 2002, pp. 212-213). A second strand also described itself as Marxist and similarly stressed the need for closer links between social workers, clients and trade unions but placed greater stress on consciousness raising in work with clients on the one hand and on working within the official structures of the Labour Party and the Trade Union Movement on the other (Corrigan and Leonard, 1978). A third strand was a libertarian or hippy stand, influenced by ideas of the 'counter culture' (Roszak, 1995). Pearson, in his critique of radical social work, probably exaggerates the importance of this strand, at times seeming to suggest that it was a dominant current within radical social work. In relation to the rising unemployment of the 1970s, for example, he writes that 'unemployment was not merely ignored within these [that is, radical social work] discourses, it was actively promoted as a "progressive" and "liberating" lifestyle' (Pearson, 1989, p. 21). Given that some of the leading supporters of *Case Con* were actively involved in campaigns such as the *National Right to Work Campaign,* which sought to challenge growing unemployment, this seems a rather skewed assessment.

Despite these political and ideological differences, it is possible to identify a number of shared themes in radical social work in the 1970s. First, and most important, was the recognition that most of the problems which clients experienced were the product not of their personal failings or inadequacies but rather were the consequences of living in a society riven by inequality, oppression and class division. As Bailey and Brake put it in the introduction to their edited collection:

> Radical social work, we feel, is essentially understanding
> the position of the oppressed in the context of the social
> and economic structure they live in.
> (Bailey and Brake, 1975, p. 9)

The failure of social workers to address the material problems faced by their clients or, more generally, to understand their clients' problems in the context of the poor communities in which they lived (despite the fact that nine out of ten clients were likely to be in receipt of welfare benefits [Becker, 1997]) had been one of the key findings of *The Client Speaks* (Mayer and Timms, 1970). There were two consequences of that failure. First, it meant that material and financial problems were left unaddressed; second, it meant that problems of poverty were often interpreted as individual failings (an inability to budget, for example) or as reflecting underlying psychological problems. Not surprisingly, then, an emphasis on the structural roots of poverty – on *class* – coupled with the development of strategies aimed at alleviating that poverty, was a central theme of radical social work.

A second theme was the critique of casework. Casework was seen primarily as a means of individualising what were essentially collective problems. At best, therefore, it was ineffective; at worst, it was pathologising, since it encouraged clients to see themselves as personally responsible for the problems they were experiencing, rather than recognising that these problems were often the product of wider social and economic processes. In that sense, it was an ideological 'con'.

Third, there was the encouragement of collective approaches. In fact, the 'rediscovery' of community work as part of social work reflected a wider recognition of the limitations of individual work, shared both by mainstream authors such as Bartlett (1970) and by proponents of what were variously known as systems, ecological or unitary approaches (Pincus and Minahan, 1973; Specht and Vickery, 1977). The difference between the two approaches, however, lay in the goals for which community work approaches were employed. While systems theorists were primarily concerned with community work as a technique for restoring equilibrium between (essentially harmonious) social systems, radical social workers, drawing both on Marxist traditions and on the writing of community activists like Saul Alinsky (1971), saw 'community action' (also the title of a long-running magazine aimed at community workers) as means both of promoting political change and of securing new resources in poor communities.

Fourth, there was the critique of professionalism. The basis of that critique was succinctly summed up in the *Case Con Manifesto* as follows:

> 'Professionalism' firstly implies the acquisition of a specialism – knowledge and skills not possessed by

untrained workers. This isolates the social worker from the population at large. Secondly, social workers come to see themselves as part of an accepted specialist group on a par with doctors and lawyers. Third, it encourages the introduction of businesslike career structures, where 'correct' and 'professional' behaviour (such as 'detachment' and 'controlled emotional involvement') are rewarded with advancement. (Bailey and Brake, 1975, p. 145)

Two main consequences flowed from this critique of professionalism. First, it suggested a different kind of relationship with clients, one which emphasised the need to reduce worker-client power differentials on the one hand and the value of clients' knowledge and experience on the other. In that sense, it can be seen as a precursor to democratic models of user involvement which developed (particularly within the voluntary sector) in the 1990s (Beresford and Croft, 1995). Second, it eschewed the need for professional organisation, in the form for example of the British Association of Social Workers (BASW), arguing that such organisations both encouraged elitism and replaced a focus on achieving social change and social justice in alliance with clients and other workers with a narrow concern for the promotion of professional interests. Instead, social workers should see themselves primarily as *workers*, whose primary form of organisation was the trade union. The astonishing growth of white-collar trade unionism in the 1970s (not least among social workers) and the failure of BASW ever to recruit more than a very small percentage of the social work workforce shows that it was an argument that had a resonance well beyond the ranks of radical social workers.

Finally, as noted above, the dominant analysis within the movement was a *socialist* analysis, which saw class as central. For Bailey and Brake (1975, p. 9), for example, 'A socialist perspective is, for us, the most human approach for social workers'.

Evaluating radical social work

The shift to the right in British politics in the late 1970s, reflected in the election of a Conservative government under Margaret Thatcher in 1979, saw social work in general, and radical social work in particular, become the scapegoat of choice for the perceived deficiencies of British society (see, for example, Brewer and Lait, 1980). A discourse of failure in relation to child protection, for example, was often linked to the alleged influence of radical ideas – initially Marxism, then feminism, and latterly 'political correctness' in general (Philpot, 1999). In their attacks on anti-racist and anti-oppressive practice, a common refrain from politicians during much of the 1980s and 1990s was that social workers should be less concerned with such 'political correctness' and needed to acquire more 'common sense'. For one Conservative Health Secretary in the mid-1990s, this involved the recruitment of more 'street-wise grandmothers' as social workers, while the first Health Minister (a consultant neurologist by profession) in the newly-formed Scottish Executive opined that:

> Social work services are not about redressing the major injustices in our world. Their remit is not to battle with the major forces that drive social exclusion. It is to promote social inclusion for each individual within their circumstances.
> (Sam Galbraith, cited in *Community Care*, 22 May 2000)

Despite the marginalisation of 1970s radical social work which this sustained onslaught produced, its influence has continued to be felt in a number of different ways. First, its core ideas, in particular the notion of understanding the position of the oppressed in the context of the social and economic structure they live in, informed the development of anti-oppressive practice through the 1980s and 1990s (albeit that a frequent criticism of the tradition was its failure to adequately address issues of oppression) (Penketh, 2000). Second, its call for a much more equal relationship between workers and clients, based both on a recognition of shared interests and a valuing of the client's experience, prefigured the development of user involvement a decade later (Beresford and Croft, 1993). Third, its emphasis on collective approaches, while less and less heeded within mainstream social work, was reflected in the growth of movements of service users in the 1980s, particularly the disability movement and the mental health users' movement (though usually without direct social work involvement) (Oliver, 1996). Fourth, while radical social work largely fell off the agenda in Britain, it continued to be developed as a living tradition elsewhere, notably in Australia and Canada (see Chapters 2 and 3, this volume). In these respects, radical social work has continued to make its influence felt.

Sometimes that legacy has manifested itself, or been deployed, in unexpected and unforeseen ways. As Langan, a leading participant in the 1970s' radical social work movement, has noted:

> One of the most significant trends of the past decade has been the deployment of formerly radical themes in a new framework of regulation. The use of the term 'empowerment' and the promotion of 'anti-discriminatory' practice in social work illustrate this trend.
>
> (Langan, 2002, p. 215)

She goes on to ask

> What does empowerment now mean? It implies an individualistic conception of power, which by reducing social relationships to the interpersonal level obscures the real power relations in society. Thus the playground bully appears as a major public menace, while the state, the real seat of power in society, appears powerless. Confusing the problem, empowerment offers illusory solutions. Measures of support or counselling make coping and surviving the ultimate objectives. This is the crux of empowerment: once the perspective of social change is eliminated, just getting by becomes the zenith of aspirations.
>
> (Langan, 2002, p. 215)

The ultimate irony, she concludes, is that 'the radical commitment to liberation appears to have been transformed into a mechanism for regulation' (Langan, 2002, p. 216).

Langan is right to point to the ways in which what Butler and Pritchard (2001, p. 8) have described as 'the flexible exploitation of ambiguity' allowed the leadership of the social work profession during the 1990s to accommodate to increased marketisation and managerialism while claiming continued adherence to the core values of social work. There is, however, another side to the story. For as we shall argue below, in the changed political circumstances of the first decade of the twenty first century, when great new social movements have developed in opposition both to neo-liberalism and to war, the survival of radical social work even as a fragment within the collective memory of social work allows a new generation of social workers to draw on that tradition as one source in the construction of a social work practice committed to social justice and social change. As Butler and Drakeford rightly argue, this is not a nostalgia trip, a naive call for a return to the 1970s. Rather:

> [T]here is some advantage to be gained in reclaiming that heritage … By building into the environment a remembrance of social work's past, one builds in too a sense of possible future alternatives … the radicalism of the 1970s, 1980s, and early 1990s is a reminder that the vision of social work can be grander than is currently the case'. (Butler and Drakeford, 2001, p. 16)

Social work in the 21st century: birth of a new radicalism?

What then are the prospects for a new radical social work in the 21st century? On first examination, the signs are hardly auspicious. As Catherine McDonald argues (Chapter 2, this volume), the 'spaces' for the development of radical forms of practice have shrunk considerably since the early 1990s. In Britain, the independent social work departments created in the early 1970s, which allowed for the development both of professional identity and of strong trade union organisation, have often disappeared, merged with health, housing or education services within new 'integrated' departments where social work is often very much the junior partner. Further, the roles played by social workers within such departments have been transformed beyond recognition. The dominance of care management approaches has fragmented the social work role and also means that social workers are now much more likely to be computer-bound, with fewer opportunities for face-to-face contact with clients and consequently for the exercise of therapeutic or advocacy skills (Clarke, 1996). Finally, as a consequence of the market in social care, the misnamed 'voluntary sector', once an option for those who wished to practise in innovative ways in organisations which often encouraged a high degree of user involvement, is increasingly made up of large organisations with budgets of millions of pounds which resemble the local authority bureaucracies they were designed to replace, the difference being that the absence of strong trade union organisation means that the wages and conditions of staff are usually much worse.

It would be wrong, then, to underestimate the obstacles to the development of more radical forms of practice. But it would be equally wrong to ignore what we have called the 'resources of hope' which have emerged in recent years (Jones *et al.*, 2004). Elsewhere we have suggested four potential bases for resistance to neo-liberal social work (Ferguson and Lavalette, 2006). First, there are the limitations of what, following Howe (1996), might be called a *social work of surfaces*, which does not get to grips with the meanings and underlying issues of clients' difficulties, both personal and structural. It is noteworthy that *Changing Lives* (Scottish Executive, 2006), the report of the 21st Century Social Work Enquiry in Scotland, places great emphasis on the importance of therapeutic relationships in social work and recognises that these have been one of the main casualties of the forms of practice that have developed since the early 1990s. By itself, of course, an emphasis on relationship which does not address the conditions required to allow workers to practise in a therapeutic manner or the wider structural factors contributing to the difficulties experienced by service users does not take us very far. Nevertheless, the acknowledgement that approaches focused on narrow, behavioural change often fail to meet even their own limited objectives is useful ammunition in the struggle to develop alternatives.

Second, there is the mounting dissatisfaction among social workers at what their job has become, evidenced both in research (Jones, 2004; Scottish Executive, 2006) and also in gatherings such as the Liverpool conferences referred to in the introduction to this chapter. The lack of opportunities for face-to-face work with clients; the dominance of budgets; the management of social work by individuals whose primary concern is not with social work values but with the bottom line of the account sheet; the loss of social work identity in merged departments dominated by other, more powerful professions; the lack of resources to do the job; and a culture which increasingly blames clients for problems over which they have little or nor control are some of the main factors which increase social workers' sense of alienation and the sense that 'I didn't come into social work for this' (Ferguson and Lavalette, 2004). If it is able to find stronger forms of organisational expression than have existed to date, such widespread and intense dissatisfaction can become a powerful factor in producing change.

Third, there is the emergence since the early 1990s of collective self-organisation among people who use health and social work services. In the narrower form of 'user involvement', this development is, of course, perfectly compatible with the prevailing consumerism of the major political parties, with 'consumer choice' often a euphemism for the increased privatisation of services. In their more radical forms, however, service user movements are capable both of providing an alternative vision of what services could look like and also of developing alliances with social workers to challenge the structural oppression and discrimination which, as the social model of disability recognises, lie at the root of many of the problems which people experience.

Finally, there are the great new movements which have developed since the early 1990s. Foremost among these is the movement against neo-liberalism, the anti-capitalist or global justice movement, which came into existence following the disruption of the World Trade Organisation talks in Seattle in 1999. Since Seattle, that movement has expressed itself through more and bigger mobilisations in many parts of the world, including the UK. In July 2005, for example, a 'Make Poverty History' demonstration in Edinburgh against the meeting of the G8 leaders at Gleneagles, Scotland attracted 300,000 people, while a demonstration at Gleneagles itself a few days later drew up to 15,000 people, despite a police ban on marching. No less important has been the contribution made by movement activists to the building of the movement against war in Iraq which saw two million people demonstrating on the streets of Britain on 15 February 2003 with twelve million people marching worldwide. Even these huge numbers, however, understate the extent of opposition to neo-liberal policies on a global scale. In France, for example, the decisive victory of the 'No!' camp in the May 2005 referendum on the French Constitution reflected popular hostility to the 'British model' of privatisation of services and a residual welfare state (Kouvelakis, 2005). Elections in Germany in the same year saw a new Left party gaining 8.7 per cent of the popular vote, mirroring the emergence of parties opposed to neo-liberalism and war in almost every European country. The real epicentre of the struggle against neo-liberalism, however, has been not Europe but rather Latin America where in country after country, most notably in Venezuela and Bolivia, governments have been elected in recent years which are fiercely opposed to the neo-liberal policies of the USA, the World Trade Organisation and the International Monetary Fund.

After two decades in which the conventional wisdom was that there was 'no alternative' to the market as a basis for organising society, this profound shift in the global *zeitgeist* gives hope and opens up new possibilities for all those who would like to see society based on a very different set of values. Elsewhere in this chapter, we have argued that radical forms of social work often develop in response to, and through contact with, wider social movements and social struggles. What then might be the significance of the new movements of the 21st century, for social work and social workers?

In the UK at present, its primary impact is *ideological*. There is a growing concern, in other words, about the implications of the market in social work and social care for the value base of social work and for the way it is reshaping relationships between social workers and those who use social work services (Jones, C., 2001; Harris, J., 2003). One indication of that concern was the Liverpool conference discussed at the beginning of this chapter. A similar conference in Nottingham took place some weeks earlier on the theme: *Affirming Our Value Base in Social Work and Social Care*. According to one experienced practitioner/academic/service user:

> 'There were about 2,000 people present. This is likely to become the stuff of legend. I have just never seen so many people together all heading in one direction, all come to find out more about how to do social work and social care well and make it the user-centred service it truly can be ... Some of social care's key moral guardians, like Bill Jordan, Bob Holman and Beatrix Campbell were there to inspire. They stressed the need for social care workers to be politically engaged.' (Beresford, 2006)

Of course these are fragile developments and the odds stacked against the emergence of a new, more radical social work rooted in social justice remain high. At the same time the conviction that (in the title of the Liverpool conference) this is 'a profession worth fighting for' remains strong among many practitioners, academics, students and service users. If that conviction can be translated into new, more radical forms of practice and into stronger forms of collective organisation than have existed to date, then there is just a chance that that vision could be realised.

Chapter 2

Wizards of Oz?
The Radical Tradition in Australian Social Work (And what we can learn from Aotearoa New Zealand)

Catherine McDonald

Introduction

> Radical social workers have often been perceived as a minority within the profession and many indeed have discarded the label 'professional'. They have, however, exerted an important influence on social work, in that they have prevented social work from feeling too comfortable in a 'professional' role ... (Ife, 1997, p. 176)

Australia, a small nation by anyone's reckoning, is nevertheless home to some of the most influential 'radical' social worker authors of the current period – Jan Fook (1993, 2002), Karen Healy (2000), Jim Ife (1997) and Bob Pease (2002) – to name a few. Further in 1998, Pritchard, the then editor of the American *Journal of Progressive Human Services*, undertook a search of international social work abstracts for articles published on radical social work during the 1980s and 1990s. To his dismay, he found only nineteen over the two decades. Surprisingly, however, he established that the greatest number of articles in a single publication were six, published in *Australian Social Work*. Lamenting this state he asks:

> Have we as a profession become less committed to each person's well-being? Have we become complacent to the

exploitative realities of our capitalist society? Is it possible
that radical changes have occurred in society, most people
have achieved well-being, and, therefore there is no longer
a need to discuss these matters? ... Perhaps a more
realistic view might be that social workers are
compromising their commitments to human welfare, and
that fewer and fewer are taking seriously these
commitments to human welfare, and that fewer and fewer
are taking seriously the paradox of a people-serving
profession in a people-denying society and that social work
as a profession has sacrificed being of real service by
selling out to conventional arrangements.
(Pritchard, 1998, p. 4)

Well, what has happened to radical social work? In this chapter I pose
that question in the one context (Australia) where it *appears* to have
maintained a high profile within the profession. I advance the argument
that although Australian radical social work (in its latest manifestation as
critical social work) seems to have a strong and continuing presence (if
publications are anything to go by), that 'presence' is more fictional than
real. In reality, Pritchard is partially correct in suggesting that capitalist
triumphalism with its associated political programme of neo-liberalism
has largely defeated traditional radicalism in Australian social work.

I further advance the post-Fordist-like proposition (admittedly
untested) that social work, and the various forms that it takes, are in no
small part influenced by the regime of capital accumulation present in
any given context. Australia is now a post-industrial economy. And as
Jessop (1999, 2002) has argued, the transformation of welfare to
workfare (a shorthand term for the potent mix of policy developments
that have reconstructed welfare in most advanced industrial nations –
but especially so in the Anglophone nations), represents a re-inscription
of the roles that 'welfare' (and social work) play in late or advanced
capitalism. Elsewhere, I have characterised the shift from welfare to
workfare as institutional change (McDonald and Chenoweth, 2005;
McDonald, C.), arguing that change at this level inevitably has significant
implications for an activity such as social work which is, almost in its
entirety, contingent on its context (McDonald *et al.*, 2003).

This does not mean that all is lost. Indeed, it can be argued that developments made by indigenous social workers in Australia, but most particularly in Aotearoa New Zealand, are charting new modes of practice attuned to cultural difference which respond, in part, to the ravages of capitalist-inspired colonialism and post-colonialism. I return to this theme in some depth in Part Three of the chapter. In Part One I chart the tradition of radicalism in Australian social work, moving across the decades from the 1970s to the present, culminating in the contemporary manifestation of critical social work. In Part Two, I evaluate this latest version of 'radicalism', particularly in terms of its intellectual claims and in terms of its utility in the contemporary era. As will become clear, I conclude that in this part of the world, indigenous practice is probably the real heir to the radical tradition. The question is: does social work as a whole know that – both in Australia and beyond?

Part One: The proud tradition

The modern form of radical social work in Australia made its advent just before the electoral win of the reformist Whitlam Labor government in 1972. During the late 1960s and early 1970s, Australia discovered (or rediscovered) poverty (Henderson, 1975) and developed a degree of optimism and confidence that social progress could be made through the institutions of the state. This optimism (and the subsequent programmes that rolled out throughout the life of that ill-fated but ultimately influential government) helped create a set of intellectual and ideological conditions which allowed a radical critique to develop within the ranks of Australian social work. As Healy (1993, p. 4) recalls, despite its avowedly liberal and reformist theme, the 1971 Australian Association of Social Work (AASW) conference was 'turbulent, provocative and radicalising as it represented a vigorous challenge to the taken-for-granted professionalist assumptions of the time which gave prominence to individualistic explanations of social problems'. As he also notes, it was during that year that the first formal local statement of radical social work was made in an article *Towards a radical critique of social work and social welfare ideology* by Pemberton and Locke (1971).

As the 1970s progressed, a range of publications came out devoted to promoting a radical agenda of structural analysis and intervention in social work, particularly in the form of macro practice. In the interests of progressing radical social work, in 1974, new graduates and students in

Sydney and Brisbane developed Inside Welfare – a group specifically dedicated to socialist practice. In 1979, this group produced a bibliography for Marxist welfare workers (Inside Welfare, 1979). Some of the publications of the time were overtly polemic in nature (for example, Throssell, 1975; Tomlinson, 1977), while others were attempting to develop actual models for practice (for example, Benn, 1976; Liffman, 1978). One interesting variant of this was the early use by Australian radical social workers of militant trade unionism. The first social work strike in Australia was in 1974, provoked by the Northern Territory Community Welfare Department's inappropriate responses to indigenous children in its care, and by its disciplining of social workers who spoke out in protest (see Tomlinson, 1977, pp. 241-260 for an impassioned account). As I discuss subsequently, the use of trade unionism in the form of alliances with militant parts of the Australian union movement was to prove an innovative model of radical practice subsequently developed to great effect in the 1980s.

Overall, the 1970s were an optimistic and interesting period which undoubtedly set the foundations for subsequent, possibly more enduring and important work, about how social work should respond to, for example, indigenous issues. By encouraging critique of mainstream and reformist approaches to social work it also encouraged the development of feminist engagement and constitution of a specifically feminist form of social work practice. Importantly, the socialist radicalism of the 1970s destabilised, perhaps permanently, any capacity for hegemonic closure by the mainstream social work professional project. As the decade drew to a close though, the upsurge of socialist-inspired radicalism in social work withered. Healy (1993) nominates a number of reasons: cultural change in the face of overseas models of practice (from Britain and the United States), the collapse of the social democratic Whitlam government and its replacement by a neo-conservative government. I suggest that this latter development was particularly significant in that it represented a fundamental shift at the level of the institutions of welfare. Under the Whitlam regime, radical social work was allowed to flourish (or at least tolerated) within sites of practice *created* by social democratically-informed policy. The change of government shut down these spaces. But as I discuss subsequently, policy initiatives by the incoming government provoked radical activism in surprising ways.

During the 1980s radical social work took two primary forms – first, that pursuing the interests of oppressed populations (of which feminist practice was the most widespread and certainly the most extensively theorised), and second, forms of social activism. As elsewhere, feminism was extremely influential in radical social work during the 1980s, presenting a powerful critique to the Marxist-dominated practice models of the early activists (Healy, 2000). Further, feminist social work of the 1980s developed in and drew on the, by then mature, knowledge and practices developed by feminist activists in women-centred and alternative services during the 1970s (Alston, 2001). In terms of social work practice, feminism inspired a dual response – one in the form of developing specific feminist-inspired practice skills, and another in the form of developing an analysis of how women (as an overall population as well as various groups) interact and engage with the institutions of welfare and the consequences of their engagement. In other words, feminist social work during this period demonstrated how radical theories could be translated into actual social work practices – via developing the processes associated with transformative analyses (consciousness raising) and adapting traditional practice skills with transformative intent, for example, feminist interviewing (see McDonald, 1988).

Indeed – and again if publications are anything to go by – feminism was one of the key influences on Australian social work thinking and practice during the 1980s (see, for example, Marchant and Wearing, 1986; McDonald, 1988). This was also the heyday of the 'femocrat'; at that time a peculiar Australian form of feminist 'practice', in which liberal feminists (social workers among them) took up key positions in the Commonwealth bureaucracy in particular, and exercised considerable influence from within (Yeatman, 1990). While this form of activism was considered highly innovative at the time, not surprisingly, there were debates about whether such practice was truly 'radical' (Eisenstein, 1996). Irrespective of its pedigree, it was nevertheless a form of practice that became more or less institutionalised within the operations of Commonwealth and state governments. This feat alone, in a growing era of conservatism, is noteworthy.

The other influential strand of radical practice during the 1980s was social activism around a number of issues – for example, organising service user groups (Dimech, 1985), the beginnings of purposeful working with indigenous people and communities (see Tomlinson, 1982, 1985), and campaigning for services for young unemployed people

(Friedland, 1985). As indicated previously, one of the most exciting developments in this period was the development of joint action between social workers as community workers and the union movement. In this case, the then most militant member of the Australian union movement – the Builders Labourers Federation (BLF) – worked with inner-city (and other suburban) resident action groups to thwart the ambitions of capitalist developers (Mundy, 1981). The resultant campaigns were known as the Green Bans, and were so successful that they contributed significantly to the ultimate de-registration and dismantling of the BLF by the state. Nevertheless, despite the continuation of radical activity in these two strands of endeavour, mainstream social work was relatively unaffected. Further, the opportunity to engage using radical frameworks and practices within the institutions of welfare – the main arenas of activity for social workers – continued to shrink.

Enter the 1990s – an interesting decade in Australia. For the first half, a Labor government pursued what was essentially a neo-liberal project, but in its own rhetoric within a 'social justice framework'. That rhetoric vanished when, in 1997, Labor was voted out and replaced by an incoming neo-conservative Coalition government committed to a set of principles and an agenda completely at odds with any socialist, social democratic or even mildly progressive project.

Possibly the most important developments in 'radical' social work during the period of the Labor government were those developed by and with indigenous people. This was, explicitly, the Australian version of anti-racist social work. But like elsewhere (see Dominelli, 1989), it was nevertheless a very small voice in the overall discourse of social work. Further, it was a period when again, the institutions of the state recognised the injustices meted out to Australia's indigenous population and opened up spaces for new and innovative types of responses. Specifically, the period saw Australia's High Court effectively overturning the institutional blindness of *terra nullius* (a long-standing legal fiction that the land was empty of people when Cook landed and claimed it for England). As a result, the Labor government began to tread the path of reconciliation, albeit slowly and hesitantly. In response, the profession as a whole apologised for its part in the sorry saga of the Stolen Generation (when Aboriginal children were removed from their parents' care for no other reason than their Aboriginality). A few social workers went further and took up the challenge of interrogating social work and of developing models of anti-racist intervention (macro and micro) (Lynn and Pye, 1990; Freedman and Stark, 1993; McMahon, 1993; McMahon, 1997).

Later I discuss these developments in more depth because, as I indicated in my introductory remarks, some forms of social work by and with indigenous people represent what is probably the most important contribution to the radical tradition in Australian social work. At this stage, however, it is more appropriate to recognise that this form of work (that is, with and for indigenous people) represented only a fragment of social work overall. In other words, it was and is marginal to the overall professional project. This point is well demonstrated by McMahon (2002) who notes that of the 933 articles published in *Australian Social Work* from 1947 to 1997, sixteen were on indigenous issues. This represents a grand total of 1.7 per-cent, lower than the incidence of indigenous people in Australia's population, and far lower than the incidence of indigenous people in the various health, welfare and correctional settings and institutions where social work is practised.

The final variant of 'radical' social work is its most contemporary manifestation – critical social work. As indicated in my introductory comments, if publications are a sign of strength, critical social work is a strong theme in Australian social work. Critical social work engages with critical social theory and in some instances, post-modernism. Despite purposeful linkages to these genres of (extremely complex) social theory, contemporary critical social work practice is nevertheless just that – it is a *set of practices* and *prescriptions for action* – couched within a particular emancipatory worldview. Critical social work purposefully carries the intent or the politics of critical social theory into the realm of social work practice.

However, one version of contemporary critical practice is informed by a human rights perspective and one of the most important contemporary advocates of human rights practice is Australian – Jim Ife (1997, 2001). In 1997, Ife discussed how human rights could be employed as a conceptual framework for underpinning social work practice. He developed an argument that social work practice can be conceived as promoting a universalist view of social justice balanced by and expressed through a relativist view of human needs, varying from person to person and from context to context. It is in this relativising process that this form of critical social work recognises the complexities and diversities of people's lives and needs accentuated by contemporary theory.

Emerging out of the tradition of radical and structural social work, the other most recent developments in critical social work practice theory are found in a growing body of work informed, as indicated earlier, by both critical social theory and by post-modern theory. The mix or theoretical emphasis does, however, vary. Some authors in the genre draw more on critical social theory; others attempt to incorporate the insights of post-modern theory. Ife (1997), for example, would position his work within the critical social work tradition, but his actual engagement with post-modern theory is both limited and he is quite critical of it. Those who do engage more directly with post-modern theory represent what is promoted as a qualitatively different and significant advance, in that the dual theoretical engagement claims to shift the foundations of social work practice sufficiently to challenge the modernist professional project. Here I briefly discuss two key Australian proponents whose work falls directly into the category of social work practice theory – Healy (2000, 2001) and Fook (2002) – while acknowledging there are other important writers who fall into this category (see Napier and Fook, 2000; Pease, 2002; Allan et al., 2003).

Jan Fook (2002) represents an important example of an author who is attempting to incorporate critical social theory and contemporary theory into everyday practice. She suggests that both bodies of theory are relevant for strengthening social work practice for a range of reasons. Overall, her position is that a positive reading of contemporary theory in conjunction with critical social theory allows for a more nuanced and liberated approach to practice with marginalised people, one which, through its critique of mainstream practices, opens up the potential for new ways of engaging. In other words, her central claim is that contemporary theory augments radical approaches to social work using Marxist or neo-Marxist theory.

Another example of influential authors developing and promoting contemporary critical social work which draws on both critical social theory and contemporary theory is Healy (2000, 2001). Her specific intent is to revive the critical social work tradition by demonstrating how to overcome the split between theory and practice, a split which has seriously undermined radical and critical practice in the past. Further, her other core objectives are to understand the importance of context in social work practice, to understand the role of power and to address the challenges posed by the New Public Management-inspired developments in public administration.

The combination and impact of these authors (if we use citation rates as an indicator) appear to demonstrate that Australian critical social work is a strong candidate for being an international front runner in the most contemporary version of the radical tradition. In the next part I evaluate the proposition that contemporary critical social work as the latest iteration of the radical tradition has the capacity to sustain and nurture that tradition in the current circumstances.

Part Two: A (critical) look at critical social work

I suggest that there are at least two reasons why critical social work (or at least some forms of it) may not be able to realise its promise to revive and sustain the radical tradition in social work. There is a considerable body of critique that is regularly levelled at some versions of contemporary critical social work, particularly those which overtly use post-modern theory. It must be acknowledged that the relevance and utility of post-modern theory to social work is a highly contested issue beyond any consideration of the radical tradition. Parts of the social work academy consider its application to social work to be more characteristic of intellectual fashion, frivolous at best and nihilistic and destructive at worst; a way of thinking that the profession should not become obsessed with (see Ife, 1999; Powell, 2001; Noble, 2004).

For the most part, doubts about the application of post-modern theory arise out of concern for the status of the emancipatory potential of radical social work. Post-modern theory would, for example, suggest that social work's emancipatory potential was always more imagined than real. Because of this negativity, many are sceptical about whether post-modern theory can make any useful contribution to practice, arguing, for example, that it leads to the promotion of uncertainty, diversity and complexity (see, for example, Meinert, 1998). Furthermore it is said to undermine the entire intellectual heritage of social work (Noble, 2004). Even more worrying, the simultaneous impact of post-modern theory and neo-liberalism has silenced those public intellectuals (often social workers) who once fervently championed the interests of the poor and promoted the advancement of their welfare (Adams, 2000). Ife (1999) and Powell (2001) argue convincingly that uncritical acceptance of post-modern theory serves the interests of neo-liberal politics by its persistent undermining of analytical genres which focus attention on capitalism's worst effects, for example, the 'grand narrative' of Left political thought. Similarly, activist and feminist social workers argue that post-modern theory is counter-revolutionary and inherently conservative in that it does not acknowledge the patterns of oppression that transcend locations and historical epochs. Post-modern theory abandons the subject just when, for example, different groups of women begin to assert their right to define what the subject is (Fawcett and Featherstone, 2000). The diverse and fragmented identities of post-modern theory deny categories of class, race and gender that continue to represent virulent social divisions. Importantly for radical social work, can collective and progressive political practices be founded on the types of slippery notions of diversity promoted by post-modern theory? Finally, post-modern theory not only destabilises the emancipatory and progressive intent of social work, it also undermines specific sets of practices – particularly those social workers use when engaging in social and community development (Midgley, 1999).

In the main, the core of this body of critical commentary on post-modern theory is that theoretical developments which undermine progressive grand narratives (such as neo-Marxist understandings about the operations of class and social stratification) and undermine representational knowledge (for example, about poverty) inevitably retreats to a position where we cannot 'know' about the enduring phenomena the radical wing of the profession has traditionally been concerned about. Furthermore, its rejection of the optimism of the Enlightenment also means a rejection of related principles of great significance to radical social work arising from the same tradition, for example, social justice (Atherton and Bollard, 2002). How, it is asked, can radical social work exist if it denies its emancipatory purposes?

Indeed, the case against the application of post-modern theory is succinctly made by Australian Brian Trainor (2003), who provides a detailed account of why post-modern theory, in certain manifestations, is dangerous. Arguing that social work needs a unitary epistemology (or knowledge base), the fragmentary tendencies of post-modern theory are, he claims, inherently damaging. Reverting to a moral reassertion of an essentially humanist imperative, Trainor argues that social workers and their (knowing) clients are 'co-travellers on a truth journey', one which seeks to 'genuinely address the true or authentic needs of clients'. For Trainor, post-modern theory is intensely, indeed immorally pessimistic, and that this 'hyper-pessimism is a form of hyper-irresponsibility' (Trainor, 2003, p. 33). In many ways, the position taken by Trainor (and the other authors noted above) is correct in that the optimism of radical social work as an emancipatory practice would be severely dented, and perhaps terminally discredited as hopelessly naïve and misguided. To the extent that this is the case (and I for one am unconvinced, although space does not allow me to mount a partial defence for post-modern theory and its relevance for contemporary critical practice[1]), then those forms of contemporary critical social work which actively embrace post-modernism are, from the point of view of an emancipatory and progressive project, doomed.

However, I suggest that there is an even more fundamental issue about the attempts to mix critical practice with post-modern (and indeed critical) social theory. Both post-modern and critical social theories are essentially *analyses of society*, particularly late capitalist society. As such, both are intensely powerful, albeit in very different ways. Critical social work practice is just that – a design recipe for *practice*. Accordingly, when the specific prescriptions for practice are developed, they cannot, in reality, translate the complexities of the theoretical analyses into desirable and distinct practices. Instead the analyses are inserted *prior to* and *separate from* the practice recommendations. As such, practice guidelines differ little from what is considered good practice in mainstream professional social work.

My comments to date have focused on the moral and intellectual limits of post-modern theory, questioning whether or not critical social work which takes it up can survive with its emancipatory intent intact, or whether as a body of practice theory, it actually progresses anything new or different from the rest of the profession. However, an equally potent argument can be made which points to a very practical problem. I begin by restating that critical social work was never at the centre of social work practice broadly conceived and, despite ambit claims, is still very much at the margins. I have, in the previous section (Part One) illustrated how earlier forms of radical practice survived, in part, because the institutions of the state allowed spaces for it to develop. These forms or modes of radical practice found institutional homes, paradoxically authorised by the state (for example in the Australian Assistance Plan during the term of the Whitlam Labor government in the 1970s, mirroring developments in the British Community Development Projects, and the US Model Cities programme in the late 1960s and early 1970s). In the contemporary environment of a full-blown neo-liberal state shaped by the remorseless dictates of New Public Management, along with relentless corporatisation and outsourcing, the institutional 'spaces' for practice as conceived within the critical genre are increasingly constrained.

Today, no state-sponsored habitat for contemporary forms of radical social work exists. Rather, the spaces for practice are small, non-state, marginal and very much under threat. Nevertheless, if we think about critical practice broadly defined discursively, as an expression of a morality and a politics (or a convenient rhetoric), it will, in all likelihood, continue to occupy a larger position in the collective professional imagination than the realities of contemporary practice actually dictate. As Healy (2000) so aptly notes, critical social work like other more traditional forms of practice, awards itself a 'truth status' and a unifying orientation in which it is positioned as a possible (read 'best') form of practice for everyone. I suspect that most, if not all forms of critical practice, will continue to be vigorously advocated by its sponsors in the Australian academy if not necessarily undertaken in the field.

It has to be acknowledged, however, that such advocacy is taking place in practice contexts and welfare organisations constituted by a welfare system increasingly shaped by neo-liberal policies, drilled down into every practice by the Australian version of New Public Management. Virtually every location where social work is undertaken has been reconstituted in such ways as to dismantle any possibility for radical or critical social work practice. Instead, in Australia, as in the United States and Britain, there has been a resurgence of the traditional professional project in a retooled 'package' – for example, in the promotion of evidence-based practice. Occurring on a broader scale than social work, the renaissance of evidence or more particularly of a specific form of 'evidence' in the contemporary regime of welfare is, of course, entirely congruent with and reflective of the times. Nevertheless, evidence-based practice attempts to overlay a particular and bounded template on the diverse and extremely complex conditions of social work practice (including radical or critical practice) that may well be shaped by different sets of assumptions. Evidence-based social work cannot possibly 'see' what is going on or 'hear' the noise generated on the ground. In many contexts, such as working with indigenous people, evidence-based practice asks the wrong questions. In working with indigenous people in an acute health care setting, for example, a social worker employing an evidence-based practice framework would not consider the impact of dispossession or alienation. By not encouraging attention to such defining factors as culture or power, social work practice drawing on an evidence-based practice framework will not achieve the sorts of measurable outcomes it so desires, and is, in fact, more likely to exacerbate the presenting 'problem'. As such, developments such as the spread and take-up of contemporary prescriptions of the traditional professional project represented by developments such as evidence-based practice illustrate how mainstream social work is moving away from its radical and critical forms. But is this move inevitable and are there no alternatives?

Part Three: Indigenous practice in Australia and Aotearoa New Zealand

I have suggested previously that, in the Australian context, the true heirs to radicalism in contemporary social work practice are those working to create ways of engaging which challenge the 'whiteness' and 'colonialism' of the traditional professional project *and* of much of the early structural forms of radical practice. Indigenous social work adopts an overt anti-colonialist stance and an overt anti-racist position (Briskman, 2003). It is a form of practice which explicitly draws the links between white privilege generated at the cost of indigenous possession of the land and at the cost of indigenous sovereignty. It is a form of practice that understands the cumulative impact of settler capitalism and its successors down through the generations to the present – the impact of arson, murder and theft. And it is a form of practice which stands in marked contrast to mainstream social work, fully acknowledging the profession's appalling complicity in the dispossession and marginalisation of Australia's indigenous people. It is a stance, for example, that wholly acknowledges much of the terrible history of the stolen generations – taken from their families and placed in abusive institutions for little reason other than their race – and it is a history that *centrally implicates* social workers and social welfare organisations.

While individual and institutional racism is still widespread in Australia, and while Australian social work itself has a very patchy history of progressive engagement with indigenous people, gradually indigenous approaches to social work are developing (Gilbert, 2001). These are, at a minimum, attempting to engage with the manifest tensions between the profession and Australia's indigenous people. Mostly these occur in indigenous organisations – in the fields of health, housing, domestic violence, child welfare and legal services, for example – led by a growing band of indigenous social workers. While the formal face of social work, the professional association, publicly acknowledges its role in promoting social justice and reconciliation, the realwork is undertaken outside of the confines of conference keynotes and is documented in spaces other than the professional journals.

Briskman (2003) outlines some of the key theoretical insights developing in indigenous social work. Citing an Aotearoa New Zealand indigenous academic – Smith (1999) – she notes that an indigenous perspective in and on social work (and in fact in and on the indigenous experience) can only develop outside of and away from the totalising ontology and epistemology of Western knowledge. It does not, she argues, suggest a wholesale rejection, but more a judicious and deliberate engagement with, for example, critical social theory. Such engagement 'reads' theory and 'interprets' research from an indigenous worldview. Such a reading creates a nuanced and culturally sensitive interpretation which is able to challenge dominant readings, and in doing so, challenge the incipient colonising tendencies that accompany the development and deployment of white 'knowledge'. Ife (2001) argues robustly that traditional social work practice – where the worldview of the practitioner is assumed to be 'superior' – is in fact colonialist practice. Indigenous practice overtly rejects automatic assumptions of superiority in ways of knowing and follows that rejection with alternative assumptions which rewrite theory in culturally appropriate ways. It is a way of knowing which overturns, for example, child welfare practices which assume particular (Western) family patterns and child care arrangements. It is a way of knowing which explicitly encourages appreciation of the spiritual dimension in indigenous knowledge and experience, and its interpenetration with all aspects of daily living. It is a way of knowing which dictates culturally sensitive ways of communicating and culturally appropriate and respectful ways of engaging.

Nevertheless, while there is little doubt that indigenous social work is the Australian heir apparent to the radical tradition in social work, questions remain about the extent to which indigenous knowledge and indigenous social work practice have moved beyond a relatively small group of indigenous social workers and their supporters. Coupled with an unrelenting macro policy environment that deepens and entrenches Australia's already widespread institutional racism, any optimism that indigenous social work will revive the vigour of the radical tradition in social work must remain muted. Such a conclusion is, I suggest, supported by the findings of McMahon (2002) I referred to earlier – about the almost total silence about indigenous issues and indigenous practice in *Australian Social Work*. In acknowledging this sorry state in Australia, I cannot help but compare this country's efforts with our cousins across the Tasman, in Aotearoa New Zealand.

I fully acknowledge the limitations and inappropriateness of a white Australian talking about bi-cultural practice in Aotearoa New Zealand, but nevertheless dare to do so in the interests of helping others appreciate, even minimally, the achievements of that country and of its social workers – both Maori and non-Maori. If, at a minimum, it turns the gaze of social workers from other parts of the world on Aotearoa New Zealand, then my purpose is achieved – and this will be in spite of my manifest inadequacies.

The capacity for social workers, both Maori and non-Maori to respond proactively, to work in partnership and to promote anti-colonial bi-cultural practice draws much of its sustenance from the 'raging fires of Te Tiriti o Waitangi' (the Treaty of Waitangi) (Ruwhiu, 2001, p. 55; Oliver, 1988). In effect, interpretations of the Treaty has provided a powerful framework which, over time, has pushed Aotearoa New Zealand society and Aotearoa New Zealand social work to engage with the herculean task of fully recognising Maori as equal participants in and contributors to cross-cultural process in virtually every area of activity and engagement (see, for example, Mataira, 1985; Matahaere-Atariki and Shannon, 1999; Webber-Dreadon, 1999; Walker, 2002).

Ruwhiu (2001), along with Matahaere-Atariki *et al.*, (2001), argue that there are several aspects emerging from the Treaty that have impacted on social work. It has enabled the legitimisation of Maori conceptual, theoretical and practice wisdom/experiences as the basis for social work action with Maori. It has overtly challenged non-Maori social workers to participate fully as Treaty partners in developing Treaty-based practice. It informs all curricula and shapes actual practices. He also argues that Treaty-based bi-cultural practice has developed in specific interaction with a series of principles, or what he calls 'recognition points'. The first of these is the recognition that history speaks – that historical patterns of inter-racial power relations between Maori and non-Maori become a central plank for appreciating the present. The second point of recognition is that which understands the power of words – specifically words which represent key constructs to Maori – for example the notion of *mana* (power or prestige) – a core construct which acts as 'cultural adhesive that cements together those various dimensions (spiritual, natural, human) of Maori culture and society' (Ruwhiu, 2001, p. 60). The third recognition point centres on the notion of well-being – itself a multi-faceted acknowledgement of the multidimensional nature of Maori spirituality – a spirituality which permeates all aspects of Maori life and which is drawn from membership of Maori society with all of its genealogical inheritance and tradition.

Drawing all of the themes and insights arising from bi-cultural practice in Aotearoa New Zealand is, of course, impossible in this instance. That said, the preceding paragraphs have, I hope, given a glimpse of the richness of this form of social work practice, a richness which I believe speaks more broadly than Aotearoa New Zealand. It certainly speaks to the ongoing shame of Australian welfare practices with indigenous people. In effect, it speaks to any context where social workers and indigenous people are trying to reach some form of mutual appreciation of how to engage with each other. It is, as I have suggested throughout, the natural heir to the radical tradition in the post-colonial world and given the scope of that world, it is an heir whose legitimacy and integrity spans the North–South and East–West divides which so bedevil human progress on a global and local level.

Conclusion

Running through this chapter is the notion that contemporary radical practice – as represented by critical social work – is a development more illusory than substantive. In Part One, I discussed the modern version of radical social work as that developed in the 1970s and the 1980s, revealing a brave history and a proud tradition. In discussing the Green Bans, for example, I was able to illustrate a unique Australian contribution – the alliance between radical practitioners and the militant wing of the trade union movement. To a lesser extent, the same may be said about the rise of the femocrats in the 1980s. However, I also proposed the notion that the existence of radical practice was largely a function of the state – in that the state either created the spaces or the habitat for radical social work through the promotion of social democratically-informed social policies, or it tolerated radical activities through a stance that could be described as benign neglect. Either way, once the state shifted its policy orientation (to neo-liberalism), and once its neglectful approach to welfare was replaced with the active engagement (through New Public Management), the spaces for radical practice, at first gradually and then with increasingly rapidity, disappeared.

Recapitulating my arguments about the limitations of contemporary critical social work, the seeming heir apparent to the radical tradition, I suggested that these are both intellectual and practical. As such, I concluded that in this instance, the emperor (or the worker) has no clothes (or at a minimum, is not stoutly shod). Rather, I have, throughout, suggested that indigenous forms of practice, both in Australia but more importantly in Aotearoa New Zealand, have more to offer. Perhaps what they have to say is not immediately relevant to the entire world, but it has something of great significance to say to those parts still suffering from the impact of colonial and post-colonial capitalist practices. Further (and perhaps most importantly of all), the development of bi-cultural social work provides a model of how an essentially Western, structuralist and modernist analysis and set of practices can be indigenised and hence, transformed.

Note

1   Its utility is predominantly to be found in its ethics, in that the latter Foucault suggests that in an era such as the current one – when neo-liberalism is hegemonic – that any critique which destabilises and problematises hegemonic ideology and associated sets of practices – is sufficient of itself because it opens up the possibility of alternatives.

Chapter 3

Radical Social Work Traditions in Canada: Examining the Quebec Community Movement

Jill Hanley and Eric Shragge

Introduction

Radical social work began to appear as a concept in the Canadian literature and in social work education, as in many other places, in the mid-to late 1970s. There were two inter-related directions in the literature. The first was a critique of and an analysis of the mainstream forms of social work practice. The second was prescriptive and argued for a 'radical' practice and looked to document examples of alternatives to the dominant models. Most of the debate was within the schools of social work with an emphasis placed on analysis and prescription. Documenting practice, however, was more difficult. 'Radical practice' was hard to find, particularly because social work organisations were increasingly institutionalised and the jobs were defined within a traditional professional framework.

One place where radical practice and experimentation did take place was in the field of community organisation. Social workers were not the only actors but many played significant roles. This chapter will draw on some of these experiences to discuss radical social work. We will focus on the province of Quebec for the most part. In Canada, the provincial government is the major player in health, social services and social development in general. Therefore, community development and organising interact with provincial bodies, simultaneously being shaped by and shaping a variety of policies and practices that have historically produced the community sector in Quebec. We will trace the complex history of the evolution of the community sector from its origins as a radical practice, involving many social workers, to its recognition and stability in a neo-liberal context. Finally we will examine some new practices that have contributed to a radicalisation, once again involving social workers and social work students.

To begin we will raise issues about the radical social work tradition and whether there is any specific Canadian contribution. We will then turn to community organisation practice, examining several Quebec cases, specifically around welfare rights and cooperative housing. We will look at the links and the importance of wider social movements to the emergence of these practices. We will explore the transformation of the community sector in the context of a neo-liberal policy environment, and a renewal of oppositional practices in the context of what has been referred to as the anti-globalisation movement.

Radical social work in the Canadian literature

Social work literature in Canada has followed larger international trends in arguing for both a radical/critical analysis of social work and promoting a practice that challenges relations of domination and oppression. In this section, we will trace some of the basic themes and raise some questions about the practice of radical social work.

The early radical social work analysis was influenced by the renewal of Marxism in the mid-to late 1970s. Bookbinder (1981) provides an example of a critical analysis of social work, and argued that the social service system in Canada functions as a means of supporting inequality. He applied a Marxist analysis of the state to social services, arguing that these function to maintain social legitimation and promote capital accumulation. Further, social services are involved in relations of social control and inequality such as the treatment of women, labelling of deviants and personal adjustment rather than wider social change. This level of critique left little room for practice, either at the level of the individual or the community. The analysis implied the necessity of revolutionary change and social work, because of its location in either social agencies or in small community agencies, could only be a small player in this process. This analysis, although prominent in that period, had little impact in understanding the complexities of practice and its possibilities and was not sympathetic to the daily struggles of the social workers who had to respond to the daily consequences and expressions of life such as poverty.

Maurice Moreau (1979), who made an important contribution to advancing radical social work, was more sympathetic to the daily struggles of social agency workers. He used the term 'structural social work'. He argued:

> The central concern of structural social work is power, both personal and political. The key assessment question is the relationship between a client's 'personal' problems, dominant ideology and his material conditions in the class structure. Structural social work is concerned with the ways in which the rich and powerful in society define and constrain the poor and the less powerful – the ways in which whites define native peoples and blacks, men define women, heterosexuals define homosexuals, adults define children, the young define the aged, and the so-called normal people define the world of the deviant. (Moreau,1979, p. 78)

As opposed to Marxist analysis and critique of social work, Moreau saw many levels of oppression that included but were not limited to the structures of social class. His work is a precursor to anti-oppression work, which examines a variety of intersecting forms of domination (Bishop, 1994). Moreau saw individual work as a crucial element in the process of social change. He described the goals of a structural approach as follows:

> The central goal of structural social work is to help clients develop social praxis – that is, to help them to critically reflect on their personal/political situation and to develop consequent personal and political plans of action. (Moreau, 1979, p. 82)

Carniol (1990) draws on Moreau's work and describes three levels for radical practice. These are ' ... a) helping with immediate resources; b) helping with clients' feelings, ideas, and behaviours and c) helping with the efforts for change within social movements' (Carniol, 1990, p. 128).

The links with social movements are a central element and the work of the social worker is to help people to secure both the material and emotional conditions to participate in wider social struggles. In Wharf's edited book, *Social Work and Social Change in Canada* (1990), authors examine the relationship between social work and the women's, First Nations, and labour movements. The contribution of the women's movement is central to this collection of essays, particularly because of the connections of the personal to the political. Gilroy (1990, p. 54) reiterates the importance of this theme as central for radical social work:

> 'The personal is political', a famous slogan of the women's movement, captures another unifying theme. Women began to see that problems such as physical abuse, which had been considered as individual and unique, were in fact common and widespread, and were rooted in women's social and political subordination. 'Political' is used here in the sense of having to do with power.

In relation to Aboriginal people in Canada, it is important to acknowledge the contribution of social work to their oppression and the assimilation strategies (attempted cultural genocide) of government and the church. Social work was part of the colonial structures and relationships. However, many Aboriginal social workers and their allies have engaged in the struggle for reclaiming and building local institutions to address social issues such as child welfare. This has been a key question in Canadian social work literature, particularly relating to how non-Aboriginal social workers can act as allies and participate in supporting the redressing of these historical injustices (Howse and Stalwick, 1990; Wharf, 1992; Brown, *et al.*, 2002). This question is part of the issue of race and oppression and the roles played by social work in perpetuating and challenging these relations.

We have outlined some of the perspectives on radical social work in Canada. This introduction is not comprehensive but outlines the central issues of class, gender and race, and the links between personal and social struggles. Wharf's (1990) book cited above, examines some of the ways in which social workers can move towards and contribute to a process of progressive social change. However, those writing and teaching radical social work in universities have had to face the limits of the institutions that employ their idealistic graduates. Wharf makes the following acknowledgement of this problem:

> For social work, the struggle is complicated by the fact that the profession is now a prisoner of its own reforms. Social workers are largely employed by state departments, which are large, hierarchical organisations providing inadequate benefits and services. These organisations are controlled by politicians and policy-makers who cherish the status-quo. (1990, p. 145)

The issue raised here is that social work is not an autonomous profession in which the work is defined independently of the institutions in which social workers are employed. There is no continuity between the calls for radical analysis and action made by academics in schools of social work versus the actual mainstream practice facing the majority of graduates. Further, there is little evidence of a radical practice actually taking place within these agencies. What are the relationships between radical social work education and institutional practice? Large social agencies are removed from broader social struggles and practices of social change taking place. They must follow specific mandates and are often overwhelmed with just that. Many individual social workers may be connected to political work and social justice movements but this tends to be outside of their official roles in their 'day jobs'.

One place where it is possible to come across radical social work practice is outside of the institutional framework. If we are looking for a practice that emphasises an individual's material needs, personal transformation, and links to social movements, perhaps the place to look is in community organisations. A radical practice concerns people having power and control over institutions that affect their lives and the ability to have some collective control over wider social processes. All of these imply collective action and organisation.

In the rest of this chapter, we will examine the role of community organisations as examples of radical practice that work to educate, empower, mobilise and advocate for the poor and other oppressed groups in our society. However, we will also acknowledge and describe the process of the institutionalisation of these organisations in Quebec.

Finally we will explore the impact of globalisation and the emergence of new movements and practices that are similar to some of the earlier practices that defined the orientation of the community movement in Quebec.

Community organising as radical practice: two case studies

The history of the community movement in Quebec has been documented extensively (Hamel, 1991; Panet-Raymond & Mayer, 1997; Shragge, 2003). Authors generally agree that it has progressed through several important stages. From the 1960s, there was a shift from local charitable services to a protest movement contesting social and urban policies, organising poor people – especially tenants and welfare recipients – and carrying out political education through citizens' committees. It was committed to grassroots democracy, and its manifestos and positions were explicitly anti-capitalist. At the same time, there were a variety of innovative services such as health clinics, daycare centres, and food cooperatives that were put in place. These organisations were governed through new forms of direct and/or participatory democracy. The legacy from this period is a tradition of local democracy in community-based organisations and a capacity to innovate and to create new solutions to many social problems.

Two different yet overlapping practices were launched in this period. The first was the organising of people to take action on specific issues, making claims on governments for better programmes or expanded benefits or services. The second was the creation of alternative services. Both types of strategies were prevalent in poor and working-class neighbourhoods in Montreal in the late 1960s and early 1970s. The commonalties of these approaches were the putting in place of organisations democratically controlled by local citizens. Through two case studies – welfare rights organising and housing cooperatives – we will illustrate the practices in this period and the roles of community organisers, many of whom were social workers.

The claim that this is radical social work remains, however, debatable, as we can see in the case of the welfare rights organising. The lead organisers of the welfare rights organisation we will present were social workers by training and came out of schools of social work. However, the ideologies and training of those programmes at the time were not supportive of their work in the late 1960s and early 1970s. Thus, we have to see the importance of social workers *despite* their training. Further, there were other political activists and welfare recipients involved in the development of the organisation who had little to do with social work and who often characterised social workers as 'baby snatchers'. Thus, it is important to acknowledge the role of certain social workers in the organising of the late 1960s and early 1970s but, at the same time, there were many tensions that will be illustrated below. The experience of welfare rights organising in Montreal did have an impact on social work education as students began to volunteer, support and do their field placements with these organisations.

The welfare rights movement: protest and contestation

The welfare rights movement was organised in both English and French communities in Montreal during the late 1960s and early 1970s. These organisations demanded an end to the discretionary powers of welfare agents and benefits as social rights. Welfare recipients also demanded a place at the table, in order to participate in decisions that affected their lives in social agencies and government policy discussions. The movement and the local organisations that grew out of it were autonomous from the state, made demands on it, and exerted pressure so that these demands could be met (Kruzynski and Shragge, 1999). The welfare rights organisations were supported by a variety of grants and foundations. Their autonomy was protected by the direct involvement of citizens, the diversity of their funding, and their outsider status in relation to state policy and service delivery. Both became transformed. The welfare rights movement ran its course as a social movement and some groups remain as advocacy and service groups.

The English-speaking welfare rights organisation, Greater Montreal Anti-Poverty Coordinating Committee (GMAPCC) was a coalition of local citizens' groups composed of the poor themselves, mainly welfare recipients.[1] Citizens from five welfare rights committees and two-full time organisers participated in the founding of the organisation in the spring of 1970 (Benello, 1972) with other neighbourhood anti-poverty groups subsequently becoming members. GMAPCC's initial mandate was one of community organising around welfare rights and advocacy:

> [GMAPCC taught] people the power of group participation through successful actions against the welfare office. It [created] a strong body of informed welfare recipients who [were] in a position to demand changes from the government over the laws which concerned their lives. (PERM, 1971)

By 1972, GMAPCC had adopted a statement of principles that covered a broad range of topics: jobs and income, housing and urban renewal, education, justice, consumer protection, mass media, democracy, women, racism, the elderly, workers and unions, language and nationalism, and big business (GMAPCC, 1972). These positions advocated redistribution of income and wealth and strong government action to reach these objectives.

GMAPCC's mandate was carried out in a number of ways. It used confrontational tactics towards winnable objectives, including disruptive tactics such as occupations, sit-ins and demonstrations of welfare offices and other institutions (Shragge, 1994). Individual advocacy was used as a way of ensuring that individuals' rights were protected from the abusive ways of the welfare institution. Advocates – citizens who were trained in the rules of the law – would accompany welfare recipients to the welfare office to demand social assistance. One of the main roles of the resource people within GMAPCC (often social workers) was to seek out, politicise and train local leadership. This was accomplished in a variety of ways such as 'kitchen meetings' where interested citizens from a particular neighbourhood would meet with the resource people to discuss issues of concern to poor people in their area. The goal of these meetings was to get citizens to participate in GMAPCC actions, and to eventually form their own local citizens' group. Education through workshops was developed to give the participants the tools with which to organise and build groups. Topics included the 'dos and don'ts' of organising, negotiating, block organising, press, tactics, and power structures.

GMAPCC enjoyed many victories around welfare rights and had a significant impact on the people who participated in its development. Thus, through their involvement in GMAPCC, not only did they have a direct impact on government policy and practice but welfare recipients had become active citizens. The poor were not 'given' rights; rather, they had claimed them. Organisations like GMAPCC argued that reform from above was not acceptable unless the poor and others who are affected by change were to have a voice in these processes. This period marks the beginning of the principle of participation of many groups in social policy development and implementation. But it is important to remember that this voice was won through organising and struggle. If the struggle is forgotten, and there is not an active participation, then the voices become weakened. Tokenism then becomes the result of representation without organisation. Thus, effective representation implies active engagement of the poor people themselves.

GMAPCC is an example of the recasting of protest movements in that period. GMAPCC played a role in the struggle for improved conditions for welfare recipients. It was not solely responsible for the gains made in that period, but it was part of a wider social movement that was pushing for social change in a period of economic expansion and social reform.

We can see from this example that radical practice was organising people who did not have a voice in the political process. The role of social workers was that of community organisers who supported the process and played an educational role. The student and the New Left movements of the period influenced some of those involved. The emphasis on participatory and direct democracy as well as non-hierarchical structures encouraged welfare recipients to have their own spokespeople and take the formal leadership of the organisations. However, even with the formal structures giving welfare activists the leadership, there were tensions because organisers still had a lot of power and influence.

Kruzynski's research (2004) illustrates this tension. She interviewed women who were active in these organisations. For many of these women, an 'outside agitator' who raised questions and issues was the first to organise them and encourage their participation and leadership. The women discussed the ambiguities of this relationship and the conflicting feelings about these outsiders. On the one hand, the women reported seeing their own power through the politics, skills and knowledge that the outsiders brought and how these opened possibilities for local residents. On the other hand, they saw relations with these outsiders as controlling and not allowing local people to be in real leadership positions. We can see both the importance and the tensions implicit in the roles of social workers and organisers. The social movements of the period, both the New Left and the women's movement, contributed ideas and energy for the organisers. However, like many successful protest movements, GMAPCC lasted only a few years and the organisers went on to build on that base and broaden their constituency.

Housing cooperatives: building alternatives

In the late 1960s, housing affordability was an important issue in Canada and, although public housing construction was at its height, government provisioning did not seem to be providing all the answers. In 1969, a federal task force confirmed that 'housing is a universal need, yet the private market on which Canadians have relied is anything but universal in its present scope and applications' (Federal Task Force on Housing and Urban Development, 1969, p.14) yet the government seemed unable to fill the void.

Housing advocate groups, with which social workers were sometimes involved (especially at the community level) were already looking for alternatives to the state-owned and managed public housing, often seen as overly bureaucratic and controlling. In March 1968, the Co-operative Union of Canada, the Canadian Union of Students and the Canadian Labour Congress had come together to form the Co-operative Housing Foundation (CHF), the first national organisation for the co-operative housing movement (Chouinard, 1990), advocating a form of social housing that was owned and managed collectively by the tenants.

Its proponents argued that cooperative housing represented an opportunity to challenge the market mechanism that traditionally controls people's access to housing. Cooperative housing is not a commodity but rather a community good that is democratically controlled, creating a parallel space for organising and solidarity within a market-dominated world. With mandates to bring together people who tend to be marginalised within broader society, a mandate which social workers helped to fulfil through community-organising initiatives, cooperative housing was hoped to become an alternative power base. Once people had settled their fundamental need for, and also right to, housing, cooperatives could serve as a place for learning skills and developing analysis that could be applied to other social struggles.

The CHF's pressure on the federal government over the next few years would change the direction of Canadian housing policy. In the early

1970s, economic conditions in Canada coalesced to create significant demand for social (that is, collectively owned, non-profit) housing. Unready to withdraw from housing provision, federal officials became interested in reducing the state's financial obligations (Morin and Dansereau, 1990, p.14) and in addressing the stigma and public concerns related to the 'concentration of poverty' created by large-scale public housing projects (Hulchanski, 1988, p. 20).

Partly in response to negotiations with the CHF – but also under pressure from the social democrat New Democratic Party (NDP) which held the balance of power in Parliament at the time (Hulchanski, 1993) – 1973 amendments to the National Housing Act changed the funding structures for public housing and allowed third-sector, or non-profit, housing initiatives to benefit from federal support (Carter, 1997). Housing co-operatives and housing owned and managed by non-profit organisations became important new providers of affordable housing.

On the local level, housing organising – in which social workers and social work students were directly involved – was also picking up. During the late 1960s and early 1970s, Montreal's urban movements, notably the Front d'action politique (FRAP), focused their efforts on the democratisation of municipal structures. Their strategy of organising on the neighbourhood level quickly led them into housing issues, particularly within the context of the ruling municipal Civic Party's lustre for urban renewal. Raising the issues of the concentration of property, the profit motive of landlords, the way that rent increases outstripped salary increases and the destruction of working-class housing and neighbourhoods for the construction of highways and highrises, the FRAP put forward the analysis that housing inequities were at once social and ethnic:

> ...We argue that there are two cities in Montreal:
> A **minority** of people, mostly Anglophone, own and control the economy (at the stock exchange, the factory, the office, the cinema and our neighbourhoods...)
> And a vast **majority**, mostly workers and tenants, and mostly among francophone and immigrant Montrealers.
> (FRAP, 1970, p. 21; emphasis original)

The early 1970s saw the creation of citizens' committees in most working-class neighbourhoods of Montreal and housing remained one of their central concerns. Tenants' association and local housing advocates shared many of their demands with FRAP: the renovation (rather than the clearance) of older working-class neighbourhoods; citizen participation in decision-making around urban planning, regulation of the private housing market and the management of social housing; stronger protections of tenants by the Rental Board; increased construction of social housing (FRAP, 1970, p. 55).

By the mid-1970s, the development of third-sector housing (cooperatives and community housing) was in full swing, with the effort to create the Milton Park Cooperative seen by many as a decisive struggle. Many central working-class neighbourhoods, such as Pointe-St-Charles, St-Henri, Little Burgundy, Centre-Sud and Hochelaga-Maisonneuve, were transformed, with the support of social work-educated community organisers, in terms of their housing stock through the 1970s and 1980s. The combination of available land, destruction of the old housing stock (fires, urban renewal) and the mobilisation of local citizens led to the construction or renovation of a great number of cooperative, community and public housing in these neighbourhoods. The organising of tenants around this housing was, and continues to be, an important source of power in these neighbourhoods.

Also during this period, towards the end of the 1970s, the 'institution' of neighbourhood-based housing committees was being consolidated. Accompanying this consolidation of neighbourhood housing committees was the creation of coalition organisations that pooled the efforts for changes around tenants' rights, social housing and urban renewal policies. The Quebec Coalition of Housing Committees and Tenants' Associations (RCLALQ) and the Popular Action Front for Urban Renewal (FRAPRU) both saw the light of day in the late 1970s.

In the 1980s, the community economic development approach began to take hold as governments began to slowly withdraw from social provisioning. In the housing sector, this was reflected through the growing sophistication of non-profit housing development and management organisations that were taking on the development of social housing. A division developed between those organisations that adopted this development approach, often with a preference for cooperative housing, and those who remained focused on tenants' rights and pressure tactics to improve housing policy. In the 1990s, with the withdrawal of the federal government from social housing development, the general trend towards 'public/private partnerships' and the official sanctioning of the 'social economy', saw an exacerbation of this split.

From opposition to service provision: becoming a player

From the case studies, we can see the important role that some social workers played in the emergence of a radical community practice through organising work and creating social alternatives. However, this practice began to shift towards service provision and the gradual professionalisation of community organisations. Often social workers played a role in initiating these social innovations and as these organisations became stable and professionalised, they provided jobs for social workers. Some of these new services were connected to wider social movements. For example, the women's movement created both shelters and rape crisis centres (Beaudry, 1984; Lamoureux, 1990). These new services embodied the values and political goals of the wider movement. Further, staff and volunteers of the shelters and rape crisis centres organised coalitions to represent the organisations, demanded recognition and support from the government, and challenged its policy directions. They succeeded in these struggles and became a significant service in communities across the province.

Similar processes occurred in other types of services as the community sector gained both power and expertise in representing its interests. At a local level, *Tables de concertation* or community councils were organised to bring local groups together to discuss common concerns (Lamoureux *et al.*, 2002). As a consequence, and over the period from the late 1970s through to the mid-1980s, community organisations, from the bottom up, formed the capacity to represent themselves and negotiate with both regional and provincial bodies on issues of funding and service provision. Throughout the 1980s the services expanded and became the primary activity of the community sector. These became increasingly professionalised, insofar as a clear division between service providers and clients was evident. Democratic practice was limited to participation on boards of directors and real power tended to rest in the hands of service providers.

Over the years, the government has recognised the expertise of community organisations. However, the power is not equal. Further, the leadership of these organisations has developed its skill and expertise in lobbying and influencing locally elected politicians and civil servants, who often started their careers in community organisations. Thus, the community sector achieved an ambiguous relation with the provincial government. Some groups still mobilised but, for the most part, the representatives of organisations – board members and staff – publicly represented the needs and interests of those they served. At other times, community organisations entered into conflict with the provincial government to protect or enhance their services and enlarge their roles and budgets. Finally, the dominant relation is perhaps that of a junior partner in service provision, with an increasingly visible role and corresponding recognition by the government.

The opposition to government policies continued to come from social movements, particularly women's organisations, with support for these campaigns coming from the community sector. Thus, there is a tension between the service and oppositional roles in the community sector. For these social actors, the tension is between the recognition by the state of a new logic of intervention, and their ability to keep at arm's length the state's local development apparatus and maintain some autonomy from it. Some groups were able to build creative, participatory alternatives that expanded democratic spheres at the local level. Others simply became managers of social programmes. However, in these processes, the community sector continued down the path of constructing more collaborative relations with government; thus reducing its critical voice.

With the economic crisis of the 1980s, shifts occurred. As with most Western governments, the first response of both the provincial-level Parti Quebecois and the federal-level Liberals was to reduce its expenses through cutbacks in government services. Along with these cutbacks came a downloading of services to the community sector. This was made possible, as we mentioned earlier, by the growing professionalisation and institutionalisation of that sector. The provincial government embarked on a policy of regionalisation, which has created a number of institutions that administer health, social services, employment and economic development programmes. These have reduced centralised power and to a limited degree have encouraged local participation in institutions and services. The model of decentralisation has provided some flexibility at the regional level, but ultimately, the policies, programmes and budgets are decided centrally. One key element is that community organisations had to apply to these regional bodies for their funds. Therefore, a key relationship for local organisations is with the provincial bodies that have shaped their activities through these processes. Further, the provincial government – through decentralisation – gave regional planning bodies powers in the allocation of resources to community and voluntary organisations. As a consequence, a mixed model developed in which the provincial government determines policy and programme direction while funding regional and local instances to carry out these directives with some flexibility. These changes have brought pressures on the community sector to become a sub-contractor of government services. The community organisation tradition of the 1960s and 1970s, based on opposition and the establishment of radical alternatives, had become transformed. These organisations, and the social workers employed within them, had become recognised by the provincial state and had begun to actively participate in service partnerships. As a sector, it was becoming highly structured and able to negotiate ongoing funding. These changes had emerged when the transformation of the late 1980s took place.

With the deepening crisis of employment and the closing of traditional industries in the 1980s, these organisations, along with their allies in the union movement, faced the following contradiction. They witnessed massive job loss; yet the conditions of the new jobs were inferior to what was lived in the earlier period. Using their traditions of social solidarity, community groups and unions tried to find ways to confront the increased poverty faced by the working class. New partnerships between the private sector, the unions, the community and the state were forged in order to find ways out of the crisis. Consensus building was designed to improve the deteriorating social and economic conditions of post-Fordist capitalism. It focused on local action and specific short-term solutions. Many organisations in the community sector entered into economic development and employability programmes. These were expressed in a variety of forms, including integrating workfare measures as part of the activities of the community initiatives. Further, the community sector adopted the ideology of social integration through wage labour as the dominant way of approaching poverty and social exclusion. This 'employability' approach created even more job opportunities for social workers.

Community organisations in Quebec play an active role in managing the problems associated with the transitions described above. Their growing professionalism and knowledge of local problems combined with their ability to use innovative strategies have contributed to their expertise. The actors in community organisations have used this approach to formulate new approaches to labour market inclusion. Often the practices begin with grassroots initiatives but then become recognised and supported by the state and become regularised and absorbed as state-community policy. One example of the type of organisation that has gone through this process is youth employment initiatives. These types of organisations began in a couple of neighbourhoods as a way to confront youth unemployment in the 1980s but grew to be present across the province. They integrate business development with training for the labour market (usually low-wage precarious work) and are called '*Entreprises d'insertions*'. We have used the expression 'training businesses' as an English translation in other work, but this translation is lacking because it does not include the dimension of inclusion and psychosocial intervention. These businesses go beyond training, but are primarily concerned with – and increasing evaluated according to – their success in job placement. The training is for people receiving social welfare, is short-term – less than a year – and provides both concrete skills and work readiness. They tend to be in the service sector and the job placements are in the low-wage sector including catering, cleaning and recycling. A couple of them are in slightly more skilled areas, but the training lacks professional credentials. At the same time as these are training businesses, many provide a community service (for example, community restaurants) or a product for that sector (for example, furniture for daycare centres).

Until its defeat in 2003, the Parti Quebecois provincial government had initiated a policy in which the community sector was to receive greater recognition and systematic support. Under the Secretariat for Autonomous Community Action (SACA), and a related inter-ministerial committee, policy for the sector was to be decided. The community sector itself was represented by an Advisory Committee for Autonomous Community Action. This committee was composed of representatives of 20 sectors and more than 130 provincial, regional and local coalitions or 'regroupements'. These structures demonstrate the way that the community sector has influenced, and is simultaneously shaped, by state policy.

The formalisation of representation allows organisations to defend their self-interest and influence policy on funding and conditions for it. The push back from the government is to define with increasing force a sub-contractual relationship between community organisations and various ministries, particularly those involved in the health social services and regional development, as the provincial government has downloaded specific functions to community organisations. For the community sector, this recognition of its professionalism promises greater stability but narrows its functions and reduces its autonomy. These issues are not resolved and with the election of a Liberal government in 2003 they are in flux once again. Of particular note is that the new government has removed the term 'Autonomous' from the name of the Secretariat. The structuring of the community sector and its relationship to the provincial government shapes the way that the local-level organisations have been able to extend their influence and democratise decision-making that affects their own support and functioning.

What are the consequences of these changes for radical social work or community development and organising? The professionalism has created opportunities and many social workers have turned to community organisations rather than state agencies for jobs. The working conditions are usually inferior to unionised and stable government jobs but often are more interesting and allow greater creativity and autonomy. However, most of the work is limited to direct service or project development. The conditions attached to funding reduce flexibility and demand measurable outcomes rather than qualitative evaluation. All of the organisations have a formal democratic structure with an elected board of directors by membership, but often these are highly routinised events. The emphasis on service provision has created relations of worker to client. Further, the pressures of everyday service work with organisations that have too few resources to fulfil their mandates have, as a consequence, kept them focused on service provision.

For the many organisations that have gone down this route, the organising processes have disappeared from their agendas. There are times when the service providers take public positions and advocate either for the interests of their organisations (for example, for better financial support) or the needs of their clients (for example, for improvements to social policy). This advocacy takes place through the 'regroupements' discussed above. However, to dismiss the radical or oppositional dimension of the community is too simple. Many of the employees and board members of the organisations are active in wider social movements and left-wing political parties, and participate in events that involve broad mobilisation such as cutbacks in state services or anti-war activities.

Community organisations: inside and outside

From the previous discussion, we can see that with growth and 'maturity' the community sector in Quebec, and the social workers within it, have lost much of their radical edge. Success has brought both increases in official recognition and participation as a 'partner' within social structures and some decision-making bodies at the local level. Although funding for some groups have been stabilised, it is still inadequate given the responsibilities taken on by these organisations. The impetus for change and mobilisation in opposition to government policies comes from either short-lived coalitions of community organisations or social movements. In the case of the former, recent examples have been the mobilisation against government policies aimed at 're-engineering' the state, implying cutbacks and privatisation of some state programmes. We will explore the latter case – social movements and new community initiatives – as a way of looking at new forms of radical practice.

International migration is one of the expressions of globalisation. Canada's recent immigrants, particularly since the early 1980s, have been from the Southern Hemisphere and their arrival has changed the racial composition of the large cities where they have settled. Despite high levels of education, they find themselves at the bottom of the labour market, earning less than native-born Canadians (except Aboriginal peoples). Canada benefits from its ecomicially-oriented immigration policies, such as the Live-In Caregiver Program (LCP) that imports domestic workers, mainly from the Philippines and often with training in fields such as nursing, to work in the homes of richer Canadians. In addition, linked to international destabilisation and local warfare, many refugees have made their way to Canada and face increasingly tough post-9/11 security regulations and deportations. On the opposition side, as in many other places, the anti-globalisation movement has been taking on issues of trade liberalisation and related policy changes. Many young activists became active in these struggles and became politicised through them. Both immigration and 'anti-globalisation' activism have converged in new forms of radical practice.

Both immigrants and refugees have begun to organise and have found allies in younger activists, some from immigrant backgrounds themselves. We will briefly present three examples: the Immigrant Workers' Centre (IWC), the March 8th Action and Coordination Committee of Women of Diverse Origins (March 8th Committee) and Solidarity Across Borders. These groups stand outside of the mainstream of the community sector and their politics explicitly challenge dominant ideologies. There are overlaps and links between these groups, and they provide examples of the intersection of community and social movements, local organising with a global consciousness.

The IWC was founded in 2000 by two trade union organisers from the Philippines and several community activists. The centre provides education to immigrant workers on their labour rights, accompanies individuals who are challenging employers, and works on campaigns on issues such as the improvement of labour standards. In addition, the centre has been involved in a corporate campaign targeting a T-shirt manufacturer for closing a newly unionised factory in Montreal and expanding production in Honduras. The IWC has not pursued the route of many community organisations that have led to recognition and funding. It has not prioritised service over social change activities and has built alliances with younger activists and trade unions through cultural activities such as MayWorks. The IWC remains at an intersection between community organisations, social movements and trade unions. This position allows it to maintain its politics and receive support and alliances but its existence and budget is precarious. It is an outsider as a community organisation but has become a meeting place for immigrant organisations, labour unions and younger activists.

The March 8th Committee involves the IWC and other grassroots women's organisations from immigrant communities. The women from these groups organised an alternative event to mainstream March 8th events because they felt that neither their issues nor their presence was taken into account by more powerful Quebec women's organisations.

The committee has organised events and marches for International Women's Day, gradually attracting more people and interest from other organisations. The content has brought forward issues such as globalisation, migration and war, with themes like the war against women here and abroad. These events raise broad political and social issues with a profound critique of both Quebec society and international issues. The organising coalition of women from immigrant communities has pushed the analysis in the wider women's movement.

Solidarity Across Borders (SAB) grew out of the work of a number of anti-globalisation activists who became concerned about the high number of deportations of refugee claimants and entered into alliance with self-organised groups of these claimants from countries such as Algeria and Palestine. There are many levels of activity including supporting specific cases, mobilisation to challenge government policy, education through a newspaper, organising and supporting sanctuary in churches as a way of resisting deportation, and public campaigns. In June of 2005, it organised a march from Montreal to Ottawa to denounce government policy and carry out public education on refugee issues and the plight of people without permanent status in Canada. SAB links the global context with local issues and brings together younger activists and refugee claimants. It is high profile and has put its politics 'into the street' using direct action tactics to support individuals threatened with deportation.

The importance of these three examples is that they represent new forms of radical practice through the community and social movements and are at the same time marginal to the mainstream community sector and its organisations. The radicalism comes out of the connections with international perspectives as well as the underlying ideologies of its members.

Conclusion: renewal or marginalisation

In this chapter, we have traced the emergence of the community movement in Quebec and examined its evolution as a highly structured sector with a strong relationship to the Quebec government. However, we are not arguing that there is a discontinuity with its more 'radical' origins. There continue to be organisations of welfare recipients, who have contested and challenged government policies and promoted alternatives. In the field of housing, there are local organisations and their coalitions that have demanded continued government support for cooperatives and social housing. The legacy of mobilising behind demands or to defend rights continues; however, service, with professionalised staff who views people as clients, remains the dominant model of practice. People with social work training, although not named as social workers, often work in them as service providers. The professionalisation of the sector has benefited social workers and those in related occupations through the creation of jobs that are outside of government agencies. These jobs are usually poorly paid and unstable but provide greater autonomy and satisfaction than jobs in government social services. Many of the graduates of social work and related programmes do enter these jobs with a social critique and at times this provides the basis of participation in wider social struggles such as defending against cutbacks in service provision.

As has happened with mobilisations elsewhere, there was a radicalisation of many younger people associated with the anti-globalisation movement and with the massive demonstration in Quebec City in 2002. The challenge is how to take this radicalism into local work. The issue of international migration and related questions of work has been one of the foci of activity. Another not discussed here is initiatives related to fair trade and the environment. The experiences of many younger people who have participated in the World Social Forum and in international solidarity work is an important source of radical renewal both within social work but also in other related fields of development. They bring a critical perspective and a commitment to local work. Many have created their own forms of action and created a variety of social alternatives. These strategies of direct action and putting in place new forms of development are similar to the strategies used in the 1960s and 1970s discussed earlier in the chapter. At the same time, these projects tend to be on the periphery of the mainstream of community organisations and remain politically outside of them. These newer initiatives represent a radical renewal, and involve many younger activists including social workers. But, so far, at least, they do not seem to have had a large impact on the mainstream of the community sector.

Note

1 This section draws on an article written by Anna Kruzynski and Eric Shragge (1999). The information about GMAPCC comes from several sources. Documents have been gathered through a community/popular archives project in Pointe-St-Charles in Montreal, and interviews with activists were carried out during the years 1993 to 1999 as assignments in courses in the School of Social Work at McGill University.

Chapter 4

The Liberatory Tradition in Nicaraguan Social Work

Maureen G. Wilson and Iris Prado Hernández

Introduction

Social work came into its own in Nicaragua in the context of the dual influences of the *sandinista* popular revolutionary movement, and of the Latin American 'reconceptualisation movement' in social work. In contrast with the experience of Western countries, it is probably fair to say that in Nicaragua the liberatory tradition has been a dominant force in social work. This chapter will tell the story of the origins, development and challenges of liberatory praxis in Nicaraguan social work.

Against the backgrounds of the popular insurrection against the Somoza dictatorship, the period of revolutionary government, the return of neo-liberal hegemony, and of the influences of the Latin America-wide 'reconceptualisation movement' in social work, we will recount and examine a number of critical moments in the shaping of Nicaraguan social work. These will include the radical transformation of social work in the 1970s; the crisis following the 1979 s*andinista* victory, when a view initially prevailed that social work would no longer be needed; the critical moment in 1990 when, after a decade of the US proxy *contra* war and economic boycott, the *sandinista* government was thrown out of power; and the continuing challenge of maintaining a liberatory approach to social work in the context of the hegemony of neo-liberal globalism. This story is co-told by a Nicaraguan social worker and scholar who has been an active participant in these events and a Canadian colleague who lived in Nicaragua through several years of this process, working with the national school of social work.

The context: a tale of British, US and Canadian imperial adventures

When the *sandinista*-led popular insurrection toppled the US-installed Somoza dictatorship in 1979, Nicaragua had for 45 years been run virtually as a private fiefdom of the Somoza family. The US had a long-standing interest in Nicaragua, having considered it a potential site for a canal across the isthmus since at least the 1830s (Close, 1998, p. 14). With the 1849 California gold rush, the British-backed US financier Cornelius Vanderbilt established a business transporting East-coast Americans to California via Nicaragua. Shortly thereafter, J.P. Morgan set up a competing company to transport goldseekers across a railway in Panama.

The first episode of US military intervention in Nicaragua came in 1855 when the adventurer William Walker, in the pay of the US-backed Morgan group, entered the civil war which had been raging between Nicaraguan Liberals and the Conservative government, in order to topple the government and put Vanderbilt out of business. Walker's forces, called the Phalanx of American Immortals, entered the fray on the side of the Liberals, vanquishing the Conservatives and naming a puppet president. In the face of a declaration of war by the four Conservative governments of Central America, Walker in June 1856 had himself elected president and sought US support by reintroducing slavery, making English the country's official language, and offering large land grants to anyone who would join him. Still unable to maintain control in the face of additional opposition from Vanderbilt money and the British Navy, Walker and his troops exited the country under a truce arranged by the US Navy, returning home to a hero's welcome.

Following a 36-year period of Conservative dominance, a Liberal government came to power led by the nationalist José Santos Zelaya. Zelaya angered the US first by giving preference to British over US banks, and then by offering the Germans and Japanese rights to build a canal through his country. Thus, when Conservatives and dissident Liberals revolted in 1909, the US dispatched the marines to 'protect American lives and property' (Black, 1981, p. 8). When Conservative elements found themselves unable to restore peace and order, in 1912 the Conservative President Díaz asked the Marines to return to help him to defeat the Liberal insurgency. The Marines remained (with a brief interruption in 1925) until 1933 when the seven-year guerrilla war against the forces led by Augusto Cesar Sandino was ended. During this period treaties were signed giving the US exclusive rights in perpetuity to build a canal, and the Nicaraguan national debt was reorganised through US banks. Control of customs, postal services, railways, harbours and the national steamship company were placed under the control of US banks and administrators, and tax and electoral laws were rewritten in accordance with US wishes.

Canadian interests were also present in Nicaragua as early as the 1880s, when Canadians participated in the gold rush to the Miskito coast. By 1918 a number of Nicaragua's gold and silver mines were controlled by Canadian interests. During the 1930s Canadian mining companies and their US counterparts became 'the financial backbone of the Somoza regime', paying a proportion of their earnings directly to President Somoza (MacFarlane, 1989, p. 10). By the 1940s, the Canadian company Falconbridge had Nicaragua's largest and one of Latin America's most productive gold mines, the La Luz mine (Wilson and Whitmore, 2000).

Before leaving Nicaragua in 1933, the US turned over the Nicaraguan National Guard it had founded, trained and equipped to Nicaraguan officers, who were to be commanded by Anastasio Somoza Garcia, a nephew-in-law of the Liberal President Sacasa. Somoza arranged his own election to the presidency in 1936, and his family ruled Nicaragua for the next 43 years. The Somoza regime was extraordinarily vicious and corrupt[1]. With the growing international demand for cotton, coffee and sugar during this period, tens of thousands of peasants and small landholders had been forced off their land. These dislocated and dispossessed people then provided a cheap pool of seasonal labour for the expanding plantations. Many migrated to marginal existences in the cities.

When the Somoza dynasty fell in 1979 to the broadly-based popular insurrection led by the *sandinistas*, Nicaragua's annual Gross National Product (GNP) per capita was a very poorly distributed US $800. Most people had annual incomes of US $200 to US $300, while the cost of living was almost as high as that in the US. With half of the country's children dying before the age of five, life expectancy was 53 years – ten years less than that for Central America as a whole and 18 years shorter than that for Cuba. Half of the population was illiterate, and livestock were more likely to receive medical treatment than were peasants.

The economy was in ruins. The war and falling international commodity prices had drastically reduced agro-export earnings, the country's major source of foreign exchange, and the country's infrastructure had been badly damaged both in the fighting and in the massive bombing ordered by the departing dictator. Further, beginning in 1981 more than half of the national budget, and the labour of much of the nation's youth, were drained off by the US-sponsored *contra* war.

In spite of all of this, the new government moved immediately to address the population's desperate needs for access to education, health care, and land. As a result, the Nicaraguan revolution 'achieved more in five years than most pre-revolutionary Latin American countries had accomplished in decades' (Walker, 1985, p. 297). A massive literacy campaign quickly reduced the illiteracy rate from approximately half of the population to about ten per cent. Health care, which had previously been available largely only to the urban and the wealthy, was extended to the entire population, and measles, diphtheria and polio were virtually eliminated. These advances were acknowledged by both the World Health Organization and the United Nations Children's Fund (UNICEF) with the granting to Nicaragua of their awards for best health achievement in the Third World and in the United Nations Educational, Scientific and Cultural Organisation's (UNESCO's) unanimous choice of Nicaragua for its Grand Prize in recognition of the literacy crusade (Barry and Preusch, 1986). As Bradford Burns (1987, p. 294) noted:

> 'Despite the hardships, war, poverty, and errors, the revolution has provided the majority of Nicaraguans with access to education, health care, and land – three primary desires of the once dispossessed.'

Social work emerges in Nicaragua

The genesis of social work in Nicaragua is best understood in the context of the need of the state to respond to social problems emerging as a consequence of the contradictions of capitalism. In the Nicaraguan context this meant seeking to create and sustain the conditions required for production and reproduction of the labour force in an agro-exportation model of capitalist development, based in the production of coffee and cotton. Thus, in 1956 social security legislation was introduced, and the

Instituto Nicaragüense de Seguridad Social (INSS: the Nicaraguan Institute of Social Security) was created, with foreign-trained social workers, to implement this legislation and deliver the first social services.

Meanwhile in the Caribbean, the Cuban revolutionary forces were gaining momentum, and their 1959 victory was to threaten US interests in Latin America. This led the US to promote a model of development in the region intended to reduce social discontent and prevent further such revolutions. Thus, at a meeting in Punta del Este, Uruguay in 1961, the J.F. Kennedy administration's Alliance for Progress was created to advance the implementation of an approach to development that would avoid radical changes in existing socio-economic structures.

At this meeting the US delegation proposed the granting of US \$20 billion in credits to Latin American countries, to be used for the development of agriculture, industry, education and health care. The US proposal involved a plan to stimulate development in Latin America through the injection of massive foreign investment, which was expected to be associated with an increase in employment opportunities, more equitable distribution of national income, stabilisation of prices of basic products, reduction of infant mortality, improvement of public health services and housing, elimination of illiteracy and expansion of vocational, secondary and higher education (Wilson, 2003).

A number of social programmes were introduced in Nicaragua in the early 1960s to take advantage of funds available through the Alliance for Progress initiative. There was now a need for social workers to handle applicants for pensions and other social benefits, and a social work education programme was established in 1961 by the Nicaraguan Institute of Social Security (Téfel, *et al.*, 1985). In 1965, just before the first class of thirteen social workers had graduated, the programme was moved to the National Autonomous University of Nicaragua (UNAN), with a senior INSS official named Director of the School.

As Prado and Palacios (2005) note, the School's curriculum in these early days reflected a social policy designed to favour conditions for capital accumulation and the continued subordination of popular sectors by the dominant classes. In this context social workers, dedicated primarily to social assistance functions, were seen as ideologically neutral professionals. During this period they were engaged largely in palliative programmes, charged with distributing eyeglasses, clothing and food through INSS, the National Social Assistance Council (JNAPS) or religious organisations, or acting as functionaries in the administration of the corrupt and restrictive system of social security benefits (Téfel, *et al.*, 1985). In the practice of community development social workers worked within poor communities, through international organisations supported by the US government, to promote a non-confrontational approach to achieving a better life (ETS, 1985).

Within a very short time it had become apparent that the Alliance for Progress programmes were not delivering their promised results. The gap between rich and poor had widened, and throughout Latin America a heavy proportion of the disbursements went 'to military regimes that had overthrown constitutional governments' (Hansen, 1967, p. 1). Few of these benefits trickled down to the mass of the people, and in Nicaragua the new programmes were serving largely as a way of providing employment and opportunities for the personal enrichment of the Somoza elite and its middle-class allies (Téfel, *et al.*, 1985; Walker, 1985). There was a growing international demand for cotton during this period, and peasants were once again driven from their land[2]. The social service bureaucracy, which might have helped address the problems of the rural dislocation and rapid urbanisation resulting from this, was so hopelessly corrupt and inept that the problems of the poor were largely neglected.

The reconceptualisation movement

> El movimiento de reconceptualización constituyó y constituye el paso más relevante de la historia del trabajo social.[3]
>
> (José Paulo Netto, cited in Alayón, 2005, p. 15)

While forces were gathering in Nicaragua to overthrow the corrupt Somoza dictatorship, throughout Latin America social workers had been engaged in a re-examination of their roles and perspectives on practice, in a search for a social work more appropriate to the Latin American reality. Out of the combined influences of dependency theory, Marxist thought, the Cuban and other revolutionary guerrilla movements, liberation theology and the work of Brazilian educator Paulo Freire, there emerged what became known as the reconceptualisation movement in social work (Alayón, 2005, p. 10; Aquín, 2005, p. 23).

This reconceptualisation involved a new emphasis on the role of social work in the promotion of social change. In this model, social workers would work more directly with the poor, facilitating groups in analysing their own positions in the historical moments in which they live, and in determining courses of action for themselves. Thus, social workers would no longer see themselves as politically neutral, but rather as actively taking the side of the poor. In their search for perspectives more appropriate to their own reality, Nicaraguan social workers and educators were drawn to this perspective.

While the interpretation and manifestations of this 'reconceptualisation' varied from place to place in Latin America, this emerging general understanding of many Latin American social workers on the role of their profession in relation to the social formation is well set out by María del Carmen Mendoza Rangel (1986) in her work *Una Opción Metodológica para los Trabajadores Sociales*. As Mendoza Rangel observes, the professional attitudes and methods of intervention of social workers in Latin America have been closely related to the historical moments in which they have found themselves. Thus, in the early stages of capitalist development the emphasis of social workers has been on *social assistance*, with 'traditional' social work methods being applied in the forms of case work, group work and community work. Corresponding to the stage of advanced capitalism, the emphasis has been on *social security*, with the expansion of social programmes to cover a larger proportion of the population, and attempts at unification and integration of these programmes. Associated with this stage is an emphasis in social work methods on administration, supervision and research.

In the historical conjuncture of a social transformation to a new society, the emphasis in social work is on the promotion of *social change*. Here social workers recognise the need to work for change in the structure of the society, and they employ a dialectical method based on a 'scientific method/theory of knowledge'. This, Mendoza Rangel notes, is a 'collective' method, incorporating the knowledge of the social sciences and employing Friere's method of popular education, or 'education for critical consciousness' (Mendoza Rangel, 1986).

This movement began in the southern cone in the mid-1960s, and Nicaraguan social workers were to soon come in contact with these ideas. Their engagement in the development of this methodology drew further impetus from the return of colleagues from Chile following the 1973 overthrow of the government of Salvador Allende (Prado and Palacios, 2005).

The transformation of Nicaraguan social work

In Nicaragua, the radical transformation of social work during this time was strongly rooted in and influenced by the broad-based *sandinista* popular movement, which aimed to replace the corrupt US-backed Somoza regime with a more egalitarian society based on social justice, self-determination, and independence from the hegemony of the US. This growing movement united a variety of social sectors, with youth and students and faculty of the universities prominent among these. Nicaraguan social workers – students, professors and practitioners alike – played very active roles in the prolonged struggle to topple the Somoza dictatorship, with important heroes and martyrs of the popular insurrection coming from among their ranks. This was fertile ground for the ideas of the reconceptualisation movement.

By 1969, dissatisfaction had begun to manifest itself among Nicaraguan students and teachers with respect to the appropriateness of their programme of social work education. In 1970 faculty members held a first seminar on reconceptualisation and between 1971 and 1973, through extensive processes of discussion, significant changes were implemented in the programme of study. In 1973, some professors who insisted upon a traditional 'social assistance' emphasis in social work were asked to resign and new professors – mostly sociologists – were hired who were to have an important influence in the search for a redefinition of social work that would be appropriate to Nicaraguan reality.

Then together, students and professors embarked upon the task of a complete review of the programme of social work education. After a term of intensive work a new plan of studies was produced, based upon a dramatically altered conception of the profession. It reflected a marked shift away from the blind *tecnicismo* that had characterised the School's curriculum throughout its first thirteen years of existence, and an emphasis on producing social workers capable of the social analysis necessary for the promotion of social transformation. In 1974, this new programme received the approval of university authorities.

Social work and the revolutionary state

Following the 1979 toppling of the Somoza dictatorship by the *sandinista* forces, social work in Nicaragua was to encounter new challenges. The social policy set out by the new *sandinista* government had the broad objectives of improving the general standard of living of the population, creating more and better jobs, and fostering popular participation to produce joint solutions to social and economic issues between the state and an organised, mobilised populace.

This new social policy was to be implemented through the mobilisation of popular capacities, so working people themselves would be the generators of the social policy for a new economy. Social programmes would be decentralised to be closer to the local level, and popular organisations and local governments would participate with the ministries and public institutions in their design and implementation, as exemplified in the operation of the popular health committees. The implementation of the various social programmes was to be prioritised, graduated, and coordinated to avoid creating expectations which could not yet be met. Health was placed at the centre of social policy, with an approach in which, through popular education and community organisation, ordinary people would build their own capacity to address basic health needs.

The setting out of these social policy objectives, advancing the interests of the popular sectors and clearly congruent with the principles of the reconceptualisation movement, naturally created hopes for a prominent role for social work. It was expected that social workers would assume an active role in the mobilisation, conscientization, participation and organisation of the population.

However, although the *sandinista* project was clearly in alignment with the perspectives of the new social work, in the context of the process of review and transformation of the system of higher education as a whole, social work entered a new period of crisis. Prevailing within the revolutionary alliance at that moment was a view that, since the traditional function of social work had been essentially to mediate between the social classes, contributing to the perpetuation of the old regime, it would no longer be needed. From this perspective, with the revolution and the emergence of a new and just society, there was no longer a need for social work. Thus, in 1980 Nicaragua's only school of social work was closed to admissions.

The national social work community quickly mobilised itself in response to this, holding a national meeting in which the social work community deliberated collectively on what should be the roles of social workers, and the content of a social work education programme, in this dramatically altered Nicaraguan reality. A new profile of the professional social worker was developed, and higher education authorities were persuaded of the need for social workers to implement the nation's new social policy[4].

After a move from the National University (UNAN) to the traditionally more conservative Universidad Centroamericana (UCA)[5], and a revision of its programme of study, in 1984 the school of social work was reopened. The new mission statement of the School declared that its graduates should be prepared to facilitate 'the democratic process of popular participation in the structural changes required to achieve a more just and egalitarian society' (ETS, 1985, p. 4). Basing a new definition of social work on service to the process of social transformation, it observed that intervention at the micro-social level must serve the interests of the popular sectors, involving 'the sensitization and organisation of these popular sectors [which] allows them to make themselves subjects of their own transformation' (ETS, 1984, p. 2).

The overriding mission of social workers, in this perspective, is to enhance 'the organised participation of the people in the development of the society ... as the practice of popular democracy' (ETS, 1984, p. 2). The methodological keys to this are to be found in the methods of popular education, which begins with people's concrete experience (practice), and facilitates reflection to develop a critical understanding of that experience (theory), enabling more strategic action based on this understanding (practice) in order to bring about positive change (Freire, 1970)[6].

Many social workers whose education had been influenced by this new conceptualisation of the work of the profession became implementers of various state programs and projects, and social workers came to be much in demand. For the first time, social workers began to work in primary health care, with the Ministry of Labour, with the national water institute, and so on. More importantly, social workers came to hold key strategic positions in some of the institutions charged with implementation of the new social policy.

Notwithstanding this favourable climate, however, it should be acknowledged that there were ways in which traditional views of social work persisted: in the narrow definition of social work in the Social Security Law, among influential actors in the health sector still inclined to ignore the social factors linked to health conditions of the population, and to some extent among the first generation of social workers. Although the majority of social workers were aligned with the revolutionary project, there were some who were apathetic or even resistant to the changes being promoted. Perhaps not coincidentally, these tended to be social workers in the agencies which had employed and educated the first social workers in the country, under an imported Western conception of social work. For some of the social workers educated prior to the process of reconceptualisation, it was more difficult to grasp the new reality and the possibility of practising a different kind of social work; the reconceptualisation was based in theoretical paradigms very different from those underlying their own education (Prado and Palacios, 2005).

Social workers educated from the perspective of the reconceptualisation movement had the benefit of a theoretical legacy that was coherent with the social processes they were experiencing. However, as with the experience of the reconceptualisation throughout Latin America, they were limited initially in their mastery of the innovative practice methods needed to accompany this theoretical sophistication to respond effectively to the demands of the new social reality. A variety of measures were taken to correct this imbalance, including internships in other Latin American contexts to provide concrete experiences for faculty members in the methods of popular education and participatory action research (Prado and Wilson, 1996).

After almost a decade of economic blockade and the US-proxy war which affected every family and caused half of the national budget to be directed toward defence, the declining availability of basic goods and services was accompanied by an erosion of support for the *sandinista* project. In the elections of 1990, the period of revolutionary government ended[7].

The return of neo-liberal hegemony

The 1990 elections, in which the *sandinistas* were defeated by a US-backed alliance of opposition parties, signalled Nicaragua's full entrance into the processes of neo-liberal globalism and structural adjustment programmes that were already in place throughout much of Latin America. This meant a profound change in the role of the state, drastic cuts to social expenditures, and the reduction of state-supported social services to an absolute minimum. The responsibility for these services then fell to non-governmental organisations: literally hundreds of new non-governmental organisations sprang up, the majority of these created by officials of the previous revolutionary government with international support and financing.

Within months, diseases which had been eradicated – through the internationally recognised programmes of immunisation and health promotion carried out by tens of thousands of volunteers mobilised during the *sandinista* era – were reappearing. Hundreds of thousands of children were now on the street, as school expenses were no longer covered by the state, and illiteracy was once again on the rise. While civic beautification projects and glitzy new restaurants and shopping malls appeared to change the face of the capital, Nicaragua was soon in a neck-and-neck race with Haiti for the distinction of most impoverished nation in the region.

This had immediate implications for the roles of social workers. Not only did the state drastically reduce the number of social work jobs, but there was a dramatic altering of both its perspectives on social problems and its preferred methods of intervention. In key state institutions, social work was going backward in terms of the practice models in operation. In the area of health, where there had been significant advances in the participation of people and communities in the health system, there was now a return to a technocratic perspective which ignored the advances that had been achieved in health care. There was now an insistence that health, education and social services could be delivered only by highly trained professionals. Family problems were now treated by looking only to the families themselves for the sources and solutions of their issues, ignoring any relationship of these difficulties to the wider environment.

These changes brought with them a return to *asistencialismo* – a focus on the social assistance function – and to a social work concerned primarily with the restoring of relationships of individuals with their immediate groups, and with the 'rehabilitation' of youths and children considered delinquent. For many social workers this meant once again confronting the old tension between their commitment to the construction of a qualitatively different society, and the conservative institutional inclinations of a system now in place that was not only capitalist, but also patriarchal and broadly exclusionist.

On the other hand, the growing non-governmental sector opened to social workers the opportunity to establish themselves in organisations seeking to maintain some of the social gains achieved in the revolutionary period. Yet the work of these organisations as well was often some distance from the reconceptualisation goals and methodologies directed to ending economic exploitation and contributing to the construction of a new society.

Members of the social work education programme, in response to the challenges of the 1990 change of government, had engaged in a process of reflection that led to a reaffirmation of their commitment to social justice and to collaboration with the most vulnerable sectors to seek solutions to their principal problems. At the same time, some curriculum reforms were introduced, in an attempt to adapt the content of the programmes to the new reality. The education of social work students in Nicaragua to the end of the 1990s was carried out by a generation of professionals strongly influenced by the Reconceptualisation Movement, in the only School of Social Work that existed to that time[8].

The current context

The first decade of the 21st century has been marked by the intensification of neo-liberal globalisation and its above-noted impacts in Nicaragua. The present reality is that of a state connected to the interests of powerful groups (particularly those in the financial sector), in which the market is viewed as sacred, and in which there is a dearth of any effective initiatives to combat poverty. The advantage of Nicaragua's debt cancellation, with its classification as among the poorest and most indebted countries, has in no way been translated into fulfilling the exercise of human needs and rights.

In this context, with the market as the essential determinant of the viability of a profession, the teaching faculty at the social work programme at the Universidad Centroamericana has an ongoing concern with the future of its program. To critically and proactively confront the dual challenges of the human impacts of the neo-liberal agenda, with its exacerbation of critical social problems in Nicaragua, and of the new demand for social workers with specific technical skills, in 1999 the curriculum was reframed around two central axes: development and social actors. The programme was renamed 'Social Work and Management of Development'.

The shift in the nature of social work opportunities that had begun in Nicaragua in the 1990s has become more pronounced. In state agencies there are fewer jobs for social workers, and that work is predominantly of a social assistance nature. With non-governmental organisations, opportunities have multiplied – in terms of both themes and social sectors of focus. By 2003, it was estimated that there were approximately 800 non-governmental organisations working in the promotion of human development in areas such as children's and women's rights, agricultural ecology, health and rehabilitation, human rights, credit, culture and citizenship (Prado and Palacios, 2005).

If in the 1990s the emphasis in social work intervention was on maintaining achievements won in the revolutionary epoch, in more recent years many of the projects emerging from civil society, and from the state itself, have begun to focus on human rights, in attempts to transcend the limitations of *asistencialismo*.

Critical factors for liberatory social work in Nicaragua

In the broader Latin American context, a number of factors have been identified as being propitious for the emergence and taking hold of a radical social work. Alayón (2005) points to the 1959 initiation of the socialist experience in Cuba, the 1968 mobilisations in France, and the 1970 election of the socialist President Salvador Allende in Chile as sources of inspiration. Chilean sociologist Diego Palma (1977) observed that the reconceptualisation movement was best able to flourish where there occurred, first, an intersection of disenchantment with traditional social service functions with the continental elevation of expectations of social transformation; second, where a certain sharpening of class struggle is achieved; and third, where the reconceptualising groups are concentrated around or linked either to universities or to churches. The Argentinian social worker/anthropologist Estela Grassi (1994) has argued that the general setting required for the reconceptualisation includes: a strong politicisation of the society in general; the development of critical currents in the social sciences – of Marxist inspiration and/or of 'national thought' (such as that of the *peronistas* in Argentina); and the establishment of a close relationship of these critical currents with concrete practice.

In the Nicaraguan case, 'traditional' social service delivery functions were too new and underdeveloped in the 1960s to have been very significant as a source of the disenchantment described by Palma. However, many of the other factors identified above can be seen to have been in play. There was undeniably a strong politicisation of the society as a whole, beginning in the 1960s through the mobilisation and inspiration of the *sandinista* popular movement, and intensifying as the *sandinistas* took and held power until 1990. This was associated with both a sharpened awareness of class conflict and a raising of hopes and expectations for transformation of the society.

Churches and universities were also factors in politicisation in Nicaragua. In the case of the churches this was complex, as there were significant divisions among both Catholic and Protestant ('evangelical') religious groups over support of the *sandinistas*, whose project was congruent with that of the reconceptualised social work. The liberation theology movement favoured the *sandinista* project; the nine-person governing council following the 1979 *sandinista* victory included four members of the clergy, and the Cabinet following the 1984 elections included three clerics, as ministers of foreign affairs, education and culture.

Universities in Latin America have traditionally been seen as places of sanctuary and, notwithstanding well-publicised raids carried out by military regimes, they have been important and comparatively safe places for the development of independent thought. In this context, critical currents in social scientific thought have made their way into thinking about a role for social work in Nicaragua. Sociology and social work have been closely linked in higher education in Nicaragua, and it was critical sociologists and social workers who together led the process of reconceptualisation in Nicaragua's national School of Social Work in the early 1970s[9].

Today a constant concern, especially among social work educators, is with the need for a clear alternative vision of development to compete with the hegemony of the strongly individualistic neo-liberal model. In their work in programmes of national and international organisations and agencies, social workers encounter slippery conceptual and methodological elements (such as social capital, social management, participation, local development), which, though they may contain valid elements for social work intervention, raise questions of what – or whose – ends are they serving. There is thus a need for a constant examination of the question of whether their work is contributing to a reproduction and revitalisation of the capitalist system in which they are immersed, or whether through their work they can contribute to the construction of a different society, one that permits the autonomy of individuals, but that at the same time generates alliances for collective action to build a society with new social relations of production. These questions, of course, are not new, but they are challenging in a new way in the current context.

In Nicaragua, a liberatory approach to social work had the unique opportunity to flower for eleven years under the protection of a sympathetic state; it has operated in the environments of both friendly and hostile governments. Will there be a return to a more hospitable environment for liberatory social work in Nicaragua? At the time of writing, left-leaning nationalist governments have been elected in Brazil, Venezuela, Chile, Bolivia, Argentina (which has emancipated itself from its International Monetary Fund control by transferring its debt to its own central bank) and Uruguay, and similar outcomes appear possible in the near future in Mexico and Nicaragua. In Nicaragua, a feud between right-wing factions[10] has strengthened *sandinista* prospects for the 2006 elections (Close, 2005; Rosales, 2006)[11]. However, regardless of these outcomes, social work in Nicaragua will continue the ongoing process of construction of its identity, positioning itself to respond to emerging realities as it challenges conventional neo-liberal wisdom and honours its own history of engagement in the creation of social and economic justice.

Notes

1   The Canadian ambassador to Chile reported:

'General Somoza ... kept photographs of Hitler and Mussolini prominently displayed on his desk. He removed them only after it became obvious that the Axis was losing the war. He was an intimate of the notorious Wilhelm von Brayman, chief of Nazi espionage in Central America'. (Ambassador Fraser Elliot, cited in MacFarlane,1989, pp. 84-85)

2   This is a scenario that had been repeated several times following the arrival of the Spaniards in 1522. With a late nineteenth-century coffee boom, for instance, had come the Pedro Joachim Chamorro Law of 1877, which drove peasants and indigenous people off the land. Five thousand rural poor were killed in a rebellion against this in 1881 in the infamous 'war of *comuneros.*'

3   'The reconceptualization movement has been and continues to be the most significant step in the history of social work' This and all translations are ours.

4   Participants in these events often observe that the 1980 closure of the School was a healthy thing for both the school and the profession. It is said to have stimulated a great deal of positive discussion and raising of consciousness among social workers and social work educators (Wilson, 2003).

5   It was hoped that the relocation of the social work programme to the UCA would help to raise social consciousness there.

6   It is interesting to note that while being grateful for the solidarity and support of the Cubans, this did not mean there was an inclination to assume the narrow, institutional definition of social work that had been adopted by the Cubans and some of their Soviet bloc allies.

7   In retrospect, according to Prado and Palacios (2005), this can in part be attributed to an overemphasis on the changing of structures at the expense of promotion of the educational dimension in the transformation of the people and groups.

8   At that point, among the dozens of new educational institutions opened by local entrepreneurs, another social work programme was opened − by people without social work training. Although some trained social workers have instructed courses there, this programme − should it survive − is not seen as a serious factor in defining social work in Nicaragua.

9   Administratively, today at the Universidad Centroamericana where the School is currently housed, sociology and social work form part of one academic unit.

10 The right-wing Liberal Party (the PLC) has been weakened by a feud

between current President Enrique Bolaños and former President Arnoldo Alemán.

11 It should be noted that the *sandinistas* (the FSLN) are hampered by divisions within their own ranks: popular former Managua Mayor Herty Lewites, expelled from the party, will now run as a candidate of a coalition of smaller parties.

Chapter 5

Resisting the New Rationale of
Social Work

Cornelia Schweppe

The new rationale of social work

Social work, especially in Western industrial countries, is presently
challenged by transformations which threaten the very nature of its
professional identity and its ethical foundations. We can mention three
aspects in particular. The first is the increasing economic rationale linked
to social work (for example, Dahme and Wohlfahrt, 2000; Otto and
Schnurr, 2000; Galuske, 2002). Market criteria, efficiency measures and
business orientation are the new essentials by which social work is
guided and judged. The financing of social work is linked to economic
efficiency and based on quantified indicators and standardised code
numbers. The demands of the market are predominant; professional
standards are of secondary importance.

The danger of linking social work to economic criteria is due to the
different rationale of social work and the economy (Thole and Cloos,
2000). The economy guides behaviour by money and power. Social
work, in opposition, is founded in communicative practices. It demands
the understanding of its clients within their social contexts. Social work
which is judged and guided by economic criteria is neither compatible
with the complex processes of communication and interaction of social
intervention nor with the singular and individually different learning
processes and developments of its clients. How, for example, can the
strengthening of self-esteem be measured by economic criteria? How
can an intervention be justified after a drug addict leaves a treatment
programme without improving their problems when economical
rationality and efficiency are the basis for social intervention? And how
far is economic efficiency compatible with the criteria of successful and

helpful intervention of social work clients?

Social work which is founded in economic rationality runs the risk of technological reductionism (Thole and Cloos, 2000). Individual life histories and life developments are pressed into quantifying indicators and code numbers; individuality is substituted by standardisation. Furthermore, there is a danger that this process will divide social work clients into those who can be helped because their problems can be improved or solved through quick – and therefore cheap – interventions and those whose problems require more complex – and therefore more expensive – interventions which by the logic of economic criteria cannot be justified.

A second danger for social work results from concepts proclaimed by models of the activating welfare state (Trube and Wohlfahrt, 2001; Dahme *et al.*, 2003). The substance of these concepts can be summarised by the formula: no rights without duties. Social support and social help are linked to duties, obligations and achievements on part of the clients. Only those clients who fulfil certain duties and obligations will receive social support. These duties, obligations and achievements are no longer a matter of dialogue or communication between the client and the social worker. They are, rather, standardised measures which are imposed upon the clients and enforced by pressure and control. For example, the obligation to work as part of social aid has become common. If force and pressure do not achieve the expected results, social benefits are reduced or cut all together. Those who do not submit themselves to the measures imposed are left to their own destiny. The co-production of social services to develop interventions according to the clients' needs is substituted by standardised measures, help is replaced by control and force. The clients' rights to autonomy do not play much of a role. Whereas social work generally considers its clients as responsible, autonomous and independent actors, these concepts maintain clients in positions of dependency by measures of force and pressure (Sturzenhecker, 2003).

A third basic threat to social work results from new mentalities and changed attitudes towards social problems. Beisenherz (2000) notes that globally as well as locally the responses to social inequality and social problems are increasingly less guided by measures and intentions of social integration and social equality. Goode and Maskovsky (2001) show that the decline of the welfare states in the USA goes along with the increase of state measures of control, surveillance and punishment. Their main targets are poor people. The authors, therefore, state that instead of speaking of a State withdrawal with regard to dealing with social problems, it is more appropriate to refer to it as a cultural reorientation which emphasises control and 'law and order' which often develops in parallel with new forms of racial discrimination.

This brief description of the present challenges to and transformations of social work shows that social work approaches which are founded in the autonomy of social work clients, their self-determination and emancipation and which are based on the principles of civil rights, social justice and social participation are under threat. In this historical context, therefore, it is of crucial importance to maintain and/or recover theoretical and professional concepts of social work in which the autonomy of social work clients is the starting and final point of social interventions and in which social support and social help is not misunderstood as an expertocratic imposition, but which are based on dialogue and communicative practices in order to strengthen self-determined life practices, to make social participation and social justice possible and which resist standardised, disciplinarian and stigmatising measures which all too often dominate societal expectations of social work.

Social work based on the daily life practices of social actors

Social work traditions and approaches which are founded in the *Lebenswelt* and in daily life practices of social actors (Thiersch, 1986, 1992, 2000) offer far-reaching perspectives with regard to the present challenges of social work. These approaches consider daily life as the main focus and context of social work. They consider and analyse social problems and life situations within the specific environment of daily life. Daily life is understood as the context where people live, where problems originate and where people find solutions to their problems. It is the context in which social actors are confronted with social demands, social needs and social structures which they have to deal with and where social actors develop their respective ways of life, their biography, their way of thinking and acting, their views of the world. Social work approaches founded in daily life practices of social actors consider social work clients as capable, resourceful and independent actors. They respect the uniqueness of each person, the uniqueness of each individual way of being and living and their problem-solving capacities. They object to standardised, disciplinarian, dominating and stigmatising interventions. Instead they emphasis the self-determination and the autonomy of a person. They are open approaches and reject the imposition of prefabricated ways of life as well as normalising definitions and solutions to social problems.

The acceptance and the respect of the experiences, the interpretations of the world, the problem-solving strategies and resources of social actors as a main element of approaches of social work founded in daily life practices, do not mean that social work merely repeats and accepts what is given. A central element is the critical understanding of daily life and daily life practices. These approaches are based on critical theories of daily life which consider daily life as contradictory and ambivalent (Thiersch, 1986). Critical theories point out the ambivalence of daily life between deception and reality, between successful coping and problem solving on the one hand and failure and pragmatism on the other. Therefore, social work needs a critical understanding and critical analysis of daily life contexts and practices in order to discover constraints, limitations and barriers and to support more satisfactory daily life practices, less suffering, pain and injustice.

These approaches to social work demand a high level of self-reflection on part of social workers. Social work interventions in the context of daily life are potentially threatened to just become part of daily life patterns and thus lose the necessary distance and critical views which are essential if social work does not want to just repeat given structures and practices or maintain the status quo.

What do these approaches demand of social work practices in order to be successful?

First, social work approaches founded in the daily life practices of social actors understand social problems as socially produced. Social problems are always embedded in a concrete and specific life reality and in social circumstances and structures. Therefore, it is necessary to analyse and understand this social context and how the material, social, cultural and institutional environment contributes to the origin and development of social problems. The analysis of a social problem within its particular social context is necessary in order to uncover the social restrictions and the social structures which prevent human beings from developing autonomous life practices, to uncover discrimination, social inequality and practices of social exclusion. It is also necessary in order to uncover resources of social support and needed changes. The analysis of a social problem within its respective social context prevents social work from individualistic and decontextualised interventions – practices which are often common to social work (Gildemeister and Robert, 1997).

Second, even though the analysis of the social context of a social problem is important, it is not sufficient if social work wants to strengthen self-determined and autonomous life practices by accepting and corresponding to singular life experiences and life perspectives of the actors it deals with. Social reality is not just shaped by social, economic, cultural and political conditions and structures. It is principally open to subjective interpretation and appropriation. Social reality is, therefore, also subjectively constructed. Through interpretation and subjective appropriation of social reality social actors attribute specific meanings to reality and develop specific patterns which guide their way of being, thinking and acting and of dealing and coping with social reality. These patterns explain why actors act the way they act and why it makes sense – from their perspective – to act the way they do. Therefore, the problems social work deals with are not only a result of specific social, cultural, political and material conditions, circumstances and structures but also contain a subjective dimension. This subjective dimension brings out a specific and singular nature of the correspondent problem. If social work wants to correspond to the singular life experiences and practices of its clients and to support self-determined life practices it is necessary to understand their subjective construction of social reality and the subjective meaning they give to social reality. It is necessary to understand their each unique and individually different life perspectives, their subjective patterns of interpreting the world, their social, cultural, biographical and material resources, the patterns of problem development and problem-solving and the subjective limits of coping with life, their experiences of exclusion, processes of suffering, and so on. Only in this way is it possible to understand how reality is experienced and shaped by them and what their unique experiences are. Only in this way clients can speak for themselves. Otherwise social work runs the risk of imposition and domination.

To understand the clients' subjectivity does not mean just repeating what clients say and express. The subjective meanings attributed to social reality often cannot be expressed and explained by the actors themselves. Subjective meanings are often embedded in routines and therefore are often not accessible to explanations. The subjective construction of social reality and the meanings actors attribute to it have to be reconstructed by means of interpretation. The reconstruction of the subjectivity is an essential and at the same time difficult task of social work. Social work often deals with behaviours, attitudes or life perspectives which are different from mainstream acting and thinking. The world and life views of social work clients often cannot immediately be understood and explained. They often appear 'strange' and do not make sense at the first instance. Instead of understanding these 'strange' and uncommon ways of thinking and acting, they are often subordinate in social work practice to subordinate under current and known patterns of thinking and acting. They are often subordinated under stereotypes or institutionally defined and accepted patterns of interpretations and worldviews. The uniqueness and individuality of the clients' life practices and life experiences are substituted by general definitions and categories. This way clients are often reduced to typical cases of social work (Schütze, 1994). Thus, hermeneutic capabilities are of crucial importance to social work (Jakob, with Wensierski, 1997).

A third important dimension for the successful realisation of social work concepts based in daily life practices is to understand the interactive nature of social work. This was particularly pointed out by theories of symbolic interaction (Schütze, 1996). The social construction of social problems does not only refer to the social and subjective dimension of social problems but also to the fact that social work takes part in this construction. Depending on how social work looks at a problem, how it defines it, what institutional resources are available, what objectives a social service pursues, this contributes to the construction and definition of a problem. Therefore, reflection of social work practice, critical distance from and analysis of social work interventions is of crucial importance. Critical reflection of one's own patterns of normality, the patterns of interactions with the clients and the adequacy of the intervention measures and procedures becomes essential in order to avoid dominating and paternalistic social work practices (Gildemeister and Robert, 1997).

Popular education and collective social practices

Social work based on daily life practices of social actors can be found in many parts of the world. Far-reaching concepts have been particularly developed particularly in Latin America countries. In this context, concepts of popular education (*educación popular*) are of special relevance (for example, Osorio, 1986; Celats, 1991). Their theoretical and practical premises are rooted in the work of Paolo Freire.

Concepts of popular education particularly refer to collective practices of poor sectors of society as they are realised by grassroots organisations or social movements. In these collective practices popular sectors (*sectores populares)* bring in their knowledge, their wisdom and their collective history to overcome problems of poverty, lack of social participation, discrimination and alienation. New grassroots organisations and social movements have originated in Latin America especially since the 1980s.

Popular soup kitchens (comedores populares) *in Lima, Peru*

An example of these grassroots organisations are popular soup kitchens (*comedores populares*) in the shanty towns of Lima and other Peruvian cities. In these organisations poor women gather in order to cook for their families and others by the principle of rotation. This is cheaper than cooking individually at home. The main aim of soup kitchens is to alleviate hunger and improve nutrition. Soup kitchens develop weekly work plans in which the tasks of the members are fixed. Each day two to three women are responsible for preparing the food, one or two women for cleaning up or buying the food. Anybody can participate in a soup kitchen as long she engages in the tasks of the soup kitchen.

All soup kitchens have more or less the same organisational structure. The highest decision-making committee is the assembly, which meets every two weeks and in which all members of a soup kitchen participate. The assembly discusses and decides all affairs of the kitchen. It establishes the weekly work plan, it decides on the appropriate sanction of members who do not carry out their tasks, it provides information on the financial situation of the kitchen, and so on. Even though the affairs of the kitchen are at the centre of the assembly meetings, they often go beyond and discuss problems of the neighbourhood, personal problems, as well as political and social issues.

The second main committee of a soup kitchen is the 'leading committee' (*comité responsable*). It consists of the leaders (*dirigentes*) of the soup kitchen who are elected each year by the assembly. It is intended that each member carries out a leading task during their membership. The function of the leading committee is to supervise the functioning of the kitchen and the achievement of its aims. The leading committee consists of five to seven leaders.

Soup kitchens have various sources of financing. The main source is the selling of the meals the kitchen prepares. Each member has to pay a certain amount for each portion it buys. Persons who are not members of the kitchen also can acquire the meals, however, the price is higher than for members. Women who prepare the food do not have to pay for the food that day. A second source of financing is food donations, for example from CARITAS.

In addition to preparing the food, many soup kitchens also organise educational programmes for their members. The topics are widely spread and contain political or social issues, gender issues, and so on.

To understand the meaning of soup kitchens it is also important to point out that they have developed a wide range of networks among themselves. These networks exists on a communal, city as well as national level. These networks aim at exchanging experiences, the organisation of educational programmes for their members, and political protest or demands towards the Peruvian government.

Even though the alleviation of hunger and the improvement of nutrition are the main aims of soup kitchens, their social significance goes beyond these aims. A case study based on an ethnographic research design shows that soup kitchens are based on social relationships that imply a potential for social change and that they contribute to the change of the situation of poor women in Peru (Schweppe, 1991, 1993). What, then, are the results of these initiatives as demonstrated by this study?

The social order of soup kitchens

The study shows that the social relationships among the members of the soup kitchen are based on equality, democracy and solidarity.

Equality among the members is shown on different levels. First, it refers to the equality of members with regard to the material benefits of the soup kitchen. A central element is the equal distribution of the meals prepared. Exact measurements are established of how to serve the food. The serving of the meals is supervised by a member of the kitchen in order to ensure equal distribution. The infringement of this rule is a matter of discussion during the assembly. Second, equality refers to equal information among the members with regard to all matters of the kitchen. The soup kitchen wants to avoid problems which originate from unequal information among the members, such as misunderstandings or power building. Third, equality means equal participation in the decision-making of the kitchen, and fourth, the equal division of labour.

The principle of equality is closely linked to the principle of democracy. In addition to the aforementioned rules and organisational structure, democracy is aimed for by the rotation of members in leading positions. The rotation of leadership aims at counterbalancing possible power building within the soup kitchen as well as at the equal distribution of work which is entailed in the functioning of the kitchen.

The principle of solidarity manifests itself by helping members who are in difficult life situations. In these situations members can be released from paying for the food for a week. If a member is in a very difficult situation the soup kitchen also organises communal activities to generate funds for the respective member. Other forms of helping are donations, home visits or the support of household activities.

The established principles of equality, democracy and solidarity are by no means easy to realise since, in many ways, they oppose the main social order of Peru. The soup kitchen wants equality in a society which is characterised by severe social inequalities. Decisions are to be taken collectively in a country where decisions are usually taken by a minority and where many are excluded from participation. Power building is to be avoided by the rotation of leaders in a country where usually these positions are carried out by a few people in order to benefit from the privileges these positions involve. And in a country where social problems are often ignored and left to the individual's destiny the soup kitchen pursues solidarity with members in difficult life situations. It is the persistent, open discussion of and confrontation with the infringements of the extablished rules and principles that make it possible that the soup kitchen approaches little by little to achieve the established aims.

The soup kitchen and the life situation of poor women

The study also shows that soup kitchens are important organisations that contribute to changing the life situation of poor women. There are various dimensions to how a woman's life changes through their participation in the soup kitchen. One change refers to their personal and family life. The women feel more self secure, they feel more capable of participating in discussions, of expressing their opinion and being more able to manage their life actively. They also report changes within their family relationships. They feel able to assert their own needs and interests within the relationship with their husband and to establish some free space from the demands of child care.

Another major change in the life of the women is that they feel less isolated. The soup kitchen for most of them provides a social network where they can share problems concerning their personal life and where they also experience moments of relaxation and joy – something which most of them lacked before.

The women also suggest the soup kitchen provides space for education and awareness-raising. It opens their eyes to social, political and gender issues. And it opens new avenues of social participation for the women. Many women report that, through their participation in the soup kitchen, they found ways to participate in other community activities and grassroots organisations which are still mainly male oriented.

In summary, the results of this study show that the soup kitchen is an effective practice to alleviate hunger as well as a microcosms of democracy, solidarity, and equality. It confirms what Tilman Evers writes about grassroots organisations: 'The innovative power of these social movements is their capacity to develop and experiment [with] other forms of daily social relationships' (Evers 1985, p. 50, translation, Cornelia Schweppe). Therefore, they manifest a potential of social change because: 'No structure of social domination can survive, if it is not represented in the social-cultural base of daily life' (Evers 1985, p. 51, translation, Cornelia Schweppe).

Popular education

Concepts of popular education that refer to collective social practices realised by grassroots organisations and social movements are intended to strengthen these practices and thus to contribute not only to the alleviation of severe social problems which result from poverty but also to contribute to a more just and democratic society.

These concepts are founded in daily life practices of popular sectors of society and are based on their knowledge, wisdom, social practices, history and experiences. Concepts of popular education consider poor people as knowledgeable and wise due to their history, social struggles and life experiences. They oppose mainstream views on poor people as ignorant and incapable. Instead of long historical traditions to suppress the history, knowledge and experiences of popular social sectors, popular education will revive and promote them in order to overcome domination and suppression. Popular education gives new meanings and a new valuation to popular culture.

Concepts of popular education are based on a specific type of social relationship between social workers and the actors they deal with. Instead of hierarchal relationships in which social workers are those who know and the clients are those who have to learn, social relationships of mutual learning are required. This does not mean that social workers are just a passive and uncritical companion of popular collective practices. Popular education realises itself through processes of dialogue. This means listening and expressing oneself, asking and responding, criticising and listening to criticism, and giving and taking (Osorio, 1986).

Concepts of popular education intend to give voice to poor and marginalised people. Based on the analysis that poor and marginalised sectors of society in Latin America are excluded from political power, collective social practices are seen as possibilities whereby marginalised and socially excluded sectors of society find new ways of social participation and articulation. Collective practices are considered as social spaces where poor sectors express their interests and social needs and conquer social spaces from which they were excluded before (for example, Borda, 1987). Therefore, the social actors engaged in these collective practices are considered as protagonists of new social relationships which object to exploitation, inequality and authoritarianism (Schweppe, 1993). These collective social practices are seen as democratic practices which contribute to the development of social structures which integrate forgotten sectors of society.

A final note

In times in which social work is threatened by a dominant economic rationale, measures of standardisation and state control, it is in danger of becoming an instrument of suppression, domination and force, of enhancing social exclusion and further social inequality. It is of fundamental importance to find ways of resistance and to maintain and strengthen those conceptions of social work which are based on social justice, democracy and equality. The described concepts of social work founded in daily life practices of social actors are one way to answer the new rationale of social work. Critical concepts of social work can be found in many parts of the world. It is necessary to unite those critical forces in order to be able to respond to neo-liberalism, enhancing inequality and social injustice by its own beliefs and convictions.

Chapter 6

Making a choice: Beyond professional social work to activism

Nalini Nayak

After doing my Masters in Social Work with a specialisation in Community Organisation at one of the most prestigious Schools of Social Work in India, in a period when social work was just being accepted as a profession, I have spent the following thirty odd years in the field fighting such professionalism. While doing so I have tried to integrate principles of community organisation with activism at the community and broader social levels. I say this from the Indian context as social work as a profession is considered an institutionalised 'job' well integrated into the mainstream of society and increasingly well paid today. My experience of working in the community necessitated a completely different approach.

Starting at the community level

It was not long after living in a community, an artisanal fishing community, that we (when I say we, it was initially a small team of four that grew larger over the years) understood the reasons for poverty in the community. This was in the early 1970s. Yes, there were numerous issues such as poor sanitation, malnutrition, unhygienic housing, illiteracy, school dropouts and the like, that could engage a social worker for an entire lifetime. While we did think it important to interact with the community through these issues, the main reason for poverty and the root cause of these other problems was exploitation and social exclusion. Exploitation by moneylenders held the fishers in a debt trap and had control of their fish catches. These moneylenders also received the patronage of the religious institutions as they also collected the church tax – representing a collusion between the economic and social structure. Moreover, because the fishers both men and women were loudly spoken, smelt of fish and came from a low social class/caste, they were excluded from mainstream society and lived at the margins both physically and socially as if condemned by fate.

My training in community organisation had given me several skills of working with people but with the basic principle being to help marginalised communities develop skills that would draw them into the mainstream and thereby reap the benefits from it. This was based on the conviction that the mainstream was the norm. But living with the fishing community, we were convinced that they were marginalised because they were exploited by people and institutions that had a prime place in the mainstream. This led us to seek tools to analyse social processes, to look at the economics of caste by developing a class perspective which is the base on which the capitalist society is constructed. The tools of social analysis developed by Francois Houtart and subsequently developed by us in India to include categories of patriarchy and situate it in an ecological perspective, have been immensely helpful since then. We also tried to integrate the methodology of Paulo Freire because the majority of people in the fishing community in the district where we worked were Christian and very religious too.

This 'consciousness raising' based on the fact that fishing and related activity was honourable and skilled work, with a body of knowledge of its own, and that people had the rights to the fruits of their labour, built up confidence to fight exploiting moneylenders and merchants and to stand up to the church for the decisions they took as the church was meant to be an institution of justice. These efforts bore fruits and evolved into creating genuine people's cooperatives that not only brought people higher incomes but helped them create institutions that were democratic and transparent and that they had the pride to manage. By the end of the 1970s these new efforts were able to convince the state government to rethink its own approach of structuring cooperatives in the coastal communities.

When the state of emergency was imposed in India in 1975, this was a sign that the Indian democracy was not sacrosanct and that the powerful ruling classes could also manipulate it. This was an 'eye-opener' that led us deeper into the analysis of political processes in India. It was evident that mere involvement in the economic processes could get derailed and could also build a petty bourgeois mentality. As the cooperatives grew as economic institutions, and as we began to observe the pressure of the fishing on the fish resources, some of us grew convinced that we needed a parallel mobilisation strategy that would give people a political vision and voice. By that time, fishing people's agitations had started in one region further north on the west coast of India, and we began to hear about the mobilisation of tribal people in other parts of India. There were also alternative forms of trade union struggles evolving when the textile industry was 'modernising' (producing widespread closures). We interacted with these groups. In fact a colleague and I took a break from work for a whole year to try to understand the new scenario that was emerging in India 25 years after independence. We could see how the divides between people and exclusion were being institutionalised and how people were responding. This break brought us deeper insights regarding the new strategies that people were developing to counter the hegemonic state, to counter the ongoing development paradigm that institutionalised the class divide. There was also a new thinking on non-party political formations with inbuilt mechanisms of transparency, accountability and democracy.

From community organisation to mobilisation

This type of initiative is what we then tried to develop back in the fishing arena. It was clear that a mobilisation strategy was necessary and only this would lead to an understanding of people's rights *vis-a-vis* the State and the rest of society. While the women in the fishing village had already created their local organisation and developed a systematic mode of functioning, they had begun to collectively discuss their problems. Their first issue was the ration shop where they were being cheated on the weights and quality of the grain they received through the public distribution system. They developed their strategy first by meeting the Collector, the official in charge of the system. Despite being assured that action would be taken, nothing was done. They then staged a sit-in, refusing to leave the ration shop until the shop owner gave them their rightful ration. Only after this did things change and, finally, the women began to run the ration shop themselves. Subsequently, they linked up with women's groups from other fishing villages and also raised the issue about the long distances they had to travel to the market carrying the fish on their heads. They were at a disadvantage reaching the market late in comparison to the men merchants who got there faster on their bicycles and thus got the better prices as well. It was in 1978 that they moved out of their local communities/villages and publicly protested on the street of the capital city demanding the right to travel on public transport. They organised all along the 30 kilometre coast of Trivandrum district, creating the Coastal Women's Forum. This organised protest caught the public eye. Here were people not asking for a dole from the government but a basic right like other citizens. Achieving such a demand was not easy and it took two years of constant protest and a lot of groundwork until the government finally created the Fishermen's Welfare Corporation and ran special buses for women fish vendors. They also organised to defend their rights in the market not only against the tax collectors extortion but also their harassment. Here again they scored success.

Organising women to demand their rights meant informing them of the way the state functioned. Facilitating their encounters with ministers and the bureaucracy meant helping them develop skills to represent their interests. This was even more difficult as it meant challenging accepted norms of for whom and what public transport was meant for – fish was considered a perishable commodity and 'dirty' too. It was a caste-bound activity and the caste was considered low. How could such women and such a commodity travel on a public bus? The women then asked the minister, *'Sir, is there any meal you eat without fish? Isn't it us women who get it to you? Why should the transport of fish by us be considered anti-social?'*

It was amazing to see the energy of the women, the resilience and will to sustain a struggle. Interacting with the State institutions, they also learnt how they functioned and how they had to deal with them.

The decade of the 1980s saw the creation of the National Fishworkers' Forum (NFF), spearheaded by the struggle of the fishers of Goa, demanding legislation to protect the rights of the coastal fishers. Subsequently, in 1981 when the fishworkers mobilised to oppose trawl fishing in Kerala, it was the women who were in the forefront. It was also they who first felt the impact of the mechanised fishing as fish prices started falling.

Growing into a political force

The state of Kerala had a tradition of Left politics. Workers of all sections, except in the fishing sector, were organised and the concept of workers' rights was well established. But like elsewhere, the Left consciousness related more to workers in the organised sector as the consciousness of 'class for itself' was conceived in the traditional frame of modernised industry. On the one hand there was the political space for more militant mobilisation of workers but on the other hand sustaining an artisanal or traditional sector was not within Left consciousness. So this was another significant breakthrough when accurate data from the sector, compiled by the cooperatives and support organisations, could prove that the artisanal fishery was more viable than the modern fishery on all economic and social counts.

It should be mentioned here that there were several support groups that were present in the coastal communities by the late 1970s. The change in the socio-political scenario, and the spontaneous mobilisation of people against injustice provided the impetus to move beyond the immediate community to the larger one, from local contradictions to those at the State level and gradually to the national level through the process of building organisation. This was a collaborative effort, the common focus being the growth of the traditional fishworkers' movement.

The process of structuring a political organisation was greatly debated. While it was clear that the political organisation of the fisher people should be independent and free from all political party affiliations, the bone of contention was whether it should be a class-based organisation including fisher people from all coastal communities, or a caste-based one. The majority of fisher folk in the southern districts of Kerala belong to the *mukkuvar* caste and are Latin Catholic (as distinct from the Syrian Catholics). This was the first big rupture in the process. What finally took off was the mobilisation of the fishworkers on a class basis and the fishing sector was gradually registered as a trade union. Those priests and religious sisters who supported such a process remained in the trade union and, in fact, the first president of the Kerala Swatantra Matsya Thozilali Federation (KSMTF) was a diocesan priest and a young fisherman, the general secretary. The Latin Catholic group grew initially but its hold gradually weakened although the issue of 'caste' also became an important feature in the KSMTF two decades later.

Registering an owner-operator fishing sector as a trade union was indeed something new. However, it gave the fishworkers an identity as workers who had rights to a livelihood. Building up a trade union consciousness in a sector that was until then considered a vote bank for the right-wing Congress party was a new step. But in Kerala, the tradition of Left politics made the trade union concept more easily acceptable. This, in fact, put the fishworkers on a par with other workers as a sector that the government had now to take seriously. But this was no automatic process. The union had to prove its strength and this was achieved through large and persistent struggles – hunger strikes and ingenious mass protests every monsoon season from 1981 to 1989. The major demand of the union was transport facilities to the market for the women, reduction of market taxes, and a ban on trawl fishing in the months of June, July and August. The protests made the government take note and sit up. They also had an impact on the traditional political party unions who were caught on the rebound on seeing the massive turn-out of people in the demonstrations. The government discussed demands at a round table with all other party unions. Right from the first struggle the KSMTF realised that the other political unions would appropriate the gains of its struggle, and that was indeed what happened. But in doing so the party unions, which otherwise unquestioningly followed a party line, were forced to take positions on crucial issues that impacted on the life of the artisanal workers that they had not done until then. Finally, only in 1989 did the government finally announce a ban on trawl fishing – and only for a mere 45 days.

I should highlight here that inputs from our social work training contributed here were important. The importance given to participatory processes, to developing the local leaders, to shared responsibility, and transparency were all important strategic considerations. There was also a need to clarify the understanding of the 'working class' and take cognisance of the role played by the unorganised sector. Supporting a people's movement while at the same time being out of it, maintaining separate identities and facilitating growth of people's leadership was an important strategy option which paid long-term dividends. While movements spontaneously take root because of the objective conditions that propel people into action, sustaining them and institutionalising the learning depends on conscious processes within. Enlightened leadership from within or support from outside is necessary for this.

As the trade union grew through mobilisation and struggles throughout the State, the government was pressurised to respond. But instead of responding to the demands of the fishworkers, the government tried to appease the union by sanctioning all kinds of welfare measures like educational grants for children, pensions, accident insurances, and so on. The Welfare Fund Act was passed in 1985 and the Fishermen's Welfare Corporation was created registering all fishworkers and the creation of the Matsyafed – a chain of fishing cooperatives on the Marianad model (a model developed by us at the village level). These were innovative structures that not only put artisanal fisheries and the fishworkers on the national map and made them an important component of the Ministry of Agriculture but also later inspired other States in the country to develop their welfare programmes for the fishworkers.

Moving to the international level

In 1984 the Food and Agriculture Organisation (FAO) organised the World Conference on Fisheries Management and Development. This was a conference that focused on the management of the 200-mile Exclusive Economic Zone as the United Nations (UN) Law of the Sea Convention (UNCLOS) had been finally ratified and became binding in 1982. The fishworkers had gathered under a separate roof – 100 fishworkers and their supporters from 34 countries. As the FAO did not pay heed to the existence of the artisanal fishers, this was their way of making their presence felt.

The initiative to organise this conference actually came from India when friends in Rome who were aware of the fishworkers struggles in India sent news about the FAO conference and suggested that the NFF ask to participate. Not being recognized as a national trade union, permission was not granted and, hence, we Indians decided that the presence of the artisanal fishers should be made visible in other ways. Spontaneously, friends from various organisations from all over the world rallied together and it was decided to organise a parallel conference of fishworkers and their supporters in Rome with one of my colleagues as the organising secretary.

This conference, besides for the first time creating a forum for the fishworkers from the coastal fishery of several countries to interact with each other, also made two very significant contributions to the international discourse in fisheries. It first of all spoke about *fishworkers* and not *fishermen*. In this way it highlighted the reality of the southern world in which fisheries were still a family business in which men, women and children were involved in different aspects of the fishery and where any development of the fishery had to take the development of the whole community into consideration. It was clear that the involvement of women in the coastal fishery is what also made it viable and sustainable. Their contribution and spaces had to be recognised and safeguarded. The second important aspect that was highlighted was the viability of the small-scale artisanal fishery. This essentially meant a fishery as a means of livelihood to thousands of coastal people, a fishery that is diversified, environmentally friendly and not only export oriented. Another important impact was that the fishworkers saw the potential of organisation and struggle for their rights and this stimulated a growth of fishworkers' organisations in other countries of the south.

What was of significance was that these positions were taken at a time when the whole world was trying to convince itself that there were large fish resources in the deep sea that the developing countries had no means to exploit, and that industrial fisheries and joint ventures were the answer. History revealed that this was a bluff, and the same FAO that gave leadership to this thinking at that time, changed its position entirely a decade later (in 1994) and then tried to lobby for a Code of Conduct of Responsible Fisheries inculcating many of the positions of the fishworkers' conference of 1984.

One of the important spin-offs of the Rome conference was the creation of the International Collective in Support of Fishworkers (ICSF) in 1986. As the name suggests, this was the response of the supporters to the suggestions of the fishworkers in Rome. Whereas the fishworkers realised that building up their national organisations was imperative for any impact on policy at national level they also expected support to tackle issues that impacted on them from the international arena. This essentially has been the role that the ICSF has played from its inception and simultaneously also succeeded to see that the artisanal fishworkers' issues found a place on the agenda of international forums.

This step took us beyond the national level to look at the issue from the international perspective as not only fisheries but the whole world was becoming increasingly integrated towards the end of the 1980s. International policy impacted on every local decision and to challenge this a united strategy at the base was necessary. Capital moved from one area to another in search of resources, cheap labour and markets. Both a local and global focus in the organisational work became imperative. While the local work was more structured through organised struggles, the international work was more flexible, made no pretense of institutionalisation but was more a network. Nevertheless, there was a concerted effort at efficient intervention in global UN forums and providing support to emerging movements at the local level.

The feminist perspective

All through the 1980s, the feminist movement that was growing in India also influenced women who worked in coastal communities where thousands of women actively participate in post-harvest fisheries. But no significance is generally attributed to this work of women when 'fisheries development' is talked about. Valorising their contributions to the community and making visible and protecting their place in the fishery was considered an important demand in the movement. This was initially done, as stated earlier, by taking up the issues that women faced as workers: their right to travel on public transport with their produce, their right to vending space in the markets, protection from exorbitant vending taxes, and so on. Later, national struggles were waged to see that women were accepted as workers in the welfare programmes of the government. These struggles certainly gave women a consciousness of their own rights and the fact that by not asserting them, they could be easily marginalised in the development process.

It was the feminist perspective that highlighted the need to focus on the nurture perspective in the fisheries and introduced this perspective in the movement. This nurture perspective, besides focusing on making women's work in the fishery visible and protecting their existing spaces in it, pushed the union to take up issues that related to daily life issues in the community – water, health facilities, education and child care, and so on. It also opened up thinking and action to conserve the fish habitat, the mangrove vegetation, the estuarine niches and recreate the destroyed habitat through artificial reefs. The feminist perspective also challenged the fact that technology and modern science are neutral. These have evolved in contexts of male dominance and the subjugation of women and nature thereby destroying the organic inter-relationships in nature and society. This paradigm of development is not life-centred and thus inherently disregards the labour of women and labour for subsistence.

From 1990 until the middle of that decade, the NFF organised formal training programmes for cadre development. One important input in the sessions was the discussion on patriarchy and a feminist perspective of fisheries development. In 1993, this led to a specific 'women in fisheries programme' in the NFF. This was part of a larger programme undertaken in different fishworkers' organisations in other parts of the world sponsored by the ICSF. This programme, which consisted in creating a core group of women leaders, taking up specific issues of women in the union and seeing how women's places in the fishery could be safeguarded, was a very important work indeed. It helped to bring some theoretical clarity by tracing the links between the development of technology and the destruction of the natural resource base and the marginalisation of women in the fishery. Besides organising specific input programmes, for the core group of women, a serious attempt was also made to collect data on women's involvement in fisheries and although this is not exhaustive, it is significant as it documents the numerous roles and spaces that women occupy in the fishery thereby making a livelihood.

This women's core group also studied and took up the issue of the injustice done to migrant women workers in the fish processing plants. Under the auspices of the NFF they organised a Public Hearing on 'Women's Struggles for Survival in Fisheries (Dossier, 1995)'[1]. Live testimonies of women workers in the fish processing plants convinced the jury that serious consideration should be given to protect the rights of these migrant women workers and the spaces of women in the fishery. Subsequently, the NFF was successfully able to intervene and see that the Department of Labour takes seriously the plight of these women and insists that the processing industry treat these women on a par with other contract and migrant labour as per the legal stipulations. Although some States did respond positively, the problem is not yet in total control.

In 1999, the NFF took up a large national struggle demanding that women be nationally considered as fishworkers and receive the welfare benefits that fishermen receive from government. In some States, such as in Orissa and West Bengal, the mobilisation around this issue challenged the accepted norm that fisheries were male domains and it appeared to take the legislators by surprise. In response to the mobilisation, the state had to accept the fact that women also earned their livelihood from fish-related activity. So as such, the NFF has succeeded to project this fact at the national level.

Despite the fact that all these attempts were made to create gender awareness in the movement, there continued to be a resistance to the more vocal and able women leaders who were emerging. The women of the core group were consistently chided and by the end of the 1990s most of them either withdrew or left. Nevertheless, the male leaders in the union, either because they were convinced about gender equity or because the general ethos of recognising women's participation was more accepted, took upon themselves to see that women's issues would still remain on the agenda. Here again the men seem more secure when they talk about women's issues than when the women talk about them. Some State unions resisted accepting an all women's union as a member of the NFF but this gradually changed because of other power conflicts.

This made us reflect on the decision that was taken in the early 1980s when the Coastal Women's Forum was asked to merge with the emerging fishermen's struggle. There were some of us women who had wanted the women's wing to be autonomous while others of us thought that both men and women should be part of the same movement. In fact the latter decision prevailed and that also brought strength to the movement. But in the long run, no matter all the attempts to build up gender consciousness and propose alternate strategies of functioning, the male power politics prevailed and frustration forced most of us women to withdraw.

These feminist perspectives got carried to other forums at the international level when the Memorial University in Newfoundland organised an international conference bringing researchers from all over the world and women from the fishing communities of Atlantic Canada together and later when the AKTEA network got researchers and women from fishworker organisations especially from Europe together. Through these interactions, women in fisheries in the developed world also understood how fisheries development in their parts of the world had marginalised them and how deep rooted is gender discrimination in the ongoing development paradigm.

The challenges of a mass base

In order to be effective and have an impact, a movement that seeks social reform should have a mass base or have mass support. The KSMTF and the NFF did pride themselves because of a substantial mass base to draw attention to the struggles. In fact the struggles were also of a creative nature and the leadership was able to draw support from different sections. All this sustained the movement that struggled for the rights of the coastal fishers. In the process, the emerging young leaders also developed skills and over the years, by the mid-1990s, the movement gained political space of its own. It was in this process, I would suggest, that two important setbacks developed. On the one hand, the mobilisation on national issues detracted from the local and the energy and time that was required to keep the base alive was substantially reduced with the result that the strength at the base dwindled. On the other hand, over the years, the distance between the cooperatives that were an economic force and the trade union that was the political force widened. The former got increasingly professionalised in operational style as its base expanded and lost the initial thrust in issue-based activism. The achievements of the trade union were therefore not translated to the base and it was as if it functioned in a vacuum. Furthermore, with the recognition as a national movement, the leaders began to vie for power and personal interest began to override the public good. Gradually, instead of the movement and its affiliated structures becoming strengthened at the base, there seemed to grow a system of patronage in order to maintain power. By the end of the 1990s, the traditional sector had grown increasingly capital intensive and had become aggressive in its fishing too. The NFF had struck deals with the trawl sector in joint struggles against the deep-sea fishing vessels and confused the members at the base. Alliance building is imperative as a movement grows from local to national but the costs have also to be collectively assessed and a balance maintained.

Conclusion

This is only a gist of a complex process that has taken place since the early 1970s. Unfortunately, since entering the 2000s, one can say with disappointment that the impact of the movement is declining. Being very closely related to these processes myself I have tried to highlight the strengths that professional tools can contribute to a process of mobilisation for people's rights but they are not sufficient. From 'non-emotional involvement with the client' as a professional social work approach, activism commences with a 'passion for the subject' that leads one to challenge the dominant mainstream and to seek justice. But activism without methodology and intervention skills can lead to anarchy and drag one into a power game. This is where community organisation skills and methodology can be useful guiding tools and principles. While such tools help one to be a facilitator, it is the spirit of activism that motivates, that reaches beyond the present and plunges into new situations created by the onward march of society.

In the neo-liberal world of today, there are large numbers that are rejected from the mainstream and others who are never integrated. In fact, they are used by the mainstream as cheap labour or as museum pieces and tourist attractions, but receive no recognition or benefits from the system. In this context it becomes increasingly important to challenge the stereotypical concepts of the homogenising mainstream and to reconceptualise social processes where cultural diversity, justice and true democracy will permit people to live in harmony.

With both the corporate sector and multinational agencies becoming increasingly involved in funding the social sector in the southern world, and with the growing concept of civil society that creates more space for non-governmental organisation activity, the strength of the people's movements gets side-tracked in making their demands on the State. Trained social workers in India are being turned out by the hundreds these days. Allured by plush jobs they easily move into this privatised sector of social service delivery. Very few have any historical or analytical perspective of social processes or are interested in the social movements. Interestingly, while movements are spontaneously growing in the Northern world, they are being contained by autocratic governments in the South. Schools of social work both in the North and the South have to therefore reassess their role and scope in the world of the 21st century.

Note

1   Public Hearing on the Struggles of women Workers in the Fish Processing Industry in India, Samudra Dossier, Women in Fisheries Series, No.1, ICSF, Chennai, 1995.

Chapter 7

Borders, Exclusions and Resistance: The Case of Slovenia

Jelka Zorn

Introduction[1]

In 1991 Slovenia separated from Yugoslavia to become an independent state. Behind the campaign for independence were demands for democracy, respect for human rights and the lure of joining the European Union (EU). However, while independence brought about a transition to parliamentary pluralism and the introduction of a fully fledged market economy it also brought about new types of exclusion and undermined the welfare state. Slovene political elites began to adhere to neo-liberal principles. As Ramesh Mishra argued, with the end of the Cold War, it appeared as if there was no alternative to capitalist neo-liberalism (Mishra, 2000).

Governmental discourse concerning the rise of social inequality, unemployment and poverty shifted from perspectives which stressed the socio-economic nature of these problems to ones that stressed 'individual failing', where deprived individuals are perceived as lacking relevant skills and an appropriate work ethic, and so on. Here, for instance, reducing social benefits is presented as a necessary control to prevent service users from abusing the welfare system. Access to most welfare services has increasingly developed around restrictive criteria based on citizenship. For example, in Yugoslavia prior to 1991, health care services were equally accessible to the whole population. Today, new criteria exist which excludes some groups of people from accessing health care services.

Citizenship status had little significance in Yugoslavia. With the transition to the independent Slovene nation state, however, both neo-liberal values and the market economy became important for the allocation of social, economic and political rights, and citizenship status became a *sine qua non* for having rights. Thus, citizenship became tied to both 'inclusion' and 'exclusion'. This is best illustrated by the concept of the 'symbolic glass floor': citizens exist above the floor and can look down on those beneath who are excluded from citizenship and are thus the most deprived in society (Shklar, in Olson, 2001). Although they face a diminishing welfare state and rising inequalities, those people above the glass floor – citizens – can be persuaded that their rights do in fact exist if they see that the rights of non-citizens or foreigners are inferior, precarious or conditioned on assimilation (Balibar, 2004, p. 37).

One can argue that 'exclusion from citizenship' has been a central theme of the Slovene state-building process. Not only was a physical boundary with the 'Balkans' (the territory of former Yugoslavia) introduced, but a symbolic boundary was also invented with the 'Balkans' typically represented in a very negative and simplified way – an irrational, backward and violent place (Močnik, 1999; Vodopivec, 2001). Long before it gained official EU status in 2004 Slovenia had become (both symbolically and physically) a 'borderland' of 'Europe'. Its 'borderland' position between 'Europe' and the 'Balkans' is most reflected in the spheres of citizenship, immigration and asylum policies.

Considering the significance of borders and 'borderlands', Balibar (2004) has argued that the term 'border' is undergoing a profound change in meaning:

> The borders of new socio-political entities, in which an attempt is being made to preserve all the functions of the sovereignty of the state, are no longer entirely situated at the outer limit of territories; they are displaced a little everywhere, wherever the movement of information, people, and things is happening and is controlled – for example in cosmopolitan cities [or in 'borderland' countries]. (Balibar, 2004, p. 1)

This means that in the attempt to preserve the sovereignty of a state, borders can result in exclusion from entry to a country as well as exclusions from membership and participation in a community. It can be argued that Slovenia as the new socio-political entity located at the new EU external border is a typical example of contradictions in Europe (simultaneously being a site of repression and democracy), especially in the field of current immigration policies.

This chapter looks at how the process of forming the new state, defining a new 'body' of citizenship and new state borders resulted in new types of exclusions. These exclusions were not only external (preventing people from entering the country legally) but also internal. Former citizens can now be treated as non-citizens, asylum seekers, undocumented immigrants and even 'erased'[2].

Focusing on the accelerated exclusions and inequalities within Slovenia and the Slovenian welfare system the chapter will also look at the growth of resistance to the continued (mis)use of state power. For the purpose of this chapter, resistance and oppression are intertwined. One can argue, that defining oppression is already a notion of resistance. Resistance in the form of struggle for social justice and respect for human rights is a core principle of social work. To be most effective it is important for social workers to identify pockets of resistance in the community and join with them in the mutual struggle for rights. Together these pockets of resistance can be identified as part of the 'new social movements' or 'movement for global justice': a local manifestation of the global movement fighting social exclusion, global inequalities and the neo-liberal onslaught on public welfare.

New borders, new exclusions

Slovenia has had a history of receiving and dealing with 'refugees' dating back to the former state of Yugoslavia. After the First World War, children from other parts of the country (Bosnia and the northern part of Serbia), who lost their parents or whose parents became destitute, were sent to Slovenia to be cared for (Zorn, 2006). Solidarity among Yugoslav nations was one of the constitutional principles of the post-war state (Bakić-Hayden and Hyden, 1992). The Ministry of Social Care was responsible for these children and attempts were made to be culturally sensitive to their needs regarding language, religion and their experiences of the war.

However, here the intention is not to discuss the quality of the service provided, but to point out the equality of treatment received by those dealt with by The Ministry of Social Care (now called the Ministry of

Labour, Family and Social Affairs) in comparison to today's refugees or asylum seekers who are almost exclusively dealt with by the Ministry of Internal Affairs (a significant shift from the 'caring' to the 'controlling' arm of the state). As a result of new immigration controls whose focus is peoples from the global South and East, and adherence to authoritarian aspects of the EU policy, a segregated and 'policing' welfare has been introduced.

In Slovenia, as elsewhere in Europe, borders have become 'essential institutions in the construction of social conditions on a global scale where the passport or identity card function as a systematic criterion' (Balibar, 2004, p. 113). For this reason Balibar defines borders as the non-democratic condition of democratic institutions (Balibar, 2004, p. 109) and speaks of a new global apartheid being put in place after the disappearance of the old colonial and postcolonial apartheids (Balibar, 2004, p. 113).

One of the symptoms of the new apartheid is the existence of institutions such as detention and deportation centres across Europe. The position of detention centres within the legal structure has been developed through the 'state of emergency' principle which permits a legal suspension of human rights and democratic norms during times when there is a need to protect the population from threats (Agamben, 1998). Their position within the legal structure is a state of exception and as such resembles concentration camps (see Agamben, 1998). However, their objective is not to deliberately murder or torture people. In comparison to concentration camps, their role is to make life in detention as 'humane' as possible. Thus, a sense of normality has been created about these institutions as well as about repressive immigration and asylum policies in general (see Cohen, 2005). Nevertheless the fact that people without criminal records are detained in the first place and that the detentions centres have become accepted as something quite normal must not be underestimated. Balibar argues that this state of exception is nothing exceptional any more. On the contrary, he argues, 'it is "banal": it permeates the functioning of social and political systems that claim or believe themselves to be "democratic"' (Balibar, 2004, p. 120).

The erasure

An unconstitutional part of Slovene immigration policy was the erasure of 18,305 people from the Register of Permanent Residents in 1992. The term 'erasure' has been developed to designate the cancellation of the legal residential status of those who did not become Slovene citizens in 1991 when the citizenship policy of Slovenia was initially designated. These people were perceived as non-Slovenes, with the vast majority of them coming to Slovenia in the 1970s as migrants from other republics of the former Yugoslavia. The consequence of the erasure from the Register of Permanent Residents, carried out by the Ministry of Internal Affairs, was the elimination of all their rights. As Blitz has argued, these individuals (who have designated themselves *The Erased*), have become *de facto* stateless:

> Like Jews in Nazi Germany, the Erased existed within a state that had robbed them of their rights but still subjected them to its jurisdiction. Like other stateless persons elsewhere, once their civil and political rights were revoked they saw their economic and social rights, including the rights to work, social security, health care and education disintegrate and were consequently subject to further abuse from third parties. (Blitz, 2006, p. 4)

This means that formally all their rights were cancelled. However, the erasure was implemented in various ways. Some lost their jobs, pensions and health insurance, others managed to regain their residential or citizenship status relatively fast – before this unexpected illegal situation would totally destroy their life. The difference in eligibility in most cases related to differences in their class position. Using Balibar's words this case of extreme exclusion in the Slovene state demonstrates the way borders 'have been transported *into the middle of political space*' together with the institutional practices that proceed from them (Balibar, 2004, p. 109, emphasis original). In his opinion, the function of the borders is social discrimination, which 'in other times we would have called this their "class function"' (Balibar, 2004, p. 113).

The exclusion had a firm legal base in the formal ascription of ethnicity to individuals, which was subsequently followed by the creation of a Slovene 'citizenship body'. Ethnicity was administratively ascribed to the whole population of Slovenia based on the 1974 Yugoslav Constitution (Dedić *et al.*, 2003). This Constitution introduced a special legal status, republican citizenship, a kind of sub-citizenship that at the time had no meaning, but which played a vital role in 1991. Once this distinction was established it could then be manipulated in various ways. Indeed, it was used against people of migrant origin.

The citizenship policy of the new state included two legal possibilities for acquiring citizenship status. Ethnic Slovenes, that is those whose names had been registered in the Slovene citizenship book, were automatically granted citizenship (that is, the *jus sanguinis* principle). For the residents of Slovenia who originated[3] from the other republics of the former Yugoslavia, citizenship was only granted on the basis of their application (according to article 40 of the Citizenship Act) (that is, the *jus soli* principle). Most of these residents of non-Slovene ethnic origin, 171,000 people, acquired Slovene citizenship this way (out of a two million Slovene population). A total of 18,305 people did not acquire Slovene citizenship. They either did not apply or their application was rejected. Consequently, these individuals were automatically and secretly erased from the Register of Permanent Residents of Slovenia by the Ministry of Internal Affairs. By this measure they were formally stripped of all their rights – social, economic and political, including the right to live in their own homes with their families. However, the erased never received any official decision or notification about the cancellation of their residential status. They learned about it individually, in various (chance) occasions. This means that a procedure for complaining did not even exist. In many cases people were 'informed' about their situation when their documents (passports, identity cards, driving licences) were made invalid (punched, cut up, defaced) at the local administrative units or town halls. Despite these illicit experiences, in general people believed that cancellation of their residential status was a temporary issue, which could be sorted out quickly. They could foresee neither the consequences nor the extent of this situation. They did not know that many other people had found themselves living under the same conditions. For example, one of the erased persons, who did not apply for Slovenian citizenship in 1991, remembered the seizure of his documents:

In 1992 I wanted to renew my driver's license in Dravograd [a small town in Slovenia]. The clerk asked me to bring my passport because she had to enter some data. She took my passport, went to another room and punched it. Since I intended to apply for citizenship anyway [under the conditions for regular naturalisation], I did not think this passport invalidation was very important. But it was strange because the passport was issued in Slovenia, in Dravograd and was valid until 1995. She said to me: 'You can't have our documents.' I was left without documents. She did not renew my driver's license but told me I'd have to renew it in my own country. I passed the driving test in Dravograd so, naturally, my driver's license was issued in Dravograd. 'You can no longer have our driver's license,' the clerk said.
(recorded interview, June 15, 2002, in Zorn, 2003)

Similar invalidations of identity cards and passports by district officials have been recounted by many other erased people (see Zorn, 2005; Blitz, 2006). This is probably one of the most common ways people learned they were no longer officially resident in Slovenia at their home addresses. Or even worse, as a consequence of becoming 'illegal', many were detained in order to be deported.

The ideological agenda behind the erasure, which made it possible and effective, was racism. Here the racism is understood in Balibar's (1991) notion of 'racism without races', meaning 'race' as a symbolic status of otherness and not (only) as skin colour. The erased included a wide range of individuals who did not have common ties to each other[4]. The only unifying factor was that these individuals were perceived as non-Slovenes, pejoratively called 'Southerners' or 'Balkans' and thus alien to Slovene 'culture' (Blitz, 2006, p. 18). This kind of racism, manifested in the form of 'anti-Balkanism' became widespread and normalised in the society. For example, hate speech against all migrants from other republics of the former Yugoslavia included public discussions about the revision and withdrawal of citizenship statuses that had already been lawfully acquired according to the application procedure (Article 40 of the Citizenship Act). Demands for revision and withdrawal of citizenship statuses were even debated in the Parliament in 1993 and 1994 (Zorn, 2005). This was a deliberate politics of deterrence.

It seemed as if the erased were being punished for not having become Slovene citizens. Despite having status as permanent residents and living in Slovenia for years or decades, suddenly they were treated as if they had just arrived in the country without any documentation or ties to the communities in Slovenia. They were not treated as legal foreigners or citizens of another state, but as pariahs, non-citizens. For example, they lost the right to employment. One of the erased, a working-class man, expressed his situation as follows:

> The state literally made a poor man out of me. I can't provide food for my children. I am on the edge of nervous breakdown, nights I can't sleep. When you just think that one ordinary paper would open up a possibility for me to get my job back. But no, they won't give it to me.
> (recorded interview, June 26, 2002, in Zorn, 2003).

These circumstances *and* not being able to support oneself and one's family resulted in a violation of human dignity, as he further expressed:

> I am ashamed in front of my neighbours. In their eyes I am young, healthy, but I don't want to work. His poor wife, they think, she has to support him. I have explained the whole problem for many years, again and again, I repeat myself like a parrot, but still at the end of the day everybody thinks it is my fault.
> (recorded interview, June 26, 2002, in Zorn, 2003).

Without legal status they were not even eligible to receive social benefits. In addition they lost their health insurance and were thus prevented from access to public health services. There were cases where individuals died due to a lack of medical assistance (Blitz, 2006; Insight News TV, 2006). Furthermore, the erased could not legally cross the state border. Being a small country and with people having relatives and friends all over the territory of the former Yugoslavia, this measure caused a great deal of stress and grievance. Some were deported and suffered great difficulties returning to their families in Slovenia.

The erasure is a curious example of a state's *production of illegality* (see Balibar, 2004). One can see how states are able to produce rather than eliminate illegality. Because of their position outside the law but still subjected to it, the erased were liable to police control. One can argue that they became the 'property of the police'. As Neocleous (2000) argues, groups that fall under this type of police regime lose their voice and power within important institutions of society and state.

From erasure to public action

The tremendous difficulties and years of suffering which these individuals and their families encountered are further described in Zorn (2005) and in Blitz (2006). However, the emphasis of this section is to highlight their collective action and resistance to the process and to look at why the oppression, the erasure, continued for so many years. Why did the oppressed individuals and their supporters, when they became outlawed in 1992, not immediately join together to fight for their rights? Simply put, the oppression was so severe that public action to fight for their rights was impossible. Or, as argued by Hannah Arendt, the fundamental violation of human rights is manifested first and above all in the 'deprivation of a place in the world which makes opinions significant and actions effective.' (Arendt, 1967, p. 296)

One of the main characteristics of the erasure was its surreptitiousness, which kept people isolated and led to these individuals feeling personally responsible for losing their status as permanent residents. Moreover, what happened to these individuals was only revealed to the public ten years later. This oppression surfaced as a result of a major joint effort of these affected people and their supporters. One of the key issues was *how to name the oppression*. Up until 2002 when the erasure became an important public question, this act did not even attract the status of the violation of human rights nor was it called the erasure from the Register of Permanent Residents. The victims of the erasure mainly did not know each other, and had attempted to regain their lost rights only individually (many of them wrote to the Ombudsman, the courts, the President, the Prime Minister, the Minister of Internal Affairs, and such like) (Zorn, 2005). Senior and junior clerks of the Ministry of Internal Affairs claimed that these people had only been transferred from one registry to another, and the media did not report on their experiences from their perspective, but only in a very bureaucratic, hostile style of language. A concealment of the traumatic experiences of the discriminated group can be defined as *cultural anaesthesia* (Adorno, in Feldman, 1996; Zaviršek, 2000). Gradually, the erased started to connect themselves within a community and founded their own non-governmental organisation (NGO) in 2002. The collective telling of life stories and sharing of experiences gradually led to the formation of a community of the erased. The links so established and the sharing of experiences contributed to their collective self-advocacy, their political action which, in the opinion of Hanna Arendt, is a special and fundamental human capability; it differs from all other activities relating to labour, art and so on, and possibly the only human activity that is capable of preventing catastrophes such as totalitarianism (Arendt, 1958).

Another important factor that contributed to the suppression of critical voices and the outcry of those who suffered violation of their rights and dignity was the constant praising of Slovenia internally, and in the international community, for being the only success story from the territory of former Yugoslavia. But there was a huge gap between the public image of Slovenia and the experiences of the erased people. For example, a young man, erased from the Register of Permanent Residents said:

> It is not the violation of our rights that hurts the most, what is even more painful is the gap between proclaimed democracy, respect for human rights and state ruled by law on the one hand and the real conditions that were thrown upon us on the other. It is painful to realise that our problems are not mentioned in public at all, because they could ruin the perfect picture of Slovenia being a democratic state. It is this silence of what happened to us that hurts the most.
> (diary record, November 2002, in Zorn, 2003)

When the silence ended in 2002 the erased were in public often referred to as public enemies of the Slovene nation. In 2003 the Slovene Constitutional Court, for the second time, ruled that the erasure from the Register of Permanent Residents was illegal because it violated the constitutional order. Nevertheless, the erased were considered to be disgraceful and deceitful in their behaviour and demands. There were attempts to block and trivialise their struggle by prominent politicians (for example, current Vice President Janez Janša). The right-wing parliamentary parties have portrayed Slovene citizens as victims who, as taxpayers, will have to pay inconceivable compensation to the erased.

When the oppression was fully brought to light through the public sharing of experiences it provoked the development of new networks with different alliances. The new coalitions turned the whole situation of oppression upside down. In the course of these events the erasure became a central point of the emerging movement for global justice in Slovenia. This movement believes that a 'better world is possible'. It continues to collectively develop arguments, raise demands and build coalitions with various activist groups and individuals, locally and internationally, in particular in nearby Italy (see www.dostje.org).

A core group of 'erased' activists went beyond fighting for their cause and began supporting other oppressed groups. Through this broader solidarity network they were able to see the injustice done to them as a part of larger context of neo-liberalism and the suspension of democracy.

Despite their exclusion from residential and citizenship *legal status* they have been engaged in public matters and thus been been participating in the *process of creating* citizenship and democracy. Although deprived of formally belonging to the community they have become an indispensable part of the community acting in solidarity and beyond national reference. Or as stated by Balibar: 'We are not "citizens", but we can "become" citizens; we can *enter into* one or several processes of creation of citizenship. And we enter all the more deeply into them the more numerous and more different (I would almost say the more *divergent*) we are.' (Balibar, 2004, p. 199)

Bosnian refugees

Another example of raising and spreading borders internally as a means of denying rights is the case of refugees fleeing the Balkan wars. However, these refugees, in contrast to the erased, came from outside the country and their misfortune provided Slovenia with an opportunity to erect and exercise the external borders.

In 1992 Croatian and Bosnian refugees sought shelter in Slovenia. At one point they numbered 45,000, which represented about two per cent of the Slovene population (Vrečer, 2005, p. 659). The number of refugees gradually reduced because many returned home or left Slovenia for other counties (that is, Western Europe, Canada, and so on), thus only a small minority have settled in Slovenia (about 1,800).

Despite the initial welcoming response of the Slovene population, which showed solidarity and empathy, the mainstream public discourse quickly shifted towards anxiety, fear and hatred. This change in attitude was, in no small part, a response to exaggerated refugee numbers presented by governmental representatives, The Red Cross and the media, who argued that the refugees represented an enormous burden on Slovene state and society (Doupona et al., 1998; Jeffs, 1999). Natalija Vrečer has argued that one of the main questions of Slovene policy and public attitude towards Bosnian refugees was: 'Why don't they return home?'. Instead of integration the government managed repatriation policies.

Nationalism, which had been one of the forces behind the secession of Slovenia, was then used against the refugees. This had very concrete consequences. The first one was the closure of the border between Slovenia and Croatia (the present EU border) to prevent more refugees gaining shelter in Slovenia. The second issue was their treatment inside the country, which can be defined as a segregation policy. They were accommodated in the collective centres across the country and the segregation measures went as far as to restrict their free movement outside these centres for certain periods of time. Besides this they were virtually excluded from the labour market. They were only allowed to work eight hours per week and as most jobs entailed a 40-hour week they simply could not compete for work. Neither the Geneva Convention on Refugees nor simple equal rights principles were applied. Initially there had been no law to define and protect their rights as refugees. When The Act on Temporary Protection was introduced in 1997 it institutionalised an already established discrimination and marginalisation of Bosnian refugees. Despite such harsh treatment many were socially and culturally very active and contributed significantly to the Slovene cultural diversity and plurality.

It would appear that closing down borders, erecting strict external immigration controls, marginalisation of refugees and spreading nationalist (anti-Balkan) discourse was the government's substitute (a symbolic glass floor) for regulation of fair employment conditions and social security for the majority of the population.

Through the first half of the 1990s there were many anti-war demonstrations organised by refugees and their supporters demanding a ceasefire in Bosnia. Only minor protests addressed the living conditions of refugees (Č elik, 1994). The refugee-led campaign gained momentum in 2002 when the government's decision to close down one of the collective centres on the outskirts of Ljubljana was strongly opposed. Despite extremely poor conditions, refugees had lived at this centre for a decade and had nowhere else to go. Their struggle was supported by a network of various activist and non-governmental groups and individuals – previously referred to as the movement for global justice (see www.dostje.org). Some of the supporters took part in active political engagement as a result of their own experience of the erasure.

Asylum seekers

One can argue that there is no more asylum in Europe, since Geneva refugee status has become so restricted. Only a small minority of asylum applications are endorsed. In Slovenia rejected asylum seekers and undocumented immigrants are most likely to be detained and deported. Those who are still involved in asylum procedures live in a segregated, institutional style of housing. The Slovene Ministry of Internal Affairs, a governmental body responsible for the implementation of asylum and immigration policies, has incorporated a form of social assistance within the two types of institutions: the *Asylum Home* and the *Detention Centre*. The police have ultimate authority and as a result, social workers cannot work independently. Thus, the role of social services in these two institutions has been more or less (but not entirely) limited to the questions of how to make a refugee without status deportable and how to make the inhumane practices of segregation, detention and deportation look as humane as possible. This and the following section look at both the role of social workers as advocates of asylum seekers' rights and also their role as (potential) collaborators of repressive police orders.

European governments claim that one of their goals is to fight illegal immigration, and to protect the human rights of 'true' refugees. According to the Slovene government, one of the strategies for vindicating the human rights of refugees is to deport those who are considered 'bogus' asylum seekers. Thus former Minister of Internal Affairs Rado Bohinc

(2004, p. 3) argued: 'A consistent implementation of measures to return individuals [who do not need international protection] to their countries of origin will prevent abuses of the asylum system'. This conceptualisation perceives refugees and undocumented immigrants as essentially two different groups with very little or nothing in common. Moreover, the real problem of selective immigration controls and the consequences that arise from both external barriers and internal discriminations is thus ignored. Promoting respect for the human rights of 'true' refugees has become a pretext for oppression of others who, according to the governmental criteria, were not tortured enough to be recognised as Geneva Convention refugees. Indeed, it is a strange world in which the human rights of 'true' refugees are vindicated by the deportation of those whose suffering and disabilities, a government has not recognized as great enough.

To normalise the exclusions and the creation of *Fortress Europe*, the media and European governments accuse asylum seekers of abusing the system. Such discourse conceals the exclusionist nature of asylum status and tries to present the problem of restrictive immigration controls as a solution. The low numbers of people obtaining refugee status in Slovenia highlights the repressive policy of the state: from 1995 to the present only 141 (out of an approximate total of 14,800) applicants have been awarded refugee status.

As Seyla Benhabib (2004, p. 2) observes, 'there is not only a tension, but often an outright contradiction, between human rights declaration and states' sovereign claims to control their borders as well as to monitor the quality and quantity of admittees'. This means that there are no objective criteria or methods of establishing 'a well-founded fear' of each individual asylum seeker. The decision-making process is inevitably the interpretation of the state employees, who are influenced by the restrictive European and national immigration policies and politics. A cursory glance into the recent history of asylum combined with the small number of granted asylums shows the extent of today's restrictive immigration politics over asylum. During the Cold War era, Eastern European refugees were generally welcomed into the Western European countries, which is no longer the case (Chimni, 1998). Today there is a culture of 'disbelief' and a designation of people as 'bogus' asylum seekers (Humphries, 2005). One could argue that the change in attitude towards refugees demonstrates the political nature of asylum. At the time of the Cold War, escapees from East to West were welcomed not only because the labour force was needed but above all because they demonstrated the failure of communist-led Europe. By accepting these refugees, Western governments affirmed that capitalism was superior.

From the middle of the 1960s until its collapse, Yugoslavia, a non-allied state, played a peculiarly interesting role for Eastern European refugees escaping to the West. It facilitated their migration to Western Europe, accommodated them in special centres or in the community, thus turning a blind eye or even driving them across the border to Italy (Č elik, 2006, pp. 92, 93). These runaways are now revered as heroes.

Today, asylum seekers are caught in a vicious circle of repressive conceptualisation: because of their poverty and/or because they have 'wrong' passports, they are criminalised through selective immigration controls. Welfare rights and benefits do not apply equally to them. They receive less and are treated differently to the extent that they are dealt with by a different governmental ministry to the rest of the population. Ed Mynott (2002) defined such composition of rights and entitlements as an 'apartheid welfare system'.

Advocacy of asylum seekers' rights

One of the constitutive moments of the movement for global justice in Slovenia has been public welcoming of asylum seekers and fighting the xenophobic responses of the government, media and some neighbourhoods. In 2000/2001 a network of individuals and groups ironically called the *Office for Intervention* (Urad za intervencije – UZI) launched an intensive campaign to support asylum seekers and to raise awareness of their plight. The Office for Intervention (in the contrast to its name) had no office, no membership, no structure, no leadership, nothing which stirred the imagination of the police spies and media (Zadnikar, 2004, p. 210). UZI organised public discussions, performances, round tables and other events such as daily 'guards' in front of the Asylum Home and the Detention Centre holding a banner 'For Solidarity!'. On 21 February 2001, popular demonstrations 'For Solidarity – Against Xenophobia' were organised in the centre of Ljubljana and more than a thousand people joined in (Zadnikar, 2004). Of course, social workers were among them.

Especially in the last couple of years, individual social workers within the Ljubljana Asylum Home have continuously advocated on behalf of asylum seekers. For example, they have facilitated complaints procedures of asylum seekers against the Asylum Home itself and to the Minister of Internal Affairs. Enormous endeavors have been made by social workers to support individual asylum seekers' inclusion into more independent, outside institutional lifestyles and in some cases, access to community social services (a women's shelter for example). Individual social workers have also connected with networks of NGOs and activists in the movement for global justice where they themselves lacked influence and power to prevent or stop mistreatment (for example, unlawful and unannounced deportations of asylum seekers at 5am).

One of the key features of the present authoritarian asylum and immigration politics in Europe is a constant revision of the legislation and adjustment of policies proceeding from laws that are increasingly more restrictive in order to deter asylum seekers (Hayter, 2004). When a Bill on asylum was introduced in Slovenia in 2005 authorising the police extensive power over asylum seekers, lawyers and NGOs launched a campaign to withdraw the Bill or revise it significantly. Social workers joined the campaign as a professional group arguing that the Bill would seriously jeopardise the human rights of asylum seekers. At the 2005 National Congress of Social Work, one of the most distinguished professional events in Slovenia, they collectively protested against the Bill by submitting a protest letter to the highest governmental bodies and the media. It received little attention by the media and was not well received by the government. Although the Bill became law with only minor revisions, this action had significant implications for the social work community. It raised awareness regarding the situation of asylum seekers, provided an opportunity for networking and a sense of professional strength.

Deportations

On average, over the past few years, Slovene police have expelled approximately 1,500 people (men, women and children) per year.

One of the discourses that seeks to legitimise repressive laws and policies is respect for human rights and human dignity. Human rights rhetoric is included in all phases of civil and police treatment of failed asylum seekers or undocumented immigrants, including their detention and deportation. What is the meaning of human rights in these cases? Is human rights only about assessing the quality of life in detention (access to food, newspapers, spending time with volunteers, and so on) and evaluating the deportations according to the level of violence used? Does the concept of human rights only go so far as looking at ensuring that inhumane policies are carried out 'humanely'?

The distortion of this discourse can only be fully grasped when understood from the perspective of the most vulnerable and oppressed – the detainees themselves. It is important for social workers to consider this perspective when looking at what changes human rights rhetoric can bring to the detainees. The police-led human rights approach includes involvement of social workers in detention centres. Thus, the role of social work has to be critically evaluated, as well.

The officially designated tasks of social workers in the Ljubljana Detention Centre are: accommodation of immigrants (which includes three no-choice meals per day), facilitating access to basic health care, providing psychosocial counselling, enrolment of children into local primary schools, facilitating onsite visits with friends and relatives, collaboration with NGOs, organising different social or 'spare-time' activities such as table games, drawing, spending time with volunteers, and so on.

The head of the main Detention Centre, a police officer, views the Centre not as being an institution of forced deportation but rather one which carries out its powers in a humane way. She calls this 'voluntary deportation' (Zorn, 2003). She explained that the role of the social workers was to ensure that detainees while waiting for deportation spend their time as usefully as possible. One of the social workers' tasks is to support immigrants in finding out what types of jobs they could do when they return to their home countries. To achieve this, the residents are given support in building self-confidence and developing social and other skills.

However, turning from the police perspective to the perspective of the asylum seekers or immigrants, advocacy and human rights remain empty concepts. The residents expressed feelings of stress and anxiety because of their imprisonment and scheduled forced removals. A young girl I met during my research had seriously injured herself and almost died when she tried to escape deportation. Others I spoke to considered the activities organised by social workers to be both cynical and humiliating (Zorn, 2003). For example, a young man from Bosnia and Herzegovina in the Detention Centre said:

> I have been here for 10 days now, waiting to be sent back home. It is horrible here, I have never been in a prison before, I never had anything to do with the police. It is as if I were a criminal. I cannot go out and this is a huge psychological pressure. It was ridiculous and tragic when the social worker brought us some drawing materials and invited us to draw pictures. I think it is silly to draw pictures here. I did not come to draw pictures together with Turks and others! Why would I do that? I feel even sillier afterwards. I left home because it is impossible to live in our country – everything has been devastated. There is no future, no hope. (diary entry, 2 March 2002, in Zorn, 2003)

Nevertheless, social workers in the Detention Centre seem to believe they are serving the immigrants, since they always have 'a door they can knock on to complain and someone trustful they can talk to', explained the head of the social workers (diary entry, December 2005, in Zorn, 2003). She added some details to a description of the method of the 'voluntary' deportation project. As explained by her, the aim of an important activity in the Detention Centre, the psychosocial counselling, was to provoke homesickness in people whose fate is deportation anyway. This task is performed by asking questions about residents' family members and others left behind, facilitating access to telephone calls to their homeland and to deal with their complaints. Due to the situation they are in, the complaints are numerous but are displaced and concern food, physical activities, and so on.

One can conclude that the role of the social service in the Detention Centre is to make the deportation as smooth as possible: preparing people to accept their return home, thus preventing violent outbursts and making life in detention bearable, not only for detainees but even more so for the employees.

Is such a role appropriate for social workers? How does it fit with the profession's values, goals and ethics? It seems the above-described attempts to humanise inhumane policies merely conceals institutionalised violence and racism and keeps the *status quo*. At best social work activities can temporarily reduce the sheer brutality of state power over the powerless and at worst they reproduce injustices and thus contradict social work's professional values.

The question for social work here is how to challenge not only such a role that has been in some cases *imposed* on social workers, but above all, the whole situation of global inequality that is reflected in Europe's immigration and asylum policies. It is a well-established fact that human rights and social justice are fundamental principles of social work. However, in relation to asylum seekers and undocumented immigrants it is unclear what rights professional social workers are prepared to advocate for. Human rights are not a static entity, fixed for all times and places, but rather they are a very contextual issue, a response to ever new manifestations and ways of exclusion, exploitation and oppression. Thus, *defining the content of human rights* and exploring questions of social justice when it comes to the undocumented is one of the important tasks of the profession of social work. Assisting people in detention or when they are deported (and even collaborating in the deportation process as some social workers are obliged to do) raises inevitable questions such as: Why can some people travel without any limitations at all, when others are completely restricted? Is the right to migrate a human right? Does every person have a right to be treated as a legal person? What does global social justice really mean? Is detention of immigrants (men, women and children) fair and morally justifiable regardless of which passport they have? What does it mean to respect asylum seekers?

For the right to stay

In comparison with other countries, such as the UK for example, the resistance against deportations has been rather small (see the National Coalition for Anti-Deportation Campaigns, 2006). It can be argued that one of the reasons for the lack of anti-deportation campaigns lies in the segregated living conditions for both asylum seekers (accommodated in Asylum Home) and people who wait to be deported (accommodated in the Detention Centre). It means that from the outset people do not have neighbours and friends in the community, but are totally confined inside the Asylum Home (see Pajnik *et al.*, 2001; Lipovec Čebron, 2002).

Because of the isolation of both groups and lack of information in the wider community the resistance has been limited to public action on principle within the movement for global justice (for example, protests in front of the fence of the Deportation Centre and in the academic context). There were only two anti-deportation campaigns to support individuals, both successful. The first in 2004 was a case of two unaccompanied minors from Ecuador who wanted to join their mother in Italy (www.dostje.org). The second, in 2005, was a case of the 'erased' Roma family; after years spent in Germany they returned to Slovenia to seek asylum. Both campaigns were successful due to the joint effort of a network of groups (among them very respectable ones such as Amnesty International), individuals and family members themselves (www.dostje.org/Prekla).

At the time of writing this chapter the activist groups and individuals have managed to establish a *Network for Permanent Visit in the Detention Centre*. Besides facilitating and promoting a campaign for the abolishment of all detention centres, their agenda is also to support individual people, and to monitor access to welfare provisions and solicitors in order to see as many people as possible being released from detention.

Denial of rights versus values of social work

As critically examined above, part of the problem are *not* the people who travel without proper documentation or who have lost their legal status, but rather internal and external selective immigration controls and repressive immigration and asylum systems. Contemporary immigration policies are about gate-keeping resources and putting people's legal status before their needs. It is a well-known fact that social workers step into the profession because of their desire to make the world a better place for all, to support people and offer information where needed. As shown in the previous section, some social workers have been drawn to a gate-keeping role and thus are not able to serve people according to their needs. However, inequality is the main issue of social work: social work is a profession that challenges inequality and structural oppression, whether perpetrated individually or socially through institutional structures and cultural norms (Dominelli, 2004, p. 71). The international document of social work ethics (IFSW/IASSW, 2006) promotes social workers' responsibility to strive for social justice in relation to society generally, and in relation to people with whom they work including:

- distributing resources equitably: social workers should ensure that resources at their disposal are distributed fairly, according to need;
- challenging unjust policies and practices – social workers have a duty to bring to the attention of their employers, policy makers, politicians and the general public, situations where resources are inadequate or where distribution of resources, policies and practices are oppressive, unfair or harmful.

To translate these demands even more precisely to the area of migration, asylum and citizenship and to work towards an inclusive society, three needs are emphasised:

(1) Every person should be treated as a legal person.
(2) A change or a 'reinvention' of welfare institutions is necessary, providing services according to need.
(3) The movement for global justice as a constitutive part of the social work struggle should be recognised.

The right of every person to be treated as a *legal* person and the right to residency along with the right to free movement of all people should be recognised as a basic human right and therefore it must be placed on the current social work agenda. This also means campaigning for the abolition of all detention and deportation centres.

Today, borders function as a prerequisite and pretext for discrimination, yet there is no ethical reason why there should be different treatment for non-citizens. Social workers should be alerted to the situation where borders create social conditions on a global scale where the passport or identity card functions as a systematic criterion of rights and dignity (Balibar, 2004, p. 113).

The second theme I raised is the need to reinvent welfare institutions, thus reinventing formal citizenship status. I will discuss this by describing an example of a special health centre for people without health insurance in the city of Ljubljana. Those who lack insurance – that is, undocumented immigrants, erased people, homeless or destitute people, asylum seekers, in some cases Bosnian refugees, and so on – cannot access mainstream health services. As a response to the increasing numbers of people who have been pushed out of the welfare system (and thus left without medical assistance of any kind) the Municipality of Ljubljana and two NGOs established a special community Health Centre for people without medical insurance.

It employed a social worker and a nurse, but all physicians are volunteers and there is a lack of proper equipment and resources for operations and other treatments. However, a variety of free-of-charge medicine is available. The most frequent reasons for people to seek medical help are chronic illnesses (such as hypertension, vein trouble), pregnancy and cancer. In the Centre people can take a shower and get clean second-hand clothes. Social workers help people to obtain health insurance in order to get access to mainstream public health services. Still, there are cases of failing to fulfil necessary conditions, especially if a person is without any legal status. The Centre was opened in 2002 and in 2003 there were already 8,101 people assisted there, 103 per cent more than in the year when it was opened. The National Action Plan against Poverty and Social Exclusion for the period 2004-2006 identified this Health Centre as an example of a good practice. Nevertheless, when taking social justice seriously, there is an issue about segregated public services having a tendency towards normalising inequality.

The fact that the introduction of the Health Centre for People without Medical Insurance was *a response* by public servants to the situation of radical exclusion of people from mainstream welfare, must not be underestimated. It provokes questions about the nature of the mainstream public services and their harsh rules when it comes to destitute or non-citizens. It is therefore appropriate to use Ed Mynott's (2002) notion of the apartheid welfare system – not on account of this local initiative resulting in a segregated and poor-quality health service, but on account of the rigorous mainstream health services and insurance system shrinking the boundaries of admittees.

Balibar was right when he wrote that interior exclusions of immigrants constitute a genuine test of welfare institutions. These exclusions show how public institutions turn against themselves. By denying services to groups of people they go against the spirit of equality, diversity and the 'rule of law' (Balibar, 2004, p. 62). The challenge for social workers is to extend *mainstream* social services and provisions to every person, also to those in precarious situations and regardless of their formal belonging (citizenship). Together we should be actively involved in reinvention towards hybrid and equally accessible welfare services.

The third theme is the necessity of establishing alliances and networks with and within the movement for global justice.

The above proposed changes are so profound that the social work profession alone is not capable of their full implementation. Social workers can effectively contribute within their own communities and to the world as a whole to become a better place for everybody, but only if they are part of a wider network of alliances. As argued in the recently published book *Globalisation, Global Justice and Social Work* (Ferguson, *et al.*, 2005), social workers around the globe are part of this relatively new movement which began in Seattle in 1999 with a vision that a better world *is* possible. This 'better world' could be achieved through a democratic, diverse and permanent struggle in our local communities, and through international sharing of experiences, solidarity and mutual actions. To address the problem at its roots, the question of neo-liberal capitalism comes to the fore. The movement for global justice has a common agenda to resist neo-liberalism which tries to reduce principles of the communities and human relations to one single rule: profit before people.

In social work this principle manifests itself as 'value for money', which means that social workers have become pressured to focus on managing budgets at the expense of meeting clients' needs (Harris, 2005). These neo-liberal demands are in blatant contradiction with social work values. The global justice movement has a major implication for social work, as argued by Ferguson and Lavalette:

> The rediscovery of the effectiveness of collective action and organisation has important implications both for social workers and for the service users with whom they work'.
> (Ferguson and Lavalette, 2005, p. 222).

Within the broad struggle against neo-liberalism and the global war on terror, the erased, asylum seekers, undocumented immigrants and many other oppressed groups in Europe as well as in Slovenia embody key pockets of resistance with very concrete demands such as 'Erase camps, not people', 'No one is illegal', 'Fight capitalist Europe', 'Social rights for all', and so on. As stated by Fahrat Kahn, one of the high-profile asylum seekers and activists in Manchester who almost got deported from the UK:

'If the Home Office would have given me a refugee status years ago, when I applied for it, maybe I wouldn't become so political' (in Zorn, 2006).

Similarly, I was wondering one Saturday in March 2006, when I marched at an anti-war demonstration in nearby Italy with a group of people who were erased from the Register of Permanent Residents: Would all these men and women of mixed generations and social backgrounds, have become so politically involved without the horrible experience of erasure? No doubt that this experience brought a huge amount of stress, anxiety and despair to their lives, however, it also provoked public action, their emancipation and helped build new networks.

This is precisely the goal of social work practice: to empower people whose rights are violated or jeopardised and to be engaged in a mutual struggle for social justice.

Conclusion

What Hannah Arendt wrote almost 40 years ago about the human rights of people who were not treated as citizens still holds true: *'The Rights of Man, supposedly inalienable, proved to be unenforceable – even in countries whose constitutions were based upon them – whenever people appeared who were no longer citizens of any sovereign state'* (Arendt, 1967, p. 293).

This chapter has looked at how borders have moved from the 'edge' to the 'centre' of public space and how external borders extend into internal ones (Balibar, 2004, p. 111). These internal borders are concentrated around the issue of citizenship, since its framework is still based on an exclusive national concept of sovereignty. In practical terms this means that immigrants or foreigners in irregular situations are deprived of fundamental social rights (Balibar, 2004, pp. 37, 163). The collapse of traditional forms of sovereignty in the face of globalisation does not prevent states from exercising a monopoly over the territory through immigration and citizenship policies (Balibar, 2004, p. 5).

Moreover, state sovereignty seems to be demonstrated with all the more ostentation to the detriment of individuals who are practically defenceless (Balibar, 2004, p. 36).

Those excluded via immigration controls (that is, particular groups of immigrants) are presented as a threat to the supposedly finite material resources of the receiving nation, as well as its 'culture' (Mynott, 2002, p. 18). It is important to recognise that as argued by Mynott (2002, p. 22), *'the systematic exclusion of "persons subject to immigration control" and the creation of apartheid welfare provision for asylum seekers takes place in the context of an unprecedented neo-liberal onslaught on the welfare state'.* The denial of rights of minority groups is simultaneous to the erosion of various provisions for the majority. It is easier to continue to accuse asylum seekers for undermining the welfare state than to closely examine a government's role in introducing market neo-liberal rules and values into public institutions (thus becoming less and less public). On the other hand, huge amounts of money are spent building an effective police system to control, detain and deport undocumented immigrants[5].

To ensure a fair and just society the current immigration situation calls for ethical considerations taking into account the role of social work with its guiding values and principles. This would lead to the 'reinvention' of welfare institutions and access to rights. Social welfare ought to be about equality and solidarity, *'a collective guarantee of individual dignified survival'* (Bauman, 1998:, p. 45). It should provide equality in need which overrides the inequality in the ability to pay (Bauman, 1998).

Contrary to this, eligibility to social benefits depends on legal status of individuals, and not on their needs. Today the right to a dignified life has become a matter of citizenship rather than universal human rights, individual needs or economic performance. For this institutional racism to be challenged, Balibar argued, *'Social state and social citizenship will have to be completely dismantled, or citizenship will have to be detached from its purely national definition so that social rights with transnational character can be guaranteed'* (Balibar, 2004, p. 113).

To rethink social justice, equality and solidarity in the local and global context, it is crucial to be *explicit about our values and interests*, thereby considering all the contradictions imposed on us. Social workers should stand together with erased people, asylum seekers and immigrants and re-establish the boundary line between police and social work. But first and above all, the immediate and most important task should be the active involvement of social workers in campaigns which demand closure of *all* detention centres.

Notes

1 This article is part of a broader research on Transnational Citizenship granted by the Slovenian Research Agency (Javna agencija za raziskovalno dejavnosti Republike Slovenije) (no. Z5-7309-0591). I am especially grateful to Iain Ferguson, who arranged my visit to the University of Stirling, and for inspiring discussions on (re)emerging radical social work and ideas around it. Also I would like to thank both Michael Lavalette and Iain Ferguson for polishing the English in this chapter.

2 Some of the ethnographic data presented in this chapter were obtained during the nine-month field research in 2002/2003 interviewing people without Slovene citizenship in the Asylum Home, the Detention Centre and at their homes. Interviews with social workers were conducted in 2002/2003 as well as in smaller-scale research in 2005.

3 The term 'originated' is used instead of 'born', because some of the erased people were actually born in Slovenia, but were not registered in the Slovene Republican Citizenship Book. The usual practice was that people were automatically registered in the Republican Citizenship Book on the basis of their birthplace. In the case where parents were migrants they could decide about formal ethnic belonging of a child. In the cases where parents did not decide, a child was registered in the Republican Citizenship Book according to their father's birthplace. This means that people born in Slovenia with their fathers born outside Slovenia could be erased. For more information see Zorn (2005).

4 The erased were a diverse group. According to Blitz (2006), the erased included Bosnians, Croats, Serbs and Roma who had migrated to Slovenia for work (especially in mines and factories), approximately 500 officers from the Yugoslav National Army, many of whom did not see active service as well as civilians born in Slovenia whose republican citizenship had been registered according to their father's birthplace in one of the other republics (Blitz, 2006, p. 18).

5 Joining the EU in May 2004 Slovenia became eligible to receive

funds for Schengen border. In the first few years of the EU membership more than 100 million Euros should be spent in Slovenia only for the police control of its part of the EU external border (Ministrstvo za notranje zadeve, 2005).

Chapter 8

Social Work and Social Activism in Post-democratic South Africa

Josephine Norma Norward

Introduction

There are varied issues and problems that have historically faced South Africa leading to the emergence of all forms of social movements since the 1950s. Social work and social welfare have also evolved over the years to respond to the problems facing the country's diverse population. To that end, the level of impact they have had in addressing the problems cannot be measured nor generalised because of the social, political, economic and educational divergences which have prevailed in this country throughout the 20th century. Of significance to this chapter are selected periods in the history of South Africa which underscore the shifts in social work practice as a result of internal and external social pressures.

In order to understand civil disobedience in South Africa during the 1950s through the late 1980s and its impact, a contextual perspective that involves an examination of the country's social, political and economic structures under the apartheid system is important. The apartheid system, which was ultimately abolished in 1994, is still considered to have been the most repressive form of government to exist in the civilised world. Built around a web of ideological beliefs and moral justifications for white supremacy, apartheid was a system of government which robbed the majority of its population of the basic rights to a decent life as articulated in the United Nations Declaration on Human Rights.

With a disregard of the inherent worth and dignity of every human being, South Africa's white minority government vigorously carried its system of oppression against black South Africans beginning in the late 1940s and escalating in the 1960s. The political and economic underpinnings of apartheid subjected black South Africans to a standard of living that was far inferior to that accorded to whites, coloureds and Indians. Though the country was rich in natural resources, its economy did not benefit the masses. Instead, myriad laws were passed to ensure that black South Africans remained on the periphery of its economy and political process. Deprived of a right to vote and to actively participate in the political process, blacks, who constituted 74% of the country's population, were denigrated to a minority status.

A set of laws was used to limit their movement and their freedom of speech. As a majority of South Africa's population, they were stripped of 90% of the land through the Land Act of 1913. Under the separate development concept, a black homeland policy during the apartheid regime, blacks were expected to establish and claim their tribal allegiances in the homelands where they could exercise their right to vote. This was a complex policy strongly disfavoured by many because its purpose was to strip the majority of blacks of their rightful claims as South Africans. Complementary to this policy was the Group Areas Act (1950, repeated 1991) which defined where blacks could live, work and congregate.

'Bantu Education', specifically designed for blacks, provided an inferior system of education compared to that of whites, Indians and coloureds. Bantu Education was solely designed to keep blacks in a subservient social position. Further, the intent of this educational system was to keep blacks from gaining employment in specific sectors of the economy through a job reservations practice which ensured certain types of jobs were not open to blacks but to whites only. Blacks were deemed not to be deserving of humane treatment. The government turned a blind eye to overcrowding, squalid living conditions, poor health, unemployment, violence and poverty which mirrored the lives of many blacks in urban and rural areas. Interestingly, when poverty became a social problem affecting whites, an organised response from the government was instituted. As we will see, the development of social welfare and social work education in South Africa was reactive to the poor White problem.

An overview of the value base of social welfare under the apartheid system

Values guide decisions about what is right and about what is wrong. Though subjective, values reflect preferences about how things are and how they ought to be. They can be influenced by occupation, race and external factors such as changing economic conditions and new norms of social behavior (Miringoff and Opdycke, 1986). Values can be reinforced through religion and patriotic messages to the extent that they become facts rather than mere subjective beliefs (Day, 1989). Ideologies then emerged from a constellation of ideas and concepts about culture, and life in general. As seen in the US, dominant societal values (Day, 1989; Tropman, 1989), ideologies and beliefs (Dobelstein, 1986) are reflected in its social welfare system. Though contradictory to each other at times, the value of work, self-determination, individualism, material comfort, morality, humanitarianism and patriotism play a major part in social welfare policies (Prigmore and Atherton, 1979). The structure of social welfare in the US demonstrates the tensions between public responsibility and individual responsibility. More importantly, political climates determine the level of funding that support residual programmes serving those who are poor. The failure to apply the work ethic is constantly under scrutiny and viewed as a character flaw. Less focus is placed on prevailing environmental and structural factors. As a result, public responsibility is less encouraged to intervene. Given the marriage between social work and social welfare, policy practice that informs advocates and questions social policies is becoming even more relevant.

South Africa's non-monolithic society suggests that its value systems are as diverse as its population. Despite its cultural and religious diversity, the values of the dominant culture composed of minority whites have, since the 1950s, served to guide decisions regarding public welfare. The belief in inequality among people based on their biological dispositions, social Darwinism, and the protestant work ethic influenced the structure of social welfare. Most importantly, self-determination as a societal value strongly emerged in the 1970s to promote separate development under the Black Homeland policy.

Societal values and beliefs which influenced policies and the social welfare system during the apartheid era, permeating all its government institutions, can be traced to a controversial secret organisation called the Broederbond, formed in the 1920s. Built on Calvinism and ethnic nationalism, this organisation saw it as its calling to protect the interests of the Afrikaner community and to make South Africa the white man's land. Members of this organisation were known to have infiltrated all segments of the government during the Malan, Herzog and Verwoerd administrations. Racial inequality as a value would therefore figure prominently in most of the policy decisions made by the minority government from the 1930s through the 1980s. As seen in the study that was commissioned by the Carnegie Foundation during the depression to investigate the Poor White Question in South Africa, its focus was solely on the issue of an impoverished white community largely composed of Afrikaans-speaking farmers commonly known as the Boers who saw themselves as God's chosen people. This study was carried out by scholars with vested interests in the future of the white community. It came as no surprise that the study in itself would ignore the massive numbers of blacks whose impoverishment far outweighed that of whites. Its findings argued for the development of a State Bureau of Social Welfare to coordinate all programmes with an aim of, 'keeping poor whites from falling behind other whites'. It also called for the training of professionals with appropriate skills to work with the poor. As a result of this study a blueprint was forged to solidify Afrikaners' economic and political dominance (Golden, 2004).

The development of social welfare was, therefore, based on the belief that the individual was primarily responsible for their own welfare, with the family coming second, then the community. The state's intervention was viewed as a last resort (Loffell, 2000). As social service programmes were being developed and expanded to address the problem of poor whites, more restrictive policies were being implemented to deal with the majority population. Another tool for the apartheid system's stronghold on social welfare emerged under Circular 29 of 1966. Articulations in these documents reinforced government's policy on the welfare organisation whose basic principle was on each population group serving its own community and discouraging any multiracial approaches to welfare organisations and delivery systems (Loffell, 2000).

Social work practice and the apartheid era

To respond to the findings of the Carnegie study for trained personnel to address the plight of the poor, the training of social workers at two-year to four-year college levels emerged within the structure of segregated educational systems. While no universal curriculum nor regulation existed, social work gradually gained recognition as a professional field of practice. The fragmentation in the social work curriculum is best described in Noyoo (2000) who observed that English-speaking universities like the Witwatersrand School of Social Work opted not to offer courses in social policy to social work majors as a way to dissociate themselves from apartheid policies.

Social work education and practice remained separated along racial lines and in keeping with the policies of the land. For example, social work practitioners who were employees of private and public organisations, regardless of their race and ethnicity, were obligated to operate within the policies of their employers. This meant that the delivery of services had to be consistent with government policies. As articulated in Circular 29 of 1966:

> 'The Government's policy on welfare organisations is based on the principle that each population group should serve its own community within the sphere of welfare'.

At the same time, there were organisations which operated independently. These organisations were mostly affiliated with church establishments. They offered opportunities to social workers to engage in social advocacy and to promote the profession's goals of social justice. On the downside, these organisations faced much scrutiny from the government and their workers would constantly be found in violation of government policies.

The paradox of wealth for whites amidst abject poverty for blacks presented dilemmas for social workers. They were witnessing the incongruence between social work's mission and practice. To those social work professionals serving the marginalised black communities, the lack of resources and injustices were overwhelming. The government's support for services to the needy blacks was very minimal, yet heavy emphasis was placed on the individuals to be self-reliant.

Everyone had to embrace the work ethic regardless of any social, economic and political constraints. Individuals who could not secure a job were described as 'shiftless' and 'work-shy'. Social work practice assumed the same approach, placing the burden on the individuals. In addition, the enforcement of apartheid policies would at times fall on the hands of social workers.

Social work practice in the South Western Townships (Soweto): a case example

In the early 1970s the policies of segregation dictated who could practice social work and with what population. In black urban townships, service delivery occurred under a three-tier structure. Black social workers were the first-line providers of direct services and those with seniority served as liaisons between direct service workers and white social workers who served as supervisors. From within, social work was not completely absolved from the ideologies of white supremacy. The general designated role of a white social worker serving a black client population was that of a supervisor often, with less if any, years of practice experience. It was common practice to find newly graduated white social workers supervising seasoned black social workers. The process of supervision in itself was complex because, by law, white supervisors could not establish an operating base in the black areas. On average, they were expected to visit Soweto once a month for supervisory purposes. Occasionally, senior workers would attend meetings with supervisors outside the townships. Following the 1976 riots, services were disrupted and safety became a major issue for any whites visiting black areas.

Typically, the problems handled by social workers in the black communities of Soweto involved overcrowding, domestic disputes, and financial difficulties due to unemployment, old age and disability. Lack of housing was one of the most pressing problems in the townships then, and the solution by both national and local governments was through the enforcement of the Bantustan policy. Therefore, to ease the housing shortage, social workers serving under the auspices of municipal superintendents were expected to coordinate the repatriation of so-called non-productive urban dwellers to 'their homelands'. None of these non-productive urban dwellers had any claim or connection with these homelands. As would be expected, social workers who were under the employment of township municipalities found themselves confronted with tough choices and ethical dilemmas. They could either be part of the problem or create solutions. Working outside the box and circumventing the system offered the best solutions than stripping individuals and families of their birth rights as citizens of South Africa in the interests of an inhumane policy.

Black social workers were presented with a paradox in the late 1970s and early 1980s. The introduction of community organisation as a method of practice was received with enthusiasm in black communities and by social workers because of its potential to promote black empowerment to communities. Local governments found it appealing because it served as a rationale for the implementation of the Bantustan policy of separate development. Under the guise of community development, urban blacks could be blackmailed into moving to the barren homelands with promises of the opportunity to exercise their rights to vote and establish themselves economically. Township municipalities in collaboration with white universities such as Rand Afrikaans Universities were offering professional development certifications in community organisation to black social workers. Despite these discerning realities, young men and women who served in these communities remained optimistic that social work was a possible vehicle to social change. They had to make their work relevant to the black struggle. By empowering clients to know their rights, municipal superintendents could not sell them as a non-existent paradise. With the support of black municipal clerks, skilful advocacy, bargaining and persuasion were used to keep families in their homes and expunge cases that were set for repatriation. Skills in community organisation would in the long run provide opportunities on smaller scales to empower communities in urban areas, providing them with tools to develop self-help projects, become socially conscience and engage in political action. By participating in a women's organisation better known as 'Zenzele', social workers were also infusing their professional knowledge and skills to promote self-reliance. They were building stronger families and communities in urban areas, negating government efforts to enforce its Bantustan policies.

Social work in pre-democratic South Africa: the influence of the women's movement and the black consciousness movement

As the entrenchment of institutional racism was tightening towards the late 1980s civil disobedience was rising to its peak. Within South Africa's borders, the oppressed were mobilising into action as witnessed in the students' riots of 1976. Commonly felt issues of disenfranchisement, injustice and a belief in equality of all people were expressed through passive resistance, peaceful demonstrations, civil disobedience, mass campaigns, boycotts and arms struggles. The voices of the forgotten and the oppressed were loudly expressed in women's movements, students' movements, the African National Congress (ANC), the Pan African Congress, labour organisations and Inkatha. External pressure from Western countries through demonstrations and economic boycotts saw segments of the white community also beginning to question the morality of a government that was destroying family lives. Whites were joining in with blacks, giving rise to a number of social movements mostly operating in exile.

Most influential to social work practice in black communities during this period were black student movements and women's movements. Legendary social workers like Helen Kuzwayo and Winnie Mandela, who were actively involved in women's movements, used their social work skills and knowledge to mobilise people into action. As an example, following the Kliptown floods and the relocation of families to men's hostels which housed mine migrant workers, Helen Kuzwayo, a prominent leader in the community, tapped into the expertise of social workers to investigate the living conditions of families in these hostels. As could be imagined, living conditions were appalling. In one instance, an individual with leprosy lived in close contact with others because of overcrowding. This type of work was external to one's regular work but it rendered true meaning to social work.

Much inspiration to social work practice in the black communities in the early 1970s came from Steven Biko's message of self-empowerment. Widely regarded as the father of the black consciousness movement, Steven Biko was a forceful voice in black universities. In his speeches on black campuses, he offered a different way of thinking and of viewing one's world. To his progeny who were struggling with misplaced pedagogy, his speeches challenged men and women to rediscover the talent and the potential within. In forming the black consciousness movement, he felt that blacks had a responsibility to begin to articulate their unique issues and chart their destiny. In his writing (Biko, 1978, p. 98) he stated:

> We have set out on a quest for true humanity, and somewhere on the distant horizon we can see the glittering prize. Let us march forth with courage and determination, drawing strength from our common plight and our brotherhood. In time, we shall be in a position to bestow upon South Africa the greatest gift – a more human face.

Followers of this movement understood the choices and risks involved. Those who chose to work from within the system to bring about change were also aware of the watchful eye of big brother. Sadly, the untimely death of Steven Biko at the hands of the oppressor brought a wave of fear and intimidation. As tensions were mounting and uncertainty engulfed black communities, culminating in the Soweto riots of 1976, social work practice found itself at a crossroads. Also, the killing of a white social work supervisor during the riots was very unsettling to both white and black social workers. Because of its marriage to government policies, social work could not completely dissociate itself from what was happening in the country. With the rise in civil disorder in the 1980s and the government's preoccupation with self-preservation, social work had to redefine its role within a broader context. It also had to contend with Afrikaaners who were opposed to any attempts at political reform. Conservative Afrikaans women's organisations like Kappiekommando and Afrikanervrouekenkrag (AVK), which was started in 1983, opposed racial integration in schools and other public places. These organisations were very vocal in their efforts at preserving white culture with its traditions and values.

Reforming social welfare in post-democratic South Africa: addressing new and old sets of social problems

When the white minority government finally yielded to make way for majority rule, freedom for South Africa's majority population came at a costly price. From the 1976 riots and its aftermath, civic disorder and chaos reigned. As the government was losing control in enforcing its laws, mayhem ruled. Black townships were mired in protests against high utility bills, denial of home ownership by municipal governments, high rental costs for houses that were poorly maintained by local municipalities, high crime waves, lack of public safety, disrupted services, public schools that were in disarray, teacher apathy and truancy. There were individuals and families who were uprooted and displaced as a result of apartheid laws and political violence. They were estimated at 500,000 (United States Committee on Refugees, 1995). In addition, homeless families that had migrated to urban areas in defiance of its Group Areas Act were organising themselves into squatter camp communities. Squatter camps were to become breeding grounds for crime, drug activities and diseases. While unemployment had always been a major problem facing blacks, the large numbers of unskilled immigrants coming from poor neighbouring countries made it worse. In 1994, South Africa had absorbed approximately one million Mozambican refugees. In addition, lawlessness characterised by the illegal occupations of abandoned apartment buildings or high-jacking of apartment buildings owned by whites was becoming a widespread solution to the housing shortage. The HIV/AIDS pandemic and its impact on families and the economy were also becoming major challenges.

The ANC's response: social development and social welfare

The African Nationalist Movement, once a liberation movement, finally took office in 1994. It also recognised the need to unify all factions. As one of the most organised political movements with a widely revered leadership, it saw itself as the only credible political organisation that could bring a wide range of social movements and other sectors of society to work together for the common good. Undoing the damage caused by years of bankrupt policies was to become one of the ANC's major challenges. To articulate a vision for a new South Africa, it utilised its blueprint referred to as the Reconstruction and Development Programme. This document would serve as a guide towards achieving equality for all South Africans. The document represented the efforts of a broad-based and inclusive constituency. It focused on seven broad problem areas, namely: violence, lack of housing, lack of jobs, inadequate education, inadequate health care, lack of democracy and a failing economy (ANC, 1994).

Following much work and the findings from the Carnegie Foundation's second study on poverty (Wilson, F. and Ramphele, M. (1989), the ANC government released its much anticipated White Paper for Social Welfare (Ministry for Welfare and Population Development, 1997). Patterned after the United Nations World Summit for Social Development (March, 1995), the White Paper for Social Welfare took on a much more comprehensive approach to correct past injustices and tackle its present challenges. It articulated its goal as the promotion of a national social development agenda that focuses on nation-building and individuals' well-being regardless of their race, ethnicity, gender, sexual orientation and religious affiliation. Its concept of social welfare and social development strongly emphasised social responsibility as described in these four areas:

- Social welfare is an integrated and comprehensive system of social services, facilities, programmes and social security aimed at promoting social development, social justice and the social functioning of people.

- Social welfare serves as a mechanism for bringing about sustainable improvement in the well-being of individuals.

- Social welfare is intrinsically linked to other social service systems through which people's needs would be met and through which people would strive to achieve their aspirations. Social welfare services will therefore serve as a range of mechanisms to achieve social development in the areas of health, nutrition, education, housing, employment, recreation, rural and urban development and land reform.

- The welfare of the population will not automatically be enhanced by economic growth. Economic development has to be accompanied by the equitable allocation and distribution of resources if it is to support social development. Social development and economic development are therefore interdependent and mutually reinforcing (Ministry for Welfare and Population Development, 1997, p. 7).

This approach to social welfare strongly recognised environmental and structural impediments to individuals' social functioning, a departure from the previous regime. Embedded in humanistic values of equity, democracy, human rights and ubuntu, (see Glossary at end of chapter) it called for a unified approach to solving the country's social problems. It also established a Department of Welfare to serve as an umbrella system that would better address social problems affecting all communities regardless of differences (Van Eeden *et al.*, 2000).

Reforming social work in post-democratic South Africa: a call for an eclectic approach to practice

The White Paper identified flaws within the current welfare system. The most glaring ones with major implications for social work practice were:

- Lack of national consensus on a welfare policy framework and its relationship to a national reconstruction and development strategy.

- Fragmentation caused by the fourteen different departments that were administering services to different population groups and homelands leading to duplication, inefficiency, and ineffectiveness in meeting the needs of individuals.

- Inappropriate approaches to service delivery that lacked a holistic approach. While some social workers had received training and practice in community development, the approach to service delivery is still rehabilitative, relying on institutional care and is not preventive and developmental (Ministry for Welfare and Population Development, 1997, p. 4).

- Unevenly distributed training opportunities throughout the country. While current social work education is generally successful in preparing practitioners for work in a therapeutic and restorative social welfare system, the courses do not equip graduates to respond appropriately to the most important social development needs in South African communities. Past government policies were not developmentally oriented and consequently no posts were subsidised for a developmental approach which impacted on the nature of academic training (Ministry for Welfare and Population Development, 1997, p.21).

Analysis and strategies

Analysis

The lack of consensus to a policy framework that is aimed at a new dispensation for the marginalised members of society and serves as a gateway to building a progressive society can be attributed to the following:

- A realisation that the policy calls for a redefinition of social work that the majority of social workers are not ready to assume.

- The process of change is a difficult one for those who have been the benefactors of an old system which stressed individual failures, rather than structural and environmental changes.

- The fundamental theme of the White Paper is towards a national collective responsibility. This possibly runs counter to the most favoured capitalistic ideologies of Social Darwinism. It is also likely to be dismissed or misconstrued as socialism.

- A community-driven and grassroots-level approach to service delivery demystifies the concept of clinical social work practice, so prevalent in social work.

- Private social welfare organisations that once enjoyed autonomy in hiring practices and choices in service delivery no longer have that power.

- Job displacement is likely to become a by-product of this policy. Resistance to the new policy might fester from those who occupied positions of power during the previous government.

Strategies

A way of moving forward is found in the International Federation of Social Workers and the International Association of Social Workers definition of social work, characterised as:

> 'a profession that promotes social changes, problem-solving in human relationships and the empowerment and liberation of people to enhance well-being. Utilizing theories of human behavior and social systems, social work intervenes at the point where people interact with their environments. Principles of human rights and social justice are fundamental to social work.' (IFSW and IASSW, 1994)

1. It is crucial for social work to adopt an eclectic approach to practice. Generalist social work practice provides such a framework. It responds to both private troubles and public issues utilising an eclectic approach. Social workers in South Africa are familiar with generalist social work. During the apartheid era, generalist social work was loosely structured, pedagogically. Its implementation was restricted and it was not universally embraced. As a result, it was ineffective. Given a political climate amicable to the accomplishment of social justice and a set of principles that are congruent with those articulated by the International Federation of Social Work and the International Association of Schools of Social Work, social workers and others involved in the human service field can serve as building blocks toward consensus building, irrespective of race and professional orientations.

2. Social workers must seize the window of opportunity to begin institutionalising a framework to practice and service delivery that is aimed at the attainment of social and economic justice. They must become social activists whose aim is to make long-term, fundamental changes in the structures of society (Brueggemann, 2006, p. 446,). Windows of opportunity are presented through political and social events or a change in personnel. Given such events, advocates ought to stand ready with their ideas because policy windows do not

stay open long. Events and personalities change, and public interest can be short-lived (Segal and Brzuzy, 1998, p. 62.).

3. Social workers regardless of differences have a prominent role to play in the implementation and realisation of the ideals articulated in the White Paper. The process begins with abandoning old values of convenience and embracing the humanistic value system of ubuntu, equity, human rights and democracy. These are values that are consistent with social work's core values of social justice and the promotion of human dignity.

A move from the old ways of perceiving and addressing social problems is needed. This is an era that calls for sustainable human development, defined as:

> 'the concern with models of material production and consumption that are replicable and desirable. It puts people at the center of development and points out forcefully that the inequities of today are so great that to sustain the present form of development is to perpetuate similar inequities for future generations …It also means that sufficient investment must be made in the education and health of today's population so as not to create a social debt for future generations.' (UNDP, 1994, pp. 13-17)

4. Embracing a multicultural perspective and actually practicing it are two different entities. A real test for all South African social workers is whether they can abandon old attitudes and beliefs and begin fully embracing a culture of equality based on humankind. There are deep-seated issues related to the past for all South Africans, whites, blacks, coloureds and Indians. To move beyond these issues, social work in South Africa must emphasise the principle of self-understanding and use of self. To have a positive impact on those who are served, it will be important for professionals to identify their own values and determine how they impact on those who are served.

5. There must be diligence in formulating proactive strategies to problems.

6. Social work is part and parcel of politics. Therefore social workers in South Africa must not alienate themselves from politics. They must take an active role in the political process to ensure that they fully represent the voices of the powerless to influence future policies. The role of advocacy to fight for those who continue to function on the periphery of the new dispensation is an important one.

Clearly social work faces an enormous task both in practice and in education. In formulating a curriculum that is reflective of the government's ideals, schools of social work can utilise three recommendations which provide a framework for charting a new course. These are covered in these following statements:

- Selection procedures for admission to the social work profession should be standardised by the training institutions.

- Social development theory and practice must provide the framework for welfare education and training programmes (Ministry for Welfare and Population Development, 1997, p. 23).

- The South African Interim Council for Social Work will deal with the required registration and licensing of social workers and the body and its terms of reference will be established after consultation with the welfare community. Consensus will be reached on a code of ethics which will set out the guiding principles and values of the social work profession (Ministry for Welfare and Population Development, 1997, p. 24).

Conclusion

The call to nation-building is a clear recognition of social work as a rightful profession to direct the course of change, and the realisation of social justice for the masses. It also provides an opportunity to self-reflect and sifts through what it takes to be a social worker in the 21st century. Clearly, change has been slow for the majority of South Africa's population and the gap between the have and the have-nots has been widening.

- Visibility and action on the part of social work is imperative.

- The ANC has not been without criticisms. It has been accused of being insensitive, apathetic, corrupt and negligent to address issues facing its poor constituency. Corruption charges against some members of the ANC have placed a closer scrutiny on the government. Claims of reverse discrimination have also been levelled against the government. Criticisms not withstanding, the government has faced many road blocks, artificial and real, as exemplified in the lack of consensus to move the welfare reform Bill. In fact, the ANC has become an enemy to some who supported it. The slow pace of change has resulted in a number of social movements springing up to protest against the government's ineptitude. There have been a number of social movements springing up since the new government took office to address issues of discourse. Many of today's social movements aimed at addressing most of these social concerns cannot be pigeon-holed into specific types. As described by Habib (2004), their approach to the struggle follows a continuum marked by radical socialists, integrationalists to those willing to work within the system to bring about change. Clearly, new social movements are being shaped by issue of the time. Socially conscious people are creating new social movements that will shape a new era.

- There is an urgent need for all of South Africa to pay close attention to the needs of its people. It cannot afford to bask in its glory nor sit back and allow anti-democratic forces to fester.

Glossary

Apartheid: an institutionalised and overt form of racial discrimination carried through a constellation of laws to subjugate the black majority population while protecting the rights of a minority white population.

Bantustan-Homelands: barren areas of land curved out of South Africa's rich lands by the minority government for the 70 per cent of Africans. Under this system, each tribal group was expected to engage in self rule and develop itself politically, economically and socially outside the white designated areas and independent of South Africa. **Blacks:** this term is used here to refer to indigenous South Africans of African descent.

Group Areas Act No. 41 of 1950: this Act designated racially segregated areas for each of the four racial groups to work and establish residence. It was deemed illegal for a member of a racial group to reside or own land in an area set aside for another race.

Non-productive individuals: this was a term used to describe the chronically unemployed, disabled people and the elderly who could no longer participate fully in the open labour market.

Ubuntu: an African adage meaning that people are people through other people. Each individual's humanity is ideally expressed through their own relationship with others. It also acknowledges both the rights and the responsibilities of every citizen in promoting individual and societal well-being.

Coloured: this is a term used to describe South Africans of mixed race.

Whites: refers to Caucasians both English and Afrikaans-speaking.

Chapter 9

The Emergence of Social Work in Palestine:

Developing Social Work in a Situation of Political Conflict and Nation Building

Jane Lindsay, Ziad Faraj and Naimeh Baidoun

Introduction

This chapter explores the emergence of the social work profession in the Occupied Palestinian Territories (OPT) in a context of ongoing political conflict and occupation, nation building, active intervention by international agencies and acute social need. First, an overview of this context is provided. The development of non-governmental organisations (NGOs) and latterly government services to meet social need is then discussed. The growth of provision of services led to the need for suitably qualified workers and the development of small-scale social work education programmes. At present there are relatively few qualified social workers in Palestine. Many social services are provided by those who have initial (Bachelors degree level) training in social work, psychology and sociology. The Palestinian Authority is currently developing regulatory policies relating to Codes of Ethics and educational requirements for workers in the sector, linked to the development of psychosocial programming and legislation related to protection, social control and service delivery. The Union of Social Workers, Sociologists and Psychologists, established in 1997, has developed its own standards and is an active participant in the debate about how to develop social work and social services in Palestine. At this time of professional and social development, this chapter argues that this is the moment for Palestinian social workers to articulate a clear radical vision of what this profession can offer and make a strong case for the development of the profession in Palestine.

The political and social context

Historical background

The OPT consists of two main and not contiguous geographical areas, the West Bank and the Gaza Strip separated by the State of Israel, which is the occupying power. Further divisions exist within the territories due to the operation of the Israeli Defence Force which has established a matrix of control within the region. Terms such as 'bantustans' and 'enclaves', drawn from other conflict zones, are often used to characterise Palestinian towns and villages which are cut off from each other by checkpoints and the 'Separation Wall'.

These lands have had a troubled and contested history for most of the 21th century until the present day. They were a part of a province of the Ottoman Empire until the end of the First World War and were then ruled by British Mandate from 1920-1948. During this period Jewish migration to Palestine increased, gaining momentum in the immediate post-Second World War period in response to the Holocaust. In 1947 a United Nations Partition Plan (UNGAR 181) proposed the establishment of a Jewish and an Arab state in historic Palestine. The proposed land division (56% Jewish, 42% Arab, plus an international zone) was not accepted by the Palestinian Arabs, who at that time constituted two-thirds of the population (Farsoun and Zacharia, 1997). On 15 May 1948, following a period of armed conflict between Jewish and Arab armies, the State of Israel was declared comprising 78% of historic Palestine (excluding the present-day OPT). The West Bank was incorporated into Jordan in 1950, with Egypt governing Gaza from 1948. In 1967 the West Bank and Gaza were occupied by Israel (the Six Days War). A United Nations (UN) Security Council resolution (242, 1967), which called on Israel to withdraw from occupied territories, was not heeded.

There have been two uprisings (Intifada) by Palestinians in the OPT against and in reaction to the Israeli occupation. The First Intifada erupted in 1987, resulted in a high number of Palestinian casualities, and continued until 1993 and the signing of the Oslo Accords (1993, 1994, 1995). The Oslo Accords were the first in a series of internationally brokered meetings aimed at securing permanent/final status. Since 1994, the Palestinian Authority has been responsible for local administration, civil jurisdiction and internal security in parts of the West Bank and Gaza, with the first elections of the President and the first Palestinian Legislative Council taking place in January,1996.

The Second Intifada (also referred to as the *Al Aqsa* Intifada), which commenced in September 2000 and continues to the present day, is often linked with popular disillusionment with the 'peace process' with Israel. Giacaman, (2004, p. 19) argues that by this point 'it was increasingly clear that the Palestinian Authority was facing a systemic crisis, a combination of internally generated problems and serious external political impediments' and allegations of corruption and 'financial diversion' were legion. The Second Intifada has been characterised by Israeli incursions into the West Bank and Gaza, curfews, closures, arrests, air strikes, targeted killings, house demolitions, destruction of orchards and expropriation of lands. Militant groups within the OPT have resisted Israeli action by tactics including carrying out suicide bombings in Israel. In 2002 Israel commenced the construction of a Separation Wall (also referred to as the Apartheid or Exclusion Wall/Fence or Barrier) in the West Bank on the pretext of security. The Wall encircles West Bank towns, has entailed land confiscations, and has separated some Palestinians from their farms, schools and other social services. In July 2004, the International Court of Justice advised Israel to discontinue and dismantle the Wall. Israel has not acted on this advice. Numbers of deaths and casualities in the Second Intifada rise daily, with the Palestinians in the West Bank and Gaza sustaining proportionally greater losses. Peace in the region and durable solutions remain elusive.

Population and refugees

The Palestinian population of the OPT is estimated to be 3.8 million, with over half the population aged less than 17 years of age (PCBS, 2005). Included within this number are over 1.6 million refugees registered with the United Nations Relief and Works Agency for Palestinian Refugees in the Near East (UNRWA). UNRWA's origins (UNGAR 302 [IV] 1949) date from the war that led to the establishment of the State of Israel in 1948 and its remit is to provide humanitarian relief and services to Palestinian refugees who were uprooted as a result of that conflict. Despite a number of UN Resolutions (for example, UNGAR 194 [III] 1948; UNSCR 242) calling for the repatriation, resettlement and rehabilitation of those refugees 'wishing to return home and live in peace with their neighbours' and the payment of compensation to 'those who chose not to return', the situation regarding the Palestinian refugees still remains intractable. The Palestinian refugee population is currently the largest refugee population in the world. UNRWA currently supports over four million registered refugees, the majority of whom live in the West Bank and Gaza, the remainder living in Jordan, Lebanon and Syria. There are 27 refugee camps within the OPT. Sizeable numbers of registered refugees live outside the refugee camps (UNRWA, 2006).

The population of the OPT also includes people who have been 'internally displaced' as a result of the Six Days War in 1967 when Israel occupied the West Bank and Gaza. Additionally, within the West Bank there is an Israeli settler population of approximately 200,000 people who are directly governed by the State of Israel. Israel withdrew its settlers from the Gaza Strip in August 2005.

Socio-economic conditions and the impact of war

The rate of economic growth in the OPT has been negatively affected by the political situation. Some Palestinian commentators (Passia, 2006) suggest that Israeli policies since 1967 sought to impede Palestinian economic development in order to create dependence on Israel, provide a market for Israeli products, and maintain a supply of cheap labour, with the question being asked: 'Can developmental frameworks address a poverty that has been structured by intent to utilise an entire civilian population as a political pressure point?' (Johnston, in Musleh and Taylor, 2005, p. 12). Roy (quoted in Musleh and Taylor, 2005, p. 12) characterises this process as 'de-development'.

Economic indicators produced by the Palestinian National Authority Bureau of Statistics show a consistent downward trend since the onset of the Second Intifada. With the closure of access to Israeli during the current Intifada for Palestinian workers, there has been a significant rise in male unemployment and decline in family incomes, with an estimated proportion of 47 per cent of households living below the poverty line and 16 per cent of the population living under the minimum level for subsistence (World Bank, 2004, in Musleh and Taylor, 2005). Refugees and those with lower educational levels appear more likely to be in irregular employment or be unemployed (Giacaman and Johnston, 2002). Hilal's (2002) analysis of the community household survey found that one in every seven households has a disabled, elderly, or chronically ill person needing help at home.

The impact of the deteriorating political and economic situation on individuals and families has been explored in a number of local studies. A poll conducted by the Palestinian Working Women's Society for Development in 2002 on violence against women in Palestine found that most (86%) respondents believed that to varying degrees the prevailing political, economic and social conditions have increased violence against women. Over half of the children in Arafat and Boothby's (2003) large-scale survey into the psychosocial needs of Palestinian children expressed the perception that their parents were not able to meet their needs for care and protection due to financial hardship and their inability to control external events. Save the Children's reports on Palestinian children to the UN Commission on Human Rights (2003, 2004) provide graphic accounts of the qualitative experience of children living behind the Separation Wall and the child detainees and argue that 'the present situation is failing to provide for the protection and development of children living within the OPT to which they have a right'. The Gaza Mental Health Centre has conducted a number of studies exploring the extent to which women and children are suffering from post-traumatic stress disorder as a result of exposure to political violence (for example Qouta, 2003). High incidence of acute symptoms were reported with a strong correlation noted between the health of mothers and their children. Giacaman *et al.*'s (2004) study of 3,500 West Bank adolescents, which focused on mental health and psychological distress, revealed a very high level of exposure of children to violent events, with boys being more likely to experience direct exposure to violence than girls, and those living in refugee camps reporting the highest levels of subjective health complaints and exposure to violence. Giacaman *et al.* (2004) make a strong call for a move away from individualised interventions to meet the needs of these young people, and call for the development of 'more effective ways of strengthening the social fabric and communal support' to promote resilience and collective coping (p. 12). This is an interesting comment which highlights the fact that the focus for psychosocial interventions is still open to debate. This point will be developed later in this chapter in discussing possible directions for the development of social work within the OPT.

The development of organised responses to community and individual need

The history and emergence of social work in Palestine has not yet been explored in the academic literature. Payne (2005, p. 11-12) identifies six aspects that may be useful in identifying the construction of the social work profession within its social networks: social issues creating need; agency, legal and organisational contexts for practice and sources for authority; occupational grouping and professions; values and philosophy; knowledge and research; and education for the profession. Payne's categories provide a framework within which to structure discussion of some of the factors that may have contributed to the emergence of social work in Palestine, and also within which to raise the question whether this profession is required in Palestine, and if so, what should be the focus of social work endeavour. The previous section has referred to some of the recent socio-political issues creating need in Palestine. This section explores the development of organised responses to meet these needs.

It is common to commence the history of the emergence of social work within a state with an account of the development of organised forms of helping others, often stemming from voluntary action, which is subsequently incorporated into the realm of state provision of services, often with the remit of creating social order and authorised by legislation. This pattern can be traced in Palestine.

Early history of philanthropic endeavour (up to 1948)

Since the early 20th century, there was some 'social work' activity in Palestine, mostly linked to philanthropic charities and missionary work. In 1914 a registration law was passed under the Ottoman regime that required organisations to register, and this legislation remained in force until 1948. During this period, the impetus to set up organisations can be traced to three main sources. First from within Palestine, second from the Arab world, often under the aegis of Islamic charitable work, and third from the international community, again often linked to Christian missionary activity. Several of the organisations set up during this period continue to provide social services in the OPT (for example, Young Women's Christian Association, initiated 1893, registered 1918).

From philanthropy to empowerment (1948-1994)

In the period from 1948, until 1994, Jordanian law regulated the establishment of organisations in the West Bank, with Egyptian law applying in Gaza in the period 1948-1967, with both areas being occupied by Israel from 1967. Governmental intervention to address psychosocial needs was limited to a 'strictly bio-medical-psychiatric model of care ... controlled by the Israeli military' (Giacaman, 2004, p. 18). International invention initially focused around the creation, establishment and support of UNRWA (from 1950) to provide humanitarian assistance to Palestine refugee families unable to meet their own basic needs. The development of UNRWA created employment opportunities in providing social services for Palestinians, who constitute the largest majority of its workforce. UNRWA's work in the social services field has developed from emergency relief in the early phases of its existence, to include a more fully articulated social development role. UNRWA's website (2006, www.un.org/unrwa/index.html) expresses its current aims in social service provision as being to 'promote self-reliance of the refugee community through community social development' which includes women's empowerment programmes, community-based rehabilitation and poverty alleviation. The changes in UNRWA's focus from merely providing emergency aid to Palestinian refugees to working towards empowerment and community development is mirrored to a certain extent in the history of the development of local Palestinian NGOs in the West Bank and Gaza.

From 1967 to 1994, Israel monitored the registration and recognition of any new and emerging local NGOs. New organisations' aims were scrutinised in terms of how they were related to political factions. It is perceived that this limited the growth of organisations in the West Bank and Gaza. Nevertheless, this period witnessed a flourishing of community voluntary action and the growth of local NGOs with a social action agenda. Local organisations developed during this period included conservative (including religious) foundations still motivated by philanthropic ideals and progressive organisations, often linked to political ideals as local political groupings started to develop legitimate extensions by using community-based organisations to reach out to recruit youth and encourage them to affiliate to political groups and to volunteer within their communities. The volunteer movement in Palestine reached its peak in the 1980s with volunteers starting to think about empowerment as a natural process. Volunteers came from the community and had the support of the community but lacked the resources to effect sustainable development. Examples of NGOs established in this period to meet social welfare and health needs, which are still extant, include the Palestine Red Crescent Society (1968), the Union of Palestinian Medical Relief Committees (1979), the Palestinian Working Women's Society for Development (1981), the Palestinian Counselling Centre (1983) and the Early Childhood Resource Centre (1985) (web addresses for each of these organisations are provided in the Bibliography). It is difficult to be confident in asserting the early aims and objectives of these organisations as easily available current accounts of their histories (as available on websites) may be framed to meet current concerns and priorities. Common themes emerge from these accounts, namely: an emphasis on an ideological position of solidarity with Palestinian national aspirations; commitment to working towards social justice, human rights and empowerment; concern for the development of a healthy Palestinian society; identification of social as well as health needs, and an emphasis on a community-based 'grassroots' level of intervention, often aimed at advancing the position of particular groups within the population (for example, women, children, those with mental health problems). Giacaman (2004) suggests that in the early phases of organisational growth, a tension existed between the 'national imperatives on one hand, and the need to address internal social issues on the other, issues which were seen by some as "rocking the boat" in the process of national liberation' (p.19).

The First Intifada (1987-1993) stimulated further local institutional development and international donor activity. The direct impact of the Intifada on young people, both as victims and participants in civil unrest prompted the growth of the disability movement, rights-based movements and psychosocial interventions first in response to those directly affected by the conflict and then generalising to recognition of the wider needs of Palestinians living under occupation. Many of these initiatives were closely linked to concurrent developments internationally in examining and responding to the impact of war on populations, growth of rights-based movements, and radical analyses of power relations within societies, communities and families. Examples of local organisations set up during this period include the Gaza Community Mental Health Programme (1990), the Women's Centre for Legal Aid and Counselling (1991) and the Defence for Children International/Palestine Section (1992) (web addresses are provided in the Bibliography). While maintaining a focus on responding to immediate needs of individuals and communities, organisations sought to influence the national agenda, for example in offering a gender analysis of patriarchal power relations and violence within families and wider community structures, and promoting the rights of children. Local and international concern about the impact of the First Intifada on young people also prompted the development of a range of youth services. The degree to which locally initiated action was and is influenced by the priorities and aims of those international donors who fund social action projects is difficult to quantify. On one hand, it has been argued (Giacaman, 2004) that during this period international donors distorted development processes to a certain extent (in focusing on youth as a 'source of violence which needs to be restrained or even controlled'(Giacaman, 2004, p.17). It can also be argued that reliance on donor assistance led to a culture of dependency at the expense of utilising community resources (to the extent that many organisations lost the ability to recruit community resources), unhelpful competition between local organisations in order to secure and control external resources, and over-reliance on single donors which led to vulnerability of organisations collapsing if donor agendas changed – a disaster for sustainability. Aspects of the interchange between local organisations and international donors during this period and ongoing have led to some positive outcomes. The activities undertaken by Palestinian organisations were legitimated as according with internationally driven rights and empowerment agendas and publicised by influential pressure groups. Interaction of local professionals with international organisations and participation in transnational research agendas promoted cross-fertilisation of ideas and approaches to intervention (for example, the Gaza Community Mental Health Programme). Limited opportunities were offered to Palestinian workers for international education, and those who have returned to Palestine are shaping current developments.

Adjusting to change: the post-Oslo period (1994-2000)

With the signing of the Oslo Accords (1993-1995), and the transfer of control of some aspects of local services administration from direct Israeli to the Palestinian National Authority (PNA), a new phase of organisational and policy development and adjustment can be distinguished, which can be broadly characterised as spanning the period from 1994 to the onset of the Second Intifada in 2000. Three main forms of institutions and their inter-relationships need to be considered in exploring the development of organisational responses to social need, namely the development of state planning and service provision under the auspices of the Palestinian Authority, the ongoing work of UNRWA, and the development of civil society initiatives in the non-governmental sector. Reliance on international donor aid and funding is a common factor in each of these sectors. In the ten-year period following the Oslo Accords (1993 to 2003), the West Bank and Gaza Strip Palestinians received the highest amount of international aid of any recipient in the world since the Second World War (from 1993 to 2003, the OPT received $6 billion in international aid). The role of international aid is controversial, with some commentators (for example, Anderson, in Keating *et al.*, 2005) asserting that donor aid without concurrent pressure being brought to bear on the Israeli government merely supports Israeli occupation policies, and others arguing that foreign funding is necessary to sustain the population and to establish the conditions for future development.

From 1994, at governmental level, Palestinian quasi-state structures started to be developed, funded and arguably influenced by international donors. This included the creation of ministries with responsibility for planning and developing national policy and legislation relevant to social, health and education services, labour, planning and international cooperation. An Agenda for Social Renewal was designed in 1995, launched in 1996 and reviewed and upgraded in 1998 with the ambition of achieving comprehensive, integrative and multi-sectoral/disciplinary planning and interventions. The transition to increased governmental strategic planning, which attracted significant amounts of international aid, changed the balance of power and arguably created some tension between those who had been developing services at a civil society level and those political leaders who returned to Palestine to take control of developing state structures. Some of those engaged in civil society work prior to the Oslo Accords perceived that. Palestinian political leadership did not fully recognise or value the contributions made by the local 'grassroots' to the national agenda of resisting occupation and developing services, people's perspectives, and the expertise and knowledge developed by local service providers in social and human development. Reflecting on the Palestinian Authority's achievements up to 1999 in relation to development of a National Plan for Action for Palestinian Children under the Agenda for Social Renewal, the Ministry of Planning and International Co-operation noted: 'Reforming and empowering these structures is an unavoidably slow and difficult process. In addition, setting up functioning ministries, training new and inexperienced staff and effectively interacting, interfacing and complementing efforts with civil society takes time'(NPA, 1999, p. 1).

One of the most significant early attempts to establish social interventions by the Palestinian Authority was the development of the post of schools counsellors (with the support of the Swedish government). Six hundred and eighty new workers (some with degree-level qualifications in social work and others with degrees in sociology or psychology) have been appointed in public schools since 1995 and other schools counsellors have been appointed in the private and UNRWA sectors. The concept, roles, responsibilities, professional interventions and strategies for this group of workers are still being evolved and their job description is developing over time. Giacaman (2004) offers a searing critique of this development noting that 'a combination of donor pressure and the starvation of funds as well as other internal considerations ... contributed to an over-rapid launching of this programme with minimal consideration given to model building ... conceptualisation of details ... such as those related to the purpose of counselling in a Palestinian context, structural changes within the school system to accommodate this new project and the human resources [and] ... the management system needed for implementation' (p. 19).

In the post-Oslo period (1994 to 2000), UNRWA continued to be the main provider of services to the refugee population, viewing their relationship with the new Palestinian Authority as being similar to their relationship with other host governments (Jordan, Lebanon and Syria).

UNRWA liaises with the relevant ministries within the Palestinian Authority on matters concerning their operations and the provision of services to the Palestine refugees. The Palestinian Authority supports the continuation of UNRWA's operations. UNRWA's position is that until the refugee issue is solved, and as long as there is a need for relief, UNRWA will continue providing services to the refugees in the West Bank and Gaza. UNRWA developed and implemented several projects under the Peace Implementation Programme, which was introduced following the signing of the Israeli–Palestinian Declaration of Principles in 1993. These included programmes aimed at the promotion of non-violent conflict resolution and human rights. UNRWA is supported by international donor aid. Keating *et al.* (2005) highlight that one of the consequences of the Oslo Accords was that international donors diverted financial support from UNRWA to the Palestinian Authority.

The creation of the Palestinian Authority created a new window for new initiatives and the evolvement and development of civil society. In 1994 the first attempt was made to draft a law for registration of charitable organisations, with Palestinian Legislative Council passing the Law of Charitable Associations and Community Organisations on 16 January 2000 (*Law 1*). According to the publications of the Palestinian Independent Commission of Human Rights in 2002 and the statistics of the Ministry of Interior in 2004, the number of recognised organisations prior to 1994 was approximately 292; between 1994 and 2000 this increased by 348; and between 2000 and 2004 it increased by 1,246 organisations. The total of registered NGOs by September 2004 was 1,886 organisations providing a range of services and support to those in need. Giacaman's 2004 study (conducted 2002-2003) of the embryonic system of psychosocial and mental health care in the OPT describes an 'institutional maze' which ranges from very small organisations with often only one or two employees working in the psychosocial field, to large-scale organisations which focus on provision of services to specific groups within the population (for example, women, children, disabled people, older people). At the point of her survey Giacaman found that several smaller registered organisations had ceased to exist, pointing to the vulnerability of smaller organisations and an environment where only the fittest can survive. Within the field of psychosocial programmes, after excluding organisations with less than two operational employees in the psychosocial sector, she identified 50

NGOs operating in this sector, over half of which had been established before 1994. Factors supporting the survival and development of these organisations appear to be their ability to transform themselves to meet emerging need, donor interest in civil society organisations and to a certain extent, their ability to act collectively.

The Palestinian NGO Network (PNGO), an umbrella organisation, was set up in 1993, after the signing of the Oslo Accords, 'with the objective of enhancing coordination, consultation and cooperation among the different sectors of civil society' (PNGO, 2006). It currently represents 92 of the larger locally based NGOs working in different developmental fields. PNGO asserts that it 'has become an important component of Palestinian society and serves as an essential coordination mechanism for the NGO sector at the local, regional and international level' (PNGO, 2006). Its mission statement includes 'advocating for the rights of the Palestinian people locally, regionally and globally [and] ... for responsible and appropriate legislation and public policies' and 'strengthening coordination within the NGO sector ... democratic values within society   [and] civil society's organisational capacities' (PNGO, 2006). Recent analysis raises questions about the role of NGOs and to what extent they represent Palestinian society and local needs. Nabulsi (in Keating *et al.*, 2005) suggests that Palestinian NGOs receive enough funding to give them a level of legitimacy that permits them to address international audiences and 'act' on behalf of Palestinian society. He argues that the role of donor-driven NGOs has become as highly politicised as other facets of the Israeli–Palestinian conflict, highlighting the competition among NGOs for foreign funding and 'connection-corruption'. A further underlying question is the impact of the international donor community on the nature of programme development and to what extent social programming provided by local NGOs is being driven by local analysis of need or by the need to generate funds and secure employment by creating programming to meet international donor agendas.

The Second Intifada and national planning for the development of social and health services (2000-2006)

The intensity and severity of the Israeli response to the Second Intifada (as outlined above) led to a refocusing of social programming from longer-term development programmes to emergency relief. During the early phase of the Second Intifada, international donor organisations promoted and imported a variety of intervention methods designed to mitigate against post-traumatic stress disorder providing local staff with short training programmes and limited follow-up. The applicability and the effectiveness of some of these methods (for example, crisis debriefing) have been questioned. Other international donors incorporated a research element in their new programming, for example: the Save the Children (US)/Palestinian Authority *Classroom-Based Intervention* programme, which was provided in all government schools. Local ethical committees to approve research-based interventions do not appear to have been developed as yet in Palestine. Perhaps partially prompted by common experience of renewed war, the recent period has also seen cross-sector cooperation and participation in the development of strategic planning and the legal framework for children's and mental health services.

In relation to children's services, for example, following a process of extensive consultation, which included '112 institutions working in the field of children's rights and programming' (NPA, 2004a) and surveying and consulting with children (Arafat and Boothby, 2003), a revised National Plan for the Child was published in 2004 (NPA, 2004a), with a detailed separate plan published at the same time for Children's Psychosocial health (2004-2007) by the Secretariat of the National Plan of Action for Palestinian Children (NPA, 2004). This plan (NPA, 2004a) provides a detailed situational analysis of the impact of the Second Intifada on child development. There is a marked contrast between these plans and that devised by the Palestinian Authority in 1999 (PNA, 1999). In the current plan, the needs and aspirations of children and the policies of ministries, UNRWA and NGOs are considered and an attempt is made to be solution focused in relation to institutional coordination, with roles and responsibilities of each provider set out in the plan.

In relation to mental health services, the Palestinian Authority Ministry of Health, in collaboration with the World Health Organization and the French and Italian governments, published and disseminated a *Plan on the Organisation of Mental Health Services in the Occupied Palestinian Territories* (Steering Committee on Mental Health) in February 2004. This plan sets out a strategic services plan which has the objective of 'meeting the needs of all people with a mental health problem in the

Occupied Palestinian Territories' (paragraph 5.1.2). It stresses the need to develop community-based integrated services and the need to develop these services in partnership with all local stakeholders. Concurrently, the PNGO worked together to develop a position paper '*Building Balance*', which put forward a Palestinian approach to a social model for mental health. PNGO engaged in robust discussions with the Ministry and the World Health Organisation about their approach to developing mental health services. There is some evidence that these views have been acknowledged in planning and piloting services – for example the piloting of Family Organizations in 2004. This approach mobilises self-help groups for families who have a family member with mental health problems. Family Organisations provide mutual support, engage in advocacy and community anti-stigma education, advise policy-makers and make representations for improvement of services. The initial evaluation of this approach appears positive and culturally relevant (Brigham, 2005).

The development of legal frameworks relevant to social work under the Palestinian Authority (1994-2006)

The OPT legal structure is complex and reflects the history of government and occupation over the 20th century. Musleh and Taylor (2005) outline that at present there are several systems of laws in force in the OPT promulgated by previous rulers (including the Ottoman Empire, the British Mandate, Egyptian law [in Gaza], Jordanian law [in the West Bank], Israeli military orders) and legislation developed by the Palestinian Authority. Furthermore, certain issues are subsumed under Family Law or Personal Status Law, which may come under the jurisdiction of either Sharia or Christian religious courts or are dealt with by traditional customary law, which mediates disputes outside of the court system. Musleh and Taylor point out that this legal situation is further complicated when the implementation of international law (for example International Humanitarian Law, the Fourth Geneva Convention) and human rights conventions are considered, with Israel denying its obligations to implement international human rights conventions and the Fourth Geneva Convention in the OPT despite its ongoing presence in the area. Any mention of Palestinian legal provisions must acknowledge the level of control Israel exercises over

Palestinian lives, what has been characterised as "the elephant in the room" by the International Crisis group (quoted in Musleh and Taylor, 2005, p. 12).

As the OPT is not a state, it is not able to sign up to international conventions. The Palestinian Authority has stated its commitment to the UN Convention on the Rights of the Child and utilises other international conventions (for example, Universal Declaration of Human Rights) in framing local legislation. Legislation is being gradually developed in the OPT that is of interest in considering the legal remit of social workers, including public health (Public Health Law, 2005), law governing the provision of mental health and Family Law (in draft – developed by a number of NGOs and Ministry of Women) and law governing children's services. Child Law (2005), for example, supersedes previous legislation on the issues it addresses, with the exception of Israeli military orders over which the Palestinian legal system has no control. This legislation will be the main legal instrument for child protection in Palestinian society. Child Law explicitly lays out in Article 53(1) the responsibility of all citizens to inform the Ministry of Social Affairs' child protection social workers if they suspect a case of violence against a child. Article 53(2) requires the same thing of educators, physicians, social workers and others entrusted with the protection and care of children. In relation to the second group, reporting is mandatory with a specific penalty laid out for non-notification [Article 53(3)]. Expectations of social workers are clearly set out in these provisions. While Child Law (2005) offers a legislation framework for supporting and protecting children in the OPT, it is arguable that the majority of its provisions cannot realistically be implemented at present. Some elements of its provisions appear to echo legislative provisions (for example, mandated reporting, fostering arrangements), which have been developed in very different cultural contexts in Western countries and may evidence the influence of international advisers and donors in drafting this legislation. How applicable or acceptable such measures will be to Palestinians is yet to be determined. A public information strategy about this legislation is planned and will doubtless promote a lively debate. Of perhaps greater importance is the fact that resources and expertise properly to implement its provisions at the levels of government policy-making, within the judicial system and at the level of actual service delivery, are minimal. For example, in relation to child protection, the Secretariat for the

National Plan for the Child estimated in 2005 that the Ministry of Social Affairs had only 25 child protection social workers to a child population of 1.7 million (Musleh and Taylor, 2005, p. 87).

Developing professionals: the growth in university provision and the development of university programmes in social work and the social sciences

The period since the early 1970s has seen a rapid expansion in higher education provision to the point where there are currently eight universities in the West Bank and three in Gaza (Source: Passia, 2006). The ethos of social service and community action in support of nation building has been a strong feature of Palestinian university life, with general graduation requirements often including that all students undertake specified hours of community work as part of their undergraduate degree programme.

The first undergraduate programme in social work was established at Bethlehem University with its first graduates completing their programme of study in 1978. This programme is embedded within a liberal arts undergraduate degree structure where social work is taken as a major field of study, with four short fieldwork placements. More recently, three other universities started to offer social work programmes at undergraduate level (Al Quds University in East Jerusalem, Al Quds Open University in the West Bank and Gaza Strip and An Najah University in Nablus [the last of the three offering a combined award in Sociology and Social Work since 2003]). Examination of the curricula of these courses (Source: websites of each university) indicates both the influence of Western models of social work education and that to some level students are offered the opportunity to engage in a debate about the nature and purpose of social work in Palestine (for example, at An Najah students are required to 'discuss social work in capitalist and oriental societies' (An Najah website, 2006, www.najah.edu/). Methods of intervention taught include certain elements that reflect Palestinian priorities such as working with and mobilising community organisations, school social work, and rehabilitation work, as well as standard approaches to working with individuals, groups and communities. Staff resources to support social work degree programmes in social work are limited. It is not easy for social work programmes to draw on the expertise of lecturers in other local social work programmes because of travel restrictions between the West Bank/Gaza Strip and Jerusalem, within the West Bank and between the West Bank and Gaza Strip (restrictions imposed by Israel occupation). It would appear that Al Quds University, perhaps because of its location within Jerusalem, is better placed to secure appropriate levels of staff resources and engage in professional and academic collaboration with Palestinians working in social work education in Israel.

Birzeit University's Continuing Education Centre has provided a specialist in-service Diploma programme for school counsellors and social workers (since 1997) and a Certificate and Diploma programme in supervision (since 2004). These programmes include live supervision, direct observation and assessment in practice. Some of those trained on this Supervision programme are also acting as field educators for undergraduate social work programmes.

At present there are no Masters degree programmes in social work or standardised frameworks for continuing professional development for social workers in Palestine. Those who wish to gain this level of qualification have to go abroad to study. Those who have gained the Masters in social work overseas have normally been funded by scholarships, which are often difficult to access and may be open to political influence in terms of allocation. Al Quds Open University is currently planning to develop a Masters in social work and expand its research activities in social work (Al Quds Open University website, 2006, www.qudsopenu.edu). Bethlehem University (www.bethlehem. edu) is also moving towards the same direction. This may lead to greater equality of access to Masters-level programmes and promote workforce development. The challenge, for both universities, is a shortage of suitably qualified people to teach on these programmes.

Social work education in Palestine has been established. The next stage may be to develop a firmer conceptualisation of Palestinian professional social work education, benchmark expected outcomes of programmes at Bachelors and Masters degree levels, develop standards for fieldwork education, formulate and fund relevant research agendas and support the development of social work educators to achieve these aims. There is a strong case to be made for local universities investing in the provision of social work courses, given the demand for these qualifications, the extent of social problems, and the development of new legislation (such as Child Law, 2005) which has a specific role for the intervention of qualified social workers.

In parallel with the development of small-scale social work education programmes, there has also been a growth in university provision in other social sciences subjects, including psychology, sociology and anthropology at undergraduate level. At postgraduate level, recent relevant developments include the accreditation of a number of Masters degree programmes including community mental health (Al Quds); public health; gender, law and development; and democracy and human rights (Birzeit University, www.birzeit.edu).

What influences the decisions of young people to select social work, sociology or psychology as an initial degree choice? It is possible that as local organisations were established and were staffed, their presence and work in communities promoted a positive attitude towards these professions, seeing them as both providing employment opportunities, good remuneration and contributing positively to local need. Many of those employed in the psychosocial field see gaining Masters degrees as their passport to advancement in the profession and their occupation (Lindsay, 2005).

Occupational grouping and professions: developing professional responses, values and ethical standards of practice

The previous section has traced the development of community-based (civil society), governmental, and international organisations in the OPT whose purposes include meeting social needs, empowerment and working towards social justice. The growth in organisations demanded new professionals and created new employment opportunities as well as voluntary effort within communities. The higher education sector responded to the needs of the social sector by creating and providing a range of courses in the social field, including social work education. Questions which are worth exploring are: Who is currently providing services? What is their educational and professional background? What types of professions exist and are needed to implement planned services? How should these professionals work collaboratively to develop and deliver services? How should professionals be supervised and supported to continue to develop their professional knowledge and expertise? What ethical standards are required and how should such professions be regulated? The following section attempts to explore these issues and highlight some of the current challenges and constraints.

Who is providing social services and psychosocial care?

Giacaman's (2004) survey of psychosocial care in the West Bank and Gaza (707 workers included in this survey) provides a snapshot of employment in the sector in 2002-2003. Giacaman found that a fairly equal distribution of men (46%) and women (54%) were employed in the sector and suggests that defeminisation of the caring profession in the OPT might be explained by 'cultural necessity' (the employment of male workers to work with boys in the school counselling service). Other factors are likely to include the availability of employment opportunities in this sector in a context of high unemployment. Respondents to this survey had been employed for a relatively short time in the sector (an average of 3.98 years per worker) and for a significant number this was their first job since graduation, indicating a youthful and fairly inexperienced profession. The majority of respondents to Giacaman's survey held Bachelors degrees (92%) in psychology, sociology, social work or education obtained from local universities. She argues that these undergraduate courses of study were 'never intended to prepare graduates to work in the sector in a full professional capacity' (Giacaman, 2004, p. 7). The shortage of workers to fill social work posts in charitable organisations and public services has meant that a wide range of fresh graduates (for example, in sociology, psychology, social work and education) have been employed as 'social workers' and 'psycho-social counsellors' without the relevant professional training. Giacaman's survey indicates that workers in the sector are able to access short training programmes. These training courses appear to be provided in a seemingly haphazard way, often linked to vertical implementation of national programmes funded by international donors. This can mean that training programmes are duplicated with workers taking the same short programme more than once. Application of learning from these programmes in practice is not assessed and it is, therefore, not possible to be confident about the effectiveness of such programmes, either in terms of resource allocation or in terms of improved service delivery. The Diploma programme in schools counselling (Birzeit University) is the only known programme that attempts to address such issues systematically.

There are very few people with a Masters degree in social work in the West Bank and Gaza. It is estimated that there are approximately ten to fifteen people working in Palestine (West Bank and Gaza) who are qualified to this level in social work. There is a high demand for those with this qualification and Masters in social work holders can command relatively high salaries in large or international NGOs in administrative positions. While there are Palestinian graduates in social work at Bachelors and Masters levels from Israeli universities, there is no incentive for them to choose to work in the OPT as they can command much better salaries in Israel.

Developing an organised professional response

On 24 March 1997, at a conference hosted by the Ministry of Labour, the Union of Social Workers, Psychologists and Sociologists was formed. Elections for officers were held and eight local branches were established centred on eight towns throughout the West Bank. Since 1997 a process of collective professional action has emerged which attempts to reflect and represent the professional needs of workers within the sector, to develop professional standards and to participate in the debate about how to develop social work and social services in Palestine. This development has not been without tensions, partially because this was a new initiative and processes and structures needed to be agreed and developed and partially because of the difficulties in communication and travel between branches in the West Bank regions. This was exacerbated by one local branch (Bethlehem) obtaining international donor funding to support its activities. Some of these issues have yet to be resolved, however this process has prompted a debate about the nature and purposes of collective action in the sector. Series of workshops and conferences have been held debating standards of practice and Codes of Ethics. Some conference reports and resolutions have been published (Union of Social Workers, Psychologists and Sociologists, 2005a) and evidence concern to enhance the professionalism of workers within the sector. They address not only employment conditions and rights and professional development frameworks including developing a network which shares knowledge and resources, but also include a strong focus on the need to improve the quality and efficiency of service provision, concern to improve the psychosocial well-being of Palestinian citizens and the need to recognise and adhere to ethical standards of practice. One of the challenges faced by Union branches is the range of educational backgrounds of workers employed within the sector. The Union to date has sought to be inclusive of three main groups (those trained in psychology, sociology and social work). The question remains to be answered as to whether separate unions representing each of these disciplines might be needed in the future. At present in Palestine, each of these disciplines has acted as an entry-level qualification to employment in the sector. Much will depend on the development of regulation and licensing arrangements (see next section), however it is likely that the transition to any new set of arrangements will take some time. One of the challenges for the Union in this process has been how to define 'social work' both in way which is relevant for Palestine, and which is aligned to recent international definitions of social work (IFSW and IASSW, 2004), which is seen as necessary if social workers trained in Palestine are to have international recognition and be able to participate fully on an international stage in the global debate on social work. As a first step in this process, the Bethlehem branch of the Palestinian Union became a member of the International Federation of Social Workers (IFSW) in 2004. It is perhaps telling that IFSW (nor IASSW) has yet attempted an Arabic translation of the 2004 international definition of social work.

The development of regulatory policies relating to Codes of Ethics and educational requirements and licensing for social workers and psychologists by the Palestinian Authority

In its review of service provision in the psychosocial sector in 2004 (NPA, 2004a), the Palestinian Authority concluded that 'job titles in the sector were unclear' there was 'a lack of professional points of reference', 'no code of ethics for practice endorsed by a legally authorised body', and 'a lack of licensure for professional practice' and an 'overlap between the professional and political agenda' (p. 40-41). A work plan for the period 2004-2007 was developed by the Ministry of Planning to address these issues and included setting up coordination committees to reform current arrangements and to develop and approve a law 'for the association of psychological and social workers to be put on the agenda of the

Legislative Council' (p. 41). Within this document there is a strong focus on psychological health rather than a social action model of intervention, with 'psychological health considered a priority for decision makers' (p. 51). Additional plans also include influencing universities in terms of educational programme development based on the country's need for specialists (p. 49).

The process of development of these policies is ongoing at the time of writing (January 2006). In July 2004, the Palestinian Union of Social Workers and Psychologists (Bethlehem Branch) launched a project to develop a regulatory law, Code of Ethics and professional definitions of the different roles and titles in the field of social work and psychology. By March 2005, a draft document of the law, bylaws, Code of Ethics and definitions was produced and submitted to the Palestinian Legislative Council legal committee by July 2005. At the same time the Ministry of Planning convened its own working group to develop codes and produced draft documents. The most recent version (November 2005 by the Ministry of Planning) provides a rather obscure definition of social work and indicates that plans for social work include setting out qualifications levels (Bachelors degree level being seen as a general-level qualification and Masters degree level being accorded the title 'Specialist'). A wide range of potential social work occupational grouping are listed in the draft document including working with children and young people, women, older people, detainees, those with special needs, those with addiction problems, victims of war and their families. Social workers are seen as having the skills to address poverty and employment, including careers counselling and the ability to work in school, medical and industrial settings.

It is likely that these plans will undergo revision in debate with the Union and the universities. It is perhaps inevitable that in any process of change, power relations become obvious. There is likely to be perceptions that the status of one professional group is being privileged over another, that work within the profession to develop its own standards has not been fully acknowledged and that consultations did not take all parties' views into account. The current challenge for the Palestinian Union is to be able to provide a united response to proposed developments and to continue to develop and articulate what social work means and could mean in Palestine. A Code of Ethics was jointly agreed in December 2005.

The potential of the social work profession in Palestine: developing a vision

The social work profession in the OPT is at the point in its development where it needs to develop a strong rationale for its place within the emerging professions engaged in the field of psychosocial care and community work. The profession needs to develop an indigenous Palestinian conception of social work and be able to articulate and promote its goals and levels of operation. Resources and investment in both initial and continuing professional education and for research are required. Furthermore, social workers need to be able to define their role and remit in relation to other professionals and determine how they can best contribute to governmental planning and community development processes.

Cox and Pawar (2006), in considering the development of social work internationally, suggest that the profession has evolved to serve three main areas of practice: this framework may provide a useful device to explore a potential vision for social work in Palestine.

First, Cox and Pawar (2006) argue that in some countries, social work functions 'as an arm of the state ... with the state effectively dictating the specific field of practice on which the profession focuses' (p.10), which they characterise as having social control and protection functions (for example, child protection, social assistance, and work with those who have broken the law). In the OPT, the implementation of new legislation such as Child Law (2005) will require social workers to take on such roles as well as the executive institutions necessary to apply the law which are not in place at the time of writing (January 2006). Social workers employed by the Ministry of Social Affairs currently have a brief to provide social security and family welfare assistance. While these are important functions, the dangers of relying only on this approach to social work provision are, as Harris (1990) suggests, that social work becomes a 'state centred, not a client centred enterprise' (quoted in Cox and Pawar, 2006, p. 11).

The second area identified by Cox and Pawar (2006) sees social work as undertaking therapeutic work with individuals and families experiencing problems. Such work is essentially remedial, aimed at enhancing social functioning, and is individualised. In Palestine, the flourishing of psychosocial approaches to intervention forms part of this tradition (including counselling in schools and with particular populations such as women experiencing domestic abuse, and individuals who have experienced traumatic events during the Intifada).

Cox and Pawar's (2006) third area encompasses the field of social development. It sees the social work profession as working at a community level to promote collective well-being, and 'to some degree as the servant of the people' (p. 10). In this area, social workers work at macro levels (social policy development) and micro levels (with communities and civil society organisations) to improve the environment and societies in which people live, and promote empowerment of people within their communities. Such work is characterised as having a participative, radical, and 'futuristic orientation' whose 'goals are always related to improving the environments or societies in which people live' (p.10). This approach appears to accord well with the history of how social work and civil society organisations have emerged in Palestine. Local research (for example, Giacaman, *et. al*, 2004) emphasises the need to develop strategies for development and change based on mobilising the strengths of communities. Social workers practising such an approach can also offer a radical and questioning approach to both national policy development and international donor activity.

Clearly, in developing the conception of Palestinian social work a balance needs to be struck between each of these areas of practice. The challenge for Palestinian social workers now is to agree what constitutes social work in a Palestinian context and to articulate a strong case for the development of the profession in order to build on the achievements since the 1970s since the profession's inception in Palestine. The development of the social work profession could make a vital and radical contribution to building cohesive, healthy and empowering communities in Palestine and promote wellbeing, empowerment, social functioning and liberation, informed and guided by principles of human rights and social justice.

Chapter 10

What is to be Done?

Chris Jones

It might be useful to start with recognising that social work, especially within capitalist societies, has always been a welfare activity mired in paradox and problematic for both governments which sponsor it and for those who practise it. This also applies, to an even greater extent, to those on the receiving end – the clients.

In the British context, which I know best, although as this book reveals, it applies to many other societies, governments have sponsored social work as a means of managing and controlling some of its most vulnerable and disadvantaged people. In comparison with other forms of welfare intervention it is often the most class specific, focused almost exclusively on the poorest sections of the working class. This remains a constant and consistent theme, although over time social work practice and policy has shifted. So when we look at the Charity Organisation Society (COS) in Victorian England we note that the COS believed that social work intervention could rescue and restore the more able of the poorest (the deserving poor). Casework, in particular, was deemed to have the capacity to remoralise this section of the poor and to make them pliant and productive citizens capable of sustaining themselves and their households without slipping into destitution. This sharply contrasts with contemporary British state social work agencies which no longer have such rehabilititive ideals but are much more concerned with surveillance and rationing.

At first glance, there seems to be nothing paradoxical about this notion of social work in that its conservatism was explicit in asserting that the 'problem' of enduring poverty lay in the character of the poor themselves and was not related to any structural features concerning the character of capitalism itself. Destitution was deemed to be rooted in the immorality of the poor – their attachment to alcohol, their inability to save, their poor socialisation of their children, their lack of commitment to self-reliance, their idleness and avoidance of wage labour, and so forth.

However, from the outset, the proponents of social work had a problem for this strategy depended on a particular form of intervention that was difficult to control and manage. The heart of social work was the casework relationship, and hence the ability of individual social workers to form relationships with their clients which would be robust enough to enable them to resocialise and remoralise their clients. This was a significant departure from any other previous methods of poor relief. It required highly personalised interventions and, as the COS recognised, it was a strategy that required a form of friendship to be established in order that sufficient trust could be created which would allow for remoralisation to take place. Moreover, unlike the Poor Law, it demanded social workers who, to put it crudely, were 'nice', thoughtful, caring and empathic. Social work could not be outwardly authoritarian or bullying.

Herein lies one of the enduring and paradoxical features of social work. Despite its conservatism it relies for its possibility on social workers who must have a capacity to make enduring relationships with some of the poorest and most disadvantaged. Not only is this a relationship to cross the chasm of class difference but it is to be operationalised in the places where the poorest live – their neighbourhoods and homes. Furthermore, it requires of these social workers an ability to believe without question that the core difficulties of poverty and hardship lie within the poor themselves. However, as the COS was soon to realise, this was no easy proposition. As their social workers penetrated into the lives and the communities of their clients, significant numbers began to recognise the profound limitations of such an approach. The sheer enormity of poverty and disadvantage, for example, was both daunting and suggested that far more was at stake than immorality and poor socialisation. Not surprisingly, the COS found itself losing its social workers to other reform movements, such as the Fabians and later the Labour Party which, while not discounting individualised accounts to explain some forms of destitution, also recognised that more structural changes were required if enduring poverty was to be alleviated.

This tension between the nature of social work as a class-specific form of welfare intervention and the motivations and perspectives of the individual practitioners has, for too long, been ignored. The concern over preventing social worker 'contamination' and of ensuring that they are not radicalised by their experiences of the poor and the disadvantaged has been evident from the very origins of modern social work. Its impact on the changing nature and organisation of social work has been far ranging and has been a significant influence on the manner in which social work has changed over time. For the COS this tension was the principal reason for its development of organised social work education at the beginning of the 20th century. It was their hope that by instituting formal courses they could create a cadre of social workers who were equipped with a 'knowledge base' that would immunise the practitioners from 'subversive ideas' about the structural iniquities of capitalism and tie them into their idealist philosophy where morality was the key. Their key ideologues – Charles Loch, Bernard and Helen Bosanquet set about the production of texts and articles all intended to prove the validity of their approach and to legitimate their approach through the emerging social sciences, especially social psychology. All of their extraordinary effort was directed at their own people, to strengthen their social workers and to stop them from wavering from the path of individualism.

This emphasis on social work education is evident throughout the history and development of British social work. It is no accident that most of the leaders of the profession in Britain such as Eileen Younghusband were social work educators. They sifted and sorted through the developing social sciences to sustain a knowledge base which concurred with their highly individualised view of poverty and inequality. This informed the renowned eclecticism of social work 'theory'. They seized on only those aspects of theory which could be shaped to support their perspective (Freudian theory being a fine example) and sociology and social policy were looted in similar fashion. Moreover, during the 1950s and 1960s, when casework remained the key method, social work leaders insisted on the most elaborate systems of student selection which were intended to ensure that only those predisposed to its individualistic and family pathological perspectives were taken on the courses. And in further recognition that an intellectual knowledge base would never be sufficient to prevent social worker contamination they insisted that students must be assessed on their placements where personal suitability (that is, conformity) could be determined. And underlaying all this was the continued emphasis on the courses, that clients were unworthy, and notwithstanding all their flaws they all too often had the unwavering skill of being able to manipulate and twist the unguarded social worker.

But even this was never enough. As some of the social sciences took on a more radical perspective in the 1960s and 1970s, especially with respect to feminism and deviancy and later 'race' and racism, we see British social work education going through successive changes. Among the first casualties were sociologists who were eased out of social work education and no longer permitted to supervise social work students. Increasingly, central government intervened and through its validating systems brought employers into the management and control of professional education. By the 1980s, universities were no longer to be trusted with the exclusive control and management of social work courses and national curricula guidelines were instituted. The consequences have been far reaching and what can only be described as a process of anti-intellectualisation has taken place as courses have abandoned the social sciences and replaced them with a narrow focus on job competencies as determined by employers.

These changes have also been mirrored in the state social work agencies and are reflected in a myriad of developments epitomised by increasing managerialism and systems of control. Today, casework in its classic sense is rarely practised. Now the core tasks are rationing and surveillance. Hence the primary forms of social worker control have changed. Talk to any frontline practitioners today and you will be regaled by tales of the mountain of paperwork which they recognise as being an attempt to regulate their work with clients. Agencies simply do not want thinking and creative social workers especially as inequalities deepen under neo-liberalism. They certainly do not want those who have some of the most intense contact with those who are suffering to be speaking out and/or working in ways which undermine their attempt to keep their budgets and provision to a minimum. They certainly do not want to hear any voices which contradict their view that the problems of the most enduring poverty are anything other than due to the inadequacies of the poor!

Understanding this aspect of social work's development is crucial for thinking about what is to be done now. Not the least, that there has been such an enduring legacy of concern about social workers speaking out as they engage directly with inequality and poverty strongly suggests that this is what we must seek to do wherever and whenever we can. It also highlights that despite the attempts of established social work to present the activity as one which can be trusted to act on behalf of the capitalist state, there is within social work an enduring strand which has always rejected social work's narrow conservatism. This is all too evident when we listen to practitioners and clients. Alongside accounts of disturbing and disrespectful practice there are equally many which portray practice and interventions which are not predicated on the individual failings of clients. Social work is replete with subversive practices, whether it is accepting that clients have to subvert the benefits systems if they are to survive, of using one's own money to help people out, of looking away as fuel meters are bypassed, of refusing to condemn lifestyles, and so forth. In my own research, I have met so many practitioners who recognise that the hardships facing their clients have everything to do with the nature of contemporary neo-liberalism and nothing to with character or morality.

To my mind, we make a mistake to regard these kinds of micro-practices as radical social work. For these practitioners this is the very nature of what social work should be and they are its guardians. From their view it is their managers and social work academics who have abandoned social work and are culpable for the disgraceful state of the activity in Britain today. They are particularly critical of social work education. Quite simply the courses, with only a few exceptions, are deemed to be useless and only have value in providing the paper required for employment. They have little value otherwise. From my own experience within social work education, I share their frustrations and their criticism of social work academics, who with very few exceptions, have failed to stand up and resist so many of the changes which over thirty years have emasculated social work courses. It seemed to me at least, that too many were concerned to 'protect' social work education at any cost and to be even more blunt, were more than happy to rid themselves of any critical content which might make their lives uncomfortable. Not surprisingly, many of these academics have been more than happy to ignore and hide the critical core of social work and to marginalise it as some radical quirk.

Thankfully, we are beginning to see some more hopeful signs within British social work. Slowly more and more frontline practitioners are beginning to say enough is enough. Taking sustenance from broader oppositional movements – against the wars in Iraq and Afghanistan, anti-globalisation mobilisations, and so forth in which many are personally involved – social workers are feeling stronger and more determined.

These developments are crucial in the renewal of the oppositional spirit and encouraging people to believe that another world is possible. At the moment, this appears to be taking the form of increasing numbers of social workers coming together to speak out about what they are experiencing. They are doing so in their trade unions and within local branches of the professional association. Some are creating new forums. At this point the form of the agitation does not matter. What is much more important is that it is happening. This is a crucial first step in building solidarity as frontline practitioners recognise that their own experiences of the abandonment of social work by their agencies and managers, and their university courses are widely shared. We are now seeing for the first time in many years, groups of practitioners and students forming to discuss their ideas and their strategies.

As these groups and meetings form, new alliances are being formed between established and growing user movements and frontline practitioners. The same abandonment of social work experienced by practitioners is also central to the experience of users who find services increasingly inaccessible or totally inappropriate. Their stories are often outrageous accounts of state brutality and disdain. Moreover, rather than totally dismissive of social work, there are still many users who have experienced a social worker who has rejected their agency's imperatives and offered support and solidarity that has made a difference. Together, users and some frontline practitioners are beginning to frame a social work that is truly of value and meaning.

It is early days. In Britain at least, we have been through three decades or more where social workers and user groups who have attempted to speak out about the appalling injustices so apparent in our midst have been demonised and vilified. Both constituencies have been faced by continuous change in welfare provision and organisation which in turn has been exhausting and confusing. Both have also been let down, not least by New Labour which many hoped would be different from the Conservatives who had wreaked so much damage on state welfare between 1979 and 1997. As new grassroot mobilisations form and ferment, we can see a growing confidence among frontline practitioners, students and users. There is a growing recognition that they have a powerful understanding of what constitutes decent, just and humane social welfare. There is a new preparedness to look not upwards for support and understanding but sideways and downwards.

Groups, individuals, populations which have been demonised by the elites, often for generations, are increasingly recognised as providing profound insights and wisdoms as to what should be. Our resources are considerable and powerful.

But this is not an agenda for radical social work as though it was some form of social work which would simply sit alongside other forms of social work. We need to be more courageous and imaginative and recall all those social workers who for over a century or more have come into the occupation because they were committed to social welfare, to making lives better, and appalled by social injustice and hardship. From my own experience of social work education I can never recall students wanting to enter social work because they desired to be the moral re-educators of the working class poor. Their ambitions and hopes were quite different. They have been betrayed by their courses and their employers. We should be outraged by that betrayal. Now at least we are seeing that outrage coming to the fore. We need to cherish and support it and work together to make, at last, a social work that is worthy of its name.

Chapter 11

Social Work and Social Justice:
A Manifesto for a New Engaged Practice

Chris Jones, Iain Ferguson, Michael Lavalette and Laura Penketh

Background to the Manifesto

In 2004 the four of us met in Preston, in the North of England, to discuss what steps we could take to address the growing feeling of crisis in British state social work. We were all undertaking research into social work and working beside practitioners – and we were all aware of a growing unease and the toll neo-liberalism, marketisation and managerialism were taking on practitioners and service users.

We decided to write the Manifesto that is reproduced below, to 'upload' it onto the internet and try and organise a few meetings on the themes contained in it. We were unsure what would happen next.

The response has been dramatic. Close to 500 people have 'signed up' to the Manifesto online (at www.socialworkfuture.org). It has been reproduced in the national media and discussed at various gatherings of academic and professional social workers.

Since it was written, we have been involved in establishing a loose network of social workers in Scotland called SWAN (social work action network) and spoken at a series of meetings. In April 2006 we organised a highly successful conference called 'A Profession Worth Fighting For?' and it was agreed this should become an annual event. The conference provided space for practitioners (the majority of the conference goers) to talk and discuss 'what needs to be done'.

The Manifesto is presented below. We believe it offers a framework for further discussion about what an engaged, committed and 'ethical' social work might look like.

Social work today

Social work in Britain today has lost direction. This is not new. Many have talked about social work being in crisis for over 30 years now. The starting point for this Manifesto, however, is that the 'crisis of social work' can no longer be tolerated. We need to find more effective ways of resisting the dominant trends within social work and map ways forward for a new engaged practice.

Many of us entered social work – and many still do – out of a commitment to social justice or, at the very least, to bring about positive change in people's lives. Yet increasingly the scope for doing so is curtailed.

Instead, our work is shaped by managerialism, by the fragmentation of services, by financial restrictions and lack of resources, by increased bureaucracy and workloads, by the domination of care-management approaches with their associated performance indicators and by the increased use of the private sector. While these trends have long been present in state social work, they now dominate the day-to-day work of frontline social workers and shape the welfare services that are offered to clients. The effect has been to increase the distance between managers and frontline workers on the one hand, and between workers and service users on the other. The main concern of too many social work managers today is the control of budgets rather than the welfare of service users, while worker–client relationships are increasingly characterised by control and supervision rather than care.

Unless the fundamental direction of social work changes, then neither a new social work degree nor new bodies such as the Social Care Councils will do anything to improve the current situation. These are no more than 'technical fixes' for deep-rooted problems. So attempts by individual local authorities to alleviate the staffing crisis by offering cash incentives – the so-called 'golden hellos' – simply move the problem around.

In the absence of an organised response to these trends, people understandably react in different individual ways. Some social workers may leave the profession, but for many this is not an option. Some workers have found ways within their workplaces to occupy spaces where they can practise a more rounded social work – in the voluntary sector, for example, or in more specialist projects – but this option is not available to most. Even in the voluntary sector the trends are increasingly mirroring the managerialist pattern of the statutory agencies.

And yet, the need for a social work committed to social justice and challenging poverty and discrimination is greater than ever. In our view, this remains a project that is worth defending. More than any other welfare state profession, social work seeks to understand the links between 'public issues' and 'private troubles' and seeks to address both. It is for this reason that many who hold power and influence in our society would be delighted to see a demoralised and defeated social work, a social work that is incapable of drawing attention to the miseries and difficulties which beset so many in our society. This alone makes social work worth fighting for.

The current degraded status of social work as a profession is inextricably related to the status and standing of those we work with. Social work clients are among some of the most vulnerable and impoverished in our society, and have benefited least from New Labour's social welfare reforms. In fact, under New Labour we have witnessed not only greater levels of material inequality, but also an intensified demonisation of asylum seekers, young people and poor families, the very groups that social workers engage with. Too frequently today social workers are often doing little more than supervising the deterioration of people's lives.

So in opposition to those who would be happy to see a defeated and silenced social work occupation, we are seeking a social work that has prevention at its heart and recognises the value of collective approaches. At the same time we also recognise that good casework has also suffered as a result of the trends referred to above. We are looking to a social work that can contribute to shaping a different kind of social policy agenda, based on our understanding of the struggles experienced by clients in addressing a range of emotional, social and material problems and the strengths they bring to these struggles.

Resources of hope

Many social workers who despair about the ways in which social work has been changed can see no way out of the current situation. Given the mauling that social work (and social workers) have taken from politicians and the tabloid media over the past 25 years, some despair or despondency is understandable, However, there is a real danger that this can blind us to the new resources of hope that have emerged in recent years and which may point the way towards a reinvigorated social work practice which plays a part in the demands for a more just and humane society.

Over the last two decades the growth of user movements (like the disability movement and the mental health users movement) have brought innovation and insight to our ways of seeing social and individual problems. These movements have developed many relevant and interesting approaches to dealing with service users' needs – collective advocacy, for example, or (in the mental health field) the Hearing Voices groups or user-led approaches such the Clubhouse model. The fact that these models have come, not from professional social work but from service users themselves, emphasises that social work needs to engage with, and learn from, these movements in ways that will allow partnerships to form and new knowledge bases and curricula to develop.

In addition, the last few years have witnessed the growth of dynamic and international global protest movements against capitalism and war. In the 1960s and 1970s, social work was profoundly influenced by the 'spirit of the sixties': the Vietnam anti-war, the black, and the women's movements. It was this that laid the basis of future anti-oppressive social work practice. Today we are seeing the rise of similar social movements. Within the anti-capitalist and anti-war movements we have 'greater resources of hope' than have been available to us for 30 years. These have been movements within which user groups and non-government organisations (NGOs) have fruitfully engaged and within which questions of social justice are paramount. They have challenged the orthodoxy of neo-liberal globalisation and its devastating impact on the poor and dispossessed across the world, on the environment and on the human costs of the privatisation of services.

The anti-capitalist movement was born out of the protests against the World Trade Organisation's Third Ministerial meeting in Seattle in 1999 and has since spread across the globe. Over the last year it has merged with the movement against war and Imperialism. In February 2003 the spirit of anti-capitalist protest dramatically came to Britain when two million people demonstrated in London against the war on Iraq. The breadth and inclusiveness of this movement in conjunction with its energy and youthfulness, has revitalised many who had fallen into despair. It has also had an impact in rejuvenating the spirit of protest within the trade union movement.

But these movements are not just against war and capitalism, they have also started to think of alternative futures. Over the last three years at various World and European Social Forums, large numbers of people have come together to share ideas and discuss what another world might look like. These debates can help us think about the shape of a modern engaged social work based around such core 'anti-capitalist' values as democracy, solidarity, accountability, participation, justice, equality, liberty and diversity.

Thus we find ourselves at a crossroads. Down one road is managerialism and increased marketisation, and with it frustration and despondency for frontline workers; while down the other there is a possibility – and it is no more than that – for a renewed and regenerated social work that engages with the resources of hope available in the new collective movements for an alternative, and better, world.

An ethical career

The enduring crisis of social work in Britain has taught us many things. It has brought us to a state of affairs that nobody in their right mind could possibly view as acceptable. It has taught us that there can be no return to a past of professional arrogance and that progressive change must involve users and all frontline workers. As agents of change senior managers have had their day. It has reminded us that budget-dominated welfare systems are cruel and destructive of human well-being. The casualties are everywhere in the social work system among clients and users and social workers. These years of turmoil have highlighted that social work has to be defined not by its function for the state but by its value base. Above all it has been a stark lesson in the need for collective organisation, both to defend a vision of social work based on social justice and also to defend the working conditions that make that possible.

As we noted at the start of this Manifesto, in the past many people entered social work because it seemed to offer a way of earning a living that did not involve oppressing or exploiting people, but on the contrary could contribute, even in a small way, to social change. It was, in other words, an ethical career. That potential for social change has all but been squeezed out of social work by the drives towards marketisation and managerialism that have characterised the last decade and a half. Yet overwhelmingly it is still the case that people enter social work not to be care-managers or rationers of services or dispensers of community punishment but rather to make a positive contribution to the lives of poor and oppressed people. If it is the widening gap between promise and reality that breeds much of the current anger and frustration among social workers, it is also the awareness that social work could be much more than it is at present that leads many of us to hang on in there.

We note that the organisation People and Planet includes social work within its 'Ethical Careers Service'. If that progressive promise is to be realised even in part, then we need to coalesce and organise around a shared vision of what a genuinely anti-oppressive social work might be like.

This *Manifesto* is a small contribution towards the process of developing that vision and that organisation.

Bibliography

Adams, A. (2000) 'Poverty – a precarious public policy idea', *Australian Journal of Public Administration*, 6 (4), pp. 89-98.

Agamben, G. (1998) *Homo Sacer: Sovereign Power and Bare Life*, Standford, CA: Standford University Press.

Alayón, N. (ed.) (2005) 'El movimiento de reconceptualización: una mirada critica', in *Trabajo Social Latinoamericano: A 40 Años de la Reconceptualización*. Buenos Aires: Espacio Editorial, pp. 9-17.

Alinsky, S. (1973) *Rules for Radicals*, New York: Vintage Books.

Allan, J., Pease, B. and Briskman, L. (eds.) (2003) *Critical Social Work: An introduction to theories and practices*, Sydney: Allen and Unqin.

Alston, M. (2001) 'Working with women', in Alston, M. and McKinnon, J. (eds.) *Social Work: Fields of Practice*, pp. 41-65, Oxford: Oxford University Press.

ANC (African National Congress) (1994) *The Reconstruction and Development Programme: A Policy Framework*, Johannesburg, South Africa: Umanyano Publications.

Aquín, N. (2005) Reconceptualización: ¿un trabajo social alternative o una alternativa al trabajo social?, in Alayón, N. (ed) *Trabajo Social Latinoamericano: a 40 Años de la Reconceptualización*, Buenos Aires: Espacio Editorial, pp. 19-33.

Arafat, C. and Boothby, N. (2003) S*ocial and Psychological Assessment of Palestinian Children,* El Bireh: NPA.

Arendt, H. (1958): *The Human Condition*, Chicago, IL: Chicago University Press.

Arendt, H. (1967) *The Origins of Totalitarianism*, London: George Allen & Unwin.

Atherton, C.R. and Bollard, K.A. (2002) 'Post-modernism: a dangerous illusion for social work', *International Social Work*, 45, pp. 421-33.

Attlee, C. (1920) *The Social Worker,* London: Heinemann.

Attlee, C. (1954) *As It Happened,* London: Heinemann.

Bailey, R. and Brake, M. (1975) *Radical Social Work*, London: Edward Arnold.

Bakić-Hayden, M. and Hayden, R.M. (1992) 'Orientalist variations on the theme "Balkans": symbolic geography in recent Yugoslav cultural politics, *Slavic Review*, 51, spring, p. 1-15.

Balibar, É. (1991) 'Is there a "Neo-Racism"?, in Balibar, É. and Wallerstein, I., *Race, Nation, Class: Ambiguous Identities*, London and New York: Verso.

Balibar, É. (2004) *We, the People of Europe? Reflections on Transnational Citizenship*, Princeton, NJ: Princeton University Press.

Bartlett, H. (1970) *The Common Base of Social Work*, Washington, DC: National Association of Social Workers.

Bauman, Z. (1998) *Modernity and the Holocaust*, Cambridge: Polity Press.

Bauman, Z. (2001) *Work, Consumerism and the New Poor*, Buckingham: Open University Press.

Beaudry, M. (1984) *Les maisons des femmes battues au Québec*, Montréal: Albert Saint-Martin.

Becker, S. (1997) *Responding to Poverty*, London: Longman.

Beisenherz, H.G. (2000) 'Kinderarmut global und lokal: armut als exklusionsrisiko', in Butterwegge, C. (ed.): *Kinderarmut in Deutschland*. Frankfurt Main: Campus Verlag, pp. 78-95.

Benello, G. (1972) 'Social animation among anglophone groups in Québec' in Lesemann, F. and Thienot, M. (eds.) *Animations sociales au Québec*, Montreal: Ecole de Service Social, Université de Montréal, p. 435-94.

Benhabib, S. (2004) *The Rights of Others: Aliens, Residents and Citizens*, Cambridge: Cambridge University Press.

Benn, C. (1976), 'A new developmental model for social work', in Boas, P.J. and Crawley, J. (eds) *Social Work in Australia: Responses to a Changing Context*, pp. 71-81, Melbourne: Australian International Press.

Beresford, P. (2006) 'Nottingham meeting gladdens the heart, *Community Care*, 15th March.

Beresford, P. and Croft, S. (1993) *Citizen Involvement*, London: Macmillan.

Beresford, P. and Croft, S. (1995) 'Whose empowerment? Equalising the competing discourses in community care', in Jack, R. (ed.) *Empowerment in Community Care*, London: Chapman and Hall.

Bernstein, H. (1978, 1985) *For their triumphs & for their tears: Women in Apartheid South Africa*, London: International Defense & Aid fund.

Biko, S. (1978) *I Write What I Like*. San Francisco, CA: Harper & Row.

Bishop, A. (1994) *Becoming an Ally: Breaking the Cycle of Oppression*, Halifax: Fernwood Press.

Black, G. (1981) *The Triumph of the People*, London: Zed.

Blitz, K. B. (2006): Statelessness and the Social (De)Construction of Citizenship: Political Restructuring and Ethnic Discrimination in Slovenia, Journal of Human Rights, 5, pp. 453-79.

Bloomberg, C. (1989) *Christian–Nationalism and the rise of the Afrikaner Broederbond in South Africa 1918-1948*, Dubow, S. (ed.), Bloomington: Indiana University Press.

Bohinc, R. (2004), Č etrta ministrska konferenca o migracijah', Govor dr. Rada Bohinca, www.mnz.si/si/1200.php?ID=361, accessed April 2005.

Bookbinder, H. (1981) 'Inequality and the Social Services', in Moscovitch, A. and Drover, G. (eds.) *Inequality: Essays on the Political Economy of Social Welfare*, Toronto: University of Toronto Press, p. 348-69.

Borda, F. (1987) 'El nuevo despertar de los movimientos sociales' in ALAETS/CELATS (eds.) XII. Seminario Latinoamericano de Trabajo Social, Medellin/Lima, pp. 11-21, Celats/Alaets.

Brewer, C. and Lait, J. (1980) *Can Social Work Survive?*, London: Temple Smith.

Brigham, B. (2005) 'Family organisations: a new development in Palestine' *Bridges: Israeli-Palestine Public Health,* 1(6), pp. 12-13.

Brigham, B., Mansour, S. and Papagallo, R. (2005) 'Community mental health development in Palestine', *Bridges: Israeli-Palestine Public Health*, 1(6), pp. 21-2.

Briskman, L. (2003) 'Indigenous Australians: postcolonial social work', in Allen, J., Pease, B. and Briskman, L. (eds.) *Critical Social Work: An Introduction to Theories and Practises*, pp. 92-106. Sydney: Allen and Unwin.

Brown, L., Haddock, L. and Kovach, M. (2002) 'Watching Over Our Families and Children: Lalum'utul' Smen'eem Child and Family Services' in Wharf, B. (ed.) *Community Work Approaches to Child Welfare*, p.131-151. Guelph: Broadview Press.

Brueggemann, W. G. (2006) *The Practice of Macro Social Work* (3rd edition) Belmont, CA: Brooks/Cole Press.

Burns, E. B.(1987) *At War in Nicaragua: The Reagan Doctrine and the Politics of Nostalgia*, New York: Harper & Row.

Butler, I. and Pritchard, C. (2002) 'Which Blair project? Communitarianism, social authoritarianism and social work', *Journal of Social Work*, 1, pp. 7-19.

Callinicos, A. (2003) *The New Mandarins of American Power*, Cambridge, Polity.

Carniol, B. (1990) 'Social work and the labour movement' in Wharf, B. (ed.), *Social Work and Social Change in Canada*, p.114-143. Toronto: McClelland and Stewart.

Carter, T. (1997) 'Current practices for procuring affordable housing: the Canadian context', *Housing Policy Debate*, 8(3): pp. 593-631.

Celats, L. (1991) Trabajo social y educación popular con ninos.

Čelik, P. (1994) *Na jüžni strani: Kronika nastajanja državne meje med Slovenijo in Hrvaško*, Ljubljana: Enotnost.

Čelik, Pavle (1994) *Policija, demonstracije, oblast: Ljubljanski nemiri v zadnjih treh desetletjih*. Ljubljana: ČZP Enotnost.

Čelik, P. (2006) *Begunstvo na Slovenskem: oris množičnih selitev domačega in tujega prebivalstva na slovenskem ozemlju v 20. stoletju zaradi vojn in revšine*. Društvo za proučevanje zgodovine, antropologije in književevnost, Ljubljana.

Charlton, J. (1999) *It Just Went Like Tinder: The Mass Movement and New Unionism in Britain 1889*, London: Redwords.

Chimni, B.S. (1998) 'The geopolitics of refugee studies: a view form the south', Journal of Refugee Studies, 11(4), pp. 355-63.

Chouinard, V. (1990) 'The Uneven Development of Capitalist States: 1. Theoretical Proposals and an Analysis of Postwar Changes in Canada's Assisted Housing Programmes' *Environment and Planning A*, 22(10), pp.1291-308.

Clarke, J. (1996) 'After social work?', in Parton, N. (ed.) *Social Theory, Social Change and Social Work*, London: Routledge.

Close, D. (1988) *Nicaragua: Politics, Economics and Society*. London: Pinter.

Close, D. (2005) 'Nicaragua and the Crisis of 2005', *Focal Point: Spotlight on the Americas*, 4(5), pp. 5-7.

Cohen, S. (2005) *Deportation is Freedom! The Orwellian World of Immigration Controls*, London: Jessica Kingsley.

Corrigan, P. and Leonard, P. (1978) *Social Work under Capitalism*,

London: Macmillan.

Cox, D. and Pawar, M. (2006) International *Social Work: Issues, Strategies and Programs*. London: Sage.

Dahme, H.-J., Otto, H.U., Wohlfahrt, N. (eds.) (2003) *Soziale Arbeit für den aktivierenden Staat*, Opladen.

Leverkusen: Leske & Budrich Verlag

Dahme, H.-J. and Wohlfahrt, N. (eds.) (2003) *Aktivierende Soziale Arbeit: Theorie – Handlungsfelder – Praxis*, Hohrengehren: Schneider Verlag.

Day, J.P. (1989) *A New History of Social Welfare*, Englewood Cliffs: Prentice Hall.

Dedić, J., Vlasta, J. and Jelka Z. (2003) The Erased: *Organised Innocence and the Politics of Exclusion*, Ljubljana: Peace Institute.

Defence for Children International/Palestine Section (DCI/PS), www.dci-pal.org/english/info/aboutus.cfm

Dietche, J. P., (1995) 'voyaging toward freedom: new voices from South Africa', *Research in African Literatures*, 26(1), pp. 61-74.

Dimech, M. (1985) 'Community work with ethnic groups', in Thorpe, R. and Petruchenia, J. (eds) *Community Work or Social Change? An Australian Perspective*, pp. 111-31. London: Routledge and Kegan Paul.

Dobelstein, A.W. (1986) *Politics, Economics and Public Welfare*. (2nd edition) Englewood Cliffs, NJ: Prentice Hall.

Dobelstein, A.W. (1996) *Social welfare policy and analysis* (2nd edition). Chicago, IL: Nelson Hall.

Dominelli, L. (1989) 'An uncaring profession: an examination of racism in social work', *New Community*, 15, pp. 391-403.

Dominelli, L. (2004) *Social Work: Theory and Practice for a Changing Profession*, Cambridge: Polity Press.

Dossier, S. (1995) *Public Hearing on the Struggles of Women Workers in the Fish Processing Industry in India*, Women in Fisheries Series, No. 1, Chennai: ICSF.

Doupona Horvat, M., Verschueren, J. and Žagar, I. Ž. (1998) *Pragmatika legitimizacije: retorika begunske politike v Sloveniji*, Ljubljana: Open Society Institute.

Drower, S.J. (1996) Social work values, professional unity, and the South African context, *Social Work*, 41(2), pp.138-146.

Early Childhood Resource Centre, www.palnet.com/~ecrc2/

Eisenstein, H. (1996), *Inside Agitators: Australian Femocrats and the State*, Sydney: Allen and Unwin.

ETS (1985) 'Práctica historica del trabajo social en Nicaragua', *Revista de Trabajo Social,*. 1, pp. 2-7.

ETS (Escuela de Trabajo Social) (1984) 'Modelo del Profesional de Trabajo Social', Managua: Facultad de Humanidades, Universidad Centroamericana.

Evers, T. (1985) Identity: the hidden side of new social movements in Latin America, in Slater, D. (ed.) *New Social Movements and the State in Latin America*. Amsterdam: Cedla.

Farsoun, S. and Zacharia, C. (1997) *Palestine and the Palestinians*, Boulder, CA: Westview Press.

Fawcett, B. and Featherstone, B. (2000) 'Setting the scene: an appraisal of notions of post-modernism, post-modernity and post-modern feminism', in Fawcett, B., Featherstone, B., Fook, J. and Rossiter, R. (eds.) *Practice and Research in Social Work: Postmodern feminist perspectives*, pp. 5-23. London: Routledge.

Federal Task Force on Housing and Urban Development (1969) *Report of the Federal Task Force on Housing and Urban Development*, Ottawa: Information Canada.

Feldman, A. (1996) "From Desert Story to Rodney King via ex-Yugoslavia: On Cultural Anesthesia" in Serementakis, N. [Ed] *The Senses Still: Memory and Perception as Material Culture*, pp. 87-107. Chicago: The University of Chigago Press.

Ferguson, I. and Lavalette, M. (2004) '"Another world is possible": social work and the struggle for social justice' in Ferguson, I., Lavalette, M. and Whitmore, E. (eds.) *Globalisation, Global Justice and Social Work*, London: Routledge.

Ferguson, I. and Lavalette, M. (2006) 'Globalization and global justice: towards a social work of resistance', *International Social Work*, 49(3), pp. 309-18.

Ferguson, I., and Lavalette, M. (2005) '"Another world is possible": social work and the struggle for social justice', in Ferguson I., Lavalette, M. and Whitmore, E. (eds.) *Globalisation, Global Justice and Social Work*, pp. 207-23, London: Routeledge.

Ferguson, I., Lavalette, M. and Whitmore, E. (eds.) (2005): *Globalisation, Global Justice and Social Work*, London and New York, Routledge.

Fook, J. (2002) *Social Work: Critical Theory and Practice*, London: Sage.

Fook, J. (1993) *Radical Casework: A Theory of Practice*, Sydney: Allen and Unwin.

FRAP (Front D'Action Populaire) (1970) *Les Salariés Au Pouvoir* Montréal: Les Presses Libres.

Freedman, L. and Stark, L. (1993) 'When the white system doesn't fit', *Australian Social Work*, 46(1), pp. 29-36.

Freire, P. (1970) *Pedagogy of the Oppressed*, New York: Seabury Press.

Friedland, J. (1985) 'The CYSS campaign: an example of collective action against cuts in services', in Thorpe, R. and Petruchenia, J. (eds) *Community Work or Social Change? An Australian Perspective*, pp. 164-78. London: Routledge and Kegan Paul.

Galuske, M. (2002) *Flexible Sozialpädagogik. Elemente einer Theorie sozialer Arbeit in der modern Arbeitsgesellschaft*, Munich: Juventa Verlag.

Gaza Community Mental Health Programme, www.gcmhp.net/, last accessed 14 September 2006.

Giacaman, R. (2004) *Psycho-social/Mental Health Care in the Occupied Palestinian Territories: The Embryonic System,* Ramallah: Birzeit University.

Giacaman, R. and Johnston, P. (2002) *Inside Palestinian Households: Initial Analysis of a Community-based Household Survey,* Ramallah: Birzeit University.

Giacaman, R., Abdul-Rahim, H.F. and Wick, L. (2003) 'Health sector reform in the Occupied Palestinian Territories: targeting the forest or the trees?', *Health Policy and Planning,* 18(1), pp. 59-67.

Giacaman, R., Saab, N., Nguyen-Gillham, V., Abdullah, A. and Naser, G. (2004) *Palestinian Adolescents Coping with Trauma,* Ramallah: Birzeit University Press.

Gilbert, S. (2001) 'Social Work with Indigenous Australians', *Social Work: Fields of Practice* in Alston, M. and McKinnon, J. (eds.), pp. 46-57, Melbourne: Oxford University Press.

Gildemeister, R. and Robert, G. (1997) '"Ich geh da von einem bestimmten Fall aus..." – Professionalisierung und Fallbezug in der Sozialen Arbeit' in Jakob, G. and Wensierski, H.-J. (eds.), *Rekonstruktive Soszialpädgogik*, pp. 23-39. Weinheim/München:

Juventa Verlag.

Gilroy, J. (1990) 'Social Work and the Women's Movement' in Wharf, B. (ed.) *Social Work and Social Change in Canada*, p.52-78. Toronto: McClelland and Stewart.

GMAPCC (Greater Montreal Anti-Poverty Coordinating Committee (unpublished, 1972) *Statement of Principles for the Greater Montreal Anti-Poverty*.

Golden, M. (2004) *Carnegie Corporation in South Africa: A difficult past leads to a commitment to change*. Carnegie Corporation of New York www.carnegie.org/results/04/index.html

Goode, J. and Maskovsky, J. [eds] (2001) *The New Poverty Studies: The Ethnography of Power, Politics and Impoverished People in the United States*, New York: New York University Press.

Gramsci, A (1917/1977) *Selections from Political Writings 1910-1920*, London: Lawrence Wishart.

Grassi, E. (1994) 'La implicancia de la investigación en la práctica del Trabajo Social', *Revista de Treball Social*, 135, pp. 43-54.

Habib, A. (2004) "State-civil society relations in post apartheid South Africa". In Daniel, J., Habib, A. and Southall, R. (eds) *State of the Nation: South Africa 2003-2004*, pp. 227-33, Cape Town: Human Science Research Council Press.

Hamel, P. (1991) *Action collective et démocratie locale: des mouvements sociaux urbains montréalais,* Montréal: Presses de l'Université de Montréal.

Hansen, S. (1967) *Five Years of the Alliance for Progress*. Washington, DC: Inter-American Affairs Press.

Harman, C. (1988) *The Fire Last time: 1968 and After,* London: Bookmarks.

Harman, C. (1999) *A People's History of the World,* London: Bookmarks.

Harris, J. (2003) 'The Social Work Business', London: Routledge.

Harris, J. (2005) 'Globalisation, neo-liberal managerialism and UK social work', in Ferguson, I., Lavalette, M. and Whitmore, E. (eds.) *Globalisation, Global Justice and Social Work*, London and New York: Routledge.

Hassim, S. (2005) "Voices, hierarchies and spaces: reconfiguring the women's movement in democratic South Africa" in South Africa Women in the 1990s. *World Factbook*, Vol. 32(2), pp. 163-175, The

Library of Congress.

Haynes, M. (1984) 'The British working class in revolt', *International Socialism* 22, pp. 87-116.

Hayter, T. (2004) *Open Borders: The Case Against Immigration Controls*, London and Ann Arbor, MI: Pluto Press.

Healy, B. (1993) 'Elements in the Development of an Australian Radical Social Work', *Australian Social Work*, 46(1), pp. 3-8.

Healy, K. (2000) *Social Work Practice: Contemporary Perspectives on Change*, London: Sage.

Healy, K. (2001) 'Reinventing Critical Social Work: Challenges from Practice, Context and Post-modernism', *Critical Social Work*, 2(1) (electronic journal).

Henderson, R. (1975) *Poverty in Australia: First Main Report*, Sydney: Australian Government Commission of Inquiry into Poverty, Australian Government Publishing Service (AGPS).

Hilal, J. (2002) 'The Burden of Care: Responsibilities for Childcare, care of the Elderly and Disabled and Domestic Chores', in Giacaman, R. and Johnston, P., *Inside Palestinian Households: Initial Analysis of a Community-based Household Survey,* pp. 147-61, Ramallah: Birzeit University.

Hobhouse, R. (1949) *Mary Hughes: Her Life for the Dispossessed,* London: Rockliff.

Howe, D. (1996) 'Surface and depth in social work practice', in Parton, N. (ed.) *Social Theory, Social Change and Social Work*, London: Routledge.

Howse, Y. and Stalwick,H. (1990) 'Social Work and the First Nation Movement: "Our Children,Our Culture"', in Wharf, B. (ed.) (1990) *Social Work and Social Change in Canada*, p. 79-113, Toronto: McClelland and Stewart.

Hulchanski, J.D. (1988) Canada's Housing and Housing Policy: An Introduction, Vancouver: University of British Columbia, School of Community and Regional Planning.

Hulchanski, J.D. (1993) 'New Forms of Owning and Renting', in Miron, J.R. (ed.) *House, Home and Community: Progress in Housing Canadians*, 1945-1986, Ottawa: CMHC.

Humphries, B. (2004) 'An Unacceptable Role for Social Work: Implementing Immigration Policy', *British Journal of Social Work*, 34, pp. 93-107.

Humphries, B. (2005) "Kako podpreti prosilce in prosilke za azil: praska in etična vprašanga za strokovnjakinje v socialnem varstvu in zdravstvu v Europi". In *Socialno delo*, pp. 277-86. Ljubljana: Fakulteta za socialno delo.

Ife, J. (1997), *Rethinking Social Work: Towards Critical Practice*, Melbourne: Longman.

Ife, J. (1999), 'Postmodernism, Critical Theory and Social Work', in Pease, B. and Fook, J. (eds.), *Transforming Social Work Practice: Postmodern Critical Perspectives*, Sydney: Allen & Unwin, pp.211-23.

Ife, J. (2001) *Human Rights and Social Work: Towards Rights-Based Practice*, Cambridge, Cambridge University Press.

Inside Welfare (1979) *An Annotated Bibliography for Marxist Welfare Workers*, Sydney: Inside Welfare.

Insight News TV (2006) documentary film, *Slovenia: The Erased People*, www.insightnewstv.com/d77, accessed 10 May 2006.

IFSW (International Federation of Social Workers) and IASSW (International Association of Schools of Social Work) (2004) Proposal for a new Ethical Document.

IFSW and IASSW (2006) www.ifsw.org/en/p38000324.htlm, accessed 25 April 2006.

Jakob, G. with Wensierski, H.-J. (1997) *Rekonstruktive Sosozialpädgogik*. Weinheim/München: Juventa Verlag.

Jeffs, N. (1999) 'Intervencija', in Zadnikar, D. (ed.) *Časopis za kritiko znanosti, Vol. XXVII, No. 195-196*. Ljubljana: Študentska založ ba, p. 29-40.

Jessop, B. (1999) 'The Changing Governance of Welfare: Recent Trends in its Primary Functions, Scale, and Modes of Coordination', *Social Policy and Administration*, 33, pp. 348-59.

Jessop, B. (2002) *The Future of the Capitalist State*, Cambridge: Polity Press.

Johnson, L.C. and Yanca, S.J. (2001) *Social Work Practice: A generalist Approach* (7th edition). Needham Heights, MA: Allyn and Bacon.

Jones, C. (1983) *State Social Work and The Working Class,* London: Macmillan.

Jones, C. (2001) *Voices from the Front-line: State Social Work and New Labour*, British Journal of Social Work, 31, pp. 547-62.

Jones, C. (2004) 'The neo-liberal assault: voices from the front-line of British social work', in Ferguson, I., Lavalette, M. and Whitmore, E. (eds.) *Globalisation, Global Justice and Social Work*, London: Routledge.

Jones, C., Ferguson, I., Lavalette, M. and Penketh, L. (2004) *Social Work and Social Justice: A Manifesto for a New Engaged Practice*, available online: www.socialworkfuture.org, last accessed 14 September 2006.

Keating, M., Le More, A. and Lowe, R. (eds) (2005) *Aid, Diplomacy, and Facts on the Ground The Case of Palestine,* London: Chatham House.

Jones, C. and Novak, T. (1993), *Social Work Today*, British Journal of Social Work, 23, pp. 195-212

Kouvelakis, S. (2005) 'France: the triumph of the political', *International Socialism*, 108, pp. 7-13.

Kruzynski, A. and Shragge, E.(1999) 'Getting Organized: Anti-poverty Organizing and Social Citizenship in the 1970s' *Community Development Journal: An International Forum*, 34(4), pp. 328-39.

Kruzynski, A.K. (2004) 'Du Silence ą l'Affirmation: Women Making History in Point St. Charles', ThŹse de doctorat, McGill Universit, Montréal.

Kurlansky, M. (2004) *1968: The Year that Rocked the World*, London: Jonathon Cape.

Lamoureux, D.(1990) 'Les services féministes: de l'autonomie ą l'extension de l'État-providence', *Nouvelles Pratiques Sociales*, 3(2), pp.33-43.

Lamoureux, H., Lavoie, J., Mayer, R and Panet-Raymond, J. (2002) *La Pratique de L'Action Communautaire*, Québec: Presses de l'Université du Québec.

Langan, M. (2002) 'The Legacy of Radical Social Work', in Adams, R., Dominelli, L. and Payne, M. (eds.), *Social Work: Themes, Issues and Critical Debates* (2nd edition), pp. 207-17, Basingstoke: Palgrave.

Lavalette, M. (2006) *George Lansbury and the Rebel Councillors of Poplar,* London: Bookmarks.

Lewis, J. (1995) *The Voluntary Sector, the State and Social Work in Britain,* Aldershot: Edward Elgar.

Liffman, M. (1978) *Power for the Poor*, Sydney: George Allen and

Unwin.

Lindsay, J. (2005) 'Evaluation Report on Implementation of NCLB Grant to the Centre of Contuining Education', Birzeit University, FOBZU (unpublished).

Lipovec Čebron, U. (ed.) (2002) *V zoni pribež n ištva: Antropološke raziskave pribež nikov v Sloveniji, Oddelek za etnologijo in kulturno antropologijo*, Ljubljana: University of Ljubljana.

Lynn, R. and Pye, R. (1990), 'Antiracist Welfare Education – Pie in the Sky?', in Petruchenia, J. and Thorpe, R. (eds.), *Social Change and Social Welfare Practice*, Sydney: Hale and Ironmonger, pp. 62-85.

McDonald, C. (1988) 'Social Work Interviewing and Feminism', *Australian Social Work*, 41, pp. 13-19.

McDonald, C. (2006) *Challenging Social Work: The Institutional Context of Practice*, Basingstoke: Palgrave Macmillan.

McDonald, C. and Chenoweth, L. (2005) 'Social Work and Workfare in Australia', *The Social Policy Journal*, Vol. 5, 2/3, pp. 109-28.

McDonald, C., Harris, J. and Wintersteen, R. (2003) 'Contingent on Context? Social work and the state in Australia, Britain and the USA', *British Journal of Social Work*, 33, pp. 191-208.

MacFarlane, P. (1989) *Northern Shadows: Canadians and Central America*, Toronto: Between the Lines.

McMahon, A. (1997) 'Child welfare and the stolen generations: time for a rethink', *Australian Social Work*, 50(4) p. 87-9.

McMahon, A. (2002) 'Writing diversity: ethnicity and race in Australian Social Work, 1947 to 1997', *Australian Social Work*, 55(3), pp. 172-83.

McMahon, T. (1990) 'Social Work and Aborigines', *Australian Social Work*, 43(3), pp. 11-14.

MacNeil, D. and Warnock, J.W. (2000) *The Disappearance of Affordable Housing in Regina*, Regina: The Council on Social Development.

Marchant, H. and Wearing, B. (eds.) (1986) *Gender Reclaimed: Women in Social Work*, Sydney: Hale and Ironmonger.

Matahaere-Atariki, D. and Shannon, P. (1999) 'The treaty and social service courses in the academy', *Social Work Review*, 11(1), pp. 16-19.

Matahaere-Atariki, D., Bertanees, C. and Hoffman, L. (2001) 'Anti-oppressive Practices in a Colonial Context', in Connolly, M. (ed.),

New Zealand Social Work: Contexts and Practices. Auckland: Oxford University Press, pp. 122-32.

Mataira, P. (1985) *A Bi-cultural Model of Social Work and Social Work Supervision*, Auckland: Massey University.

Mayer, J.E. and Timms, N. (1970) *The Client Speaks*, London: Routledge and Kegan Paul.

Mazibuko, F., McKendrick, B. and Patel, L. (1992) Social Work in South Africa: coping with apartheid and change, in Hokenstad, M.C., Khinduka, S.K. and Midgley, J. (eds.), *Profiles in International Social Work*, Washington, DC: NASW Press.

Meinert, R. (1998) 'Consequences for Professional Social Work under Conditions of Postmodernity', *Social Thought*, 18, pp. 41-54.

Mendoza Rangel, M. del C. (1986) *Una opción metodológica para los trabajadores sociales*, Mexico: DF: AMLETS.

Midgley, B. (2001) 'Issues in International Social Work', *Journal of Social Work*, 1(1), pp. 244-52.

Midgley, J. (1999) 'Postmodernism and Social Development: Implications for Progress, Intervention and Ideology', *Social Development Issues*, 21(3), pp. 5-13.

Ministrstvo za notranje zadeve (1993) *Odmevnejš pojavi in kršitve z množ ično udelež bo*, Ljubljana: Ministrstvo za notranje zadeve.

Ministry for Welfare and Population Development (1997) *White Paper for Social Welfare*, Notice 1108 of 1997, Pretaria: Department of Welfare, Republic of South Africa.

Miringoff, M.L. and Opdycke, S. (1986) *American Social Welfare: Reassessment and reform*. Englewood Cliffs, NJ: Prentice Hall.

Mishra, R.(2000) *Globalisation and the Welfare State*, London: Edward Elgar.

Močnik, R. (1999) *3 teorije. Ideologija, nacija, institucija.*cf., Ljubljana: Založ ba.

Moreau, M. (1979) 'A Structural Approach to Social Service Practice', *Canadian Journal of Social Work Education*, 5(1) p. 78-94.

Morin, R. and Dansereau, F. (1990) *L'Habitation Sociale: Les ClientŹles Et Leur Vécu, Les Modes De Gestion, Les Solutions De Rechange*, SynthŹse De La Littérature, avec la colloboration de Daniel Nadeau, Montreal: INRS-Urbanisation.

Mullaly, B. (2003) *Structural Social Work* (second edition), Oxford: Oxford University Press.

Mundy, J. (1981), *Green Bans and Beyond*, Sydney: Angus and Robertson.

Murray, A. and German, L. (2005) *Stop the War: The Story of Britain's Biggest Mass Movement,* London: Bookmarks.

Musleh, D. and Taylor, K. (2005) *Child Protection in the Occupied Palestinian Territories*: *A National Position Paper*, Palestinian Authority, Secretariat National Plan of Action for Palestinian Children. El Bireh.

Mynott, E. (2002) 'Nationalism, racism and immigration control: from anti-racism to anti-capitalism', in Cohen, S., Humphries, B. and Mynott, E. (eds.), from *Immigration Control to Welfare Control*, pp. 11-29, London and New York: Routledge.

Napier, L. and Fook, J. (eds.) (2000) *Breakthroughs in Practice: Theorising Critical Moments in Social Work*, London: Whiting and Birch.

National Action Plan against Poverty and Social Exclusion for the period 2004-2006, www.cnvos.si/mreza/clanki/?id=248pid=16, accessed 8 May 2006.

National Coalition of Anti-deportation Campaigns, www.ncadc.org.uk/resourses.ias.html, accessed 25 April 2006.

Neocleous, M. (2000) The Fabrication of Social Order. A Critical Theory of Police Power, London: Pluto Press.

Netto, J.P. (1981) 'La crítica conservadora a la Reconceptualización', *Acción Critica*, 9. Lima: CELATS.

Noble, C. (2004) 'Postmodern Thinking: where is it taking social work?', *Journal of Social Work*, 4, pp. 289-304.

Noyoo, N. (2000). 'The state of the university of the Witwatersrand social policy training in South Africa', *Journal of Social Work Education*. 36, pp. 253-56.

NPA (National Plan of Action) for Palestinian Children Secretariat (1999) *The Agenda for Social Renewal: National Plan for Palestinian Children: Revised and updated 1999-2001,* El Birch: Palestinian Authority.

NPA for Palestinian Children Secretariat (2004a) *The National Plan for Children's Psycho-social Health,* El Birch: Palestinian Authority.

NPA for Palestinian Children Secretariat (2004b) *The National Plan for the Child,* El Birch: Palestinian Authority.

Ntusi, T. (1995) 'South Africa: history of social work education', in Elliot,

D., Mayadas, N. and Watts, T.D. (eds), *International Handbook on Social Work Education*. Pretoria: Greenwood Press.

Oliver, M. (1996) *Understanding Disability: From Theory to Practice*, London: Macmillan.

Oliver, W.H. (1988) 'Social Policy in New Zealand: An Historical Overview in the Royal Commission on Social Policy', *The April Report: The Royal Commission on Social Policy*, Vol. 1, Wellington: RCSP.

Olson, J. (2001): 'A Democratic Problem of the White Citizen', in *Constellations*, 8(2), pp. 163-83.

Osorio, J. (1986) 'Educación popular en América Latina', in Asociación Latinomaericana de Escuelas de Trabajo Social/Centro Latinoamericano de Trabajo Social/Consejo Nacional de Educación en Trabajo Social/Federación Colombiana de Trabajadores Sociales/Universidad de Antioquia (eds.) *Moviminentos Sociales, Educación Popular y Trabajo Social*, Medellin: Celats/Alaets.

Otto, H.-U. and Schnurr, S. (eds.) (2000) *Privatisierung und Wettbewerb in der Jugendhilfe: marktorientierte Modernisierungsstrategien in internationaler Perspektive*, Neuwied/Kriftel: Luchterhand Verlag.

Pajnik, M., Lesjak-Tušek, P. and Gregorčič M. (2001): *Immigrants, who are you?*, Ljubljana: Peace Institute.

Palestinian Academic Society for the Study of International Affairs, www.passia.org/index_publication.htm

Palestinian Authority Ministry of Health, in collaboration with the World Health Organization and the France and Italian governments (2004) 'Plan on the Organisation of Mental Health Services in the Occupied Palestinian Territories (Steering Committee on Mental Health) (unpublished).

PCBS (Palestinian Central Bureau of Statistics) (2005) www.pcbs.org/

Palestinian Authority Ministry of Health, in collaboration with the World Health Organization and the governments of France and Italy (2004) *Plan on the Organisation of Mental Health Services in the Occupied Palestinian Territories*, Steering Committee on Mental Health (unpublished).

Palestinian Counselling Centre www.pcc-jer.org/, last accessed 14 September 2006.

Palestinian Red Crescent Society

www.palestinercs.org/prcsindepth/index.htm, last accessed 24 September 2006.

Palestinian Union of Social Workers and Psychologists www.puswp-beth.org, last accessed 24 September 2006.

Palestinian Working Women's Society for Development (2002) 'Violence Against Women in Palestine: a public opinion poll' (unpublished) www.pwwsd.org/about/about.html

Palma, D. (1977) *La Reconceptualización: Una búsqueda en AmericanaLatina*, Lima: CELATS.

Panet-Raymond, J. and Mayer, R. (1997) 'The History of Community Development in Quebec' in Wharf, B. and Clague, M. (eds.) Community Organizing: Canadian Experiences, Oxford University Press, p. 29-61.

Pankhurst, S.E. (1932/1987) *The Home Front,* London: Cresset.

Passia (2006) www.passia.org/index_publication.htm

Payne, M. (2005) *The Origins of Social Work: Continuity and Change,* Basingstoke: Palgrave.

Pearce, R. (1997) *Attlee,* London: Longman.

Pearson, G. (1975) *The Deviant Imagination*, London: Macmillan.

Pearson, G. (1989) 'Women and men without work: the political economy is personal', in Rojek, C., Peacock, G. and Collins, S. (eds.) *The Haunt of Misery: Critical Essays in Social Work and Helping*, pp. 121-32, London: Routledge.

Pease, B. and Fook, J. (eds.) (1999) *Transforming Social Work Practice: Postmodern Critical Perspectives*, Sydney: Allen and Unwin.

Pease, P. (2002) 'Rethinking empowerment: a postmodern reappraisal for emancipatory practice', *British Journal of Social Work*, (32), pp. 135-47.

Pederson, S. (2004) *Eleanor Rathbone and the Politics of Conscience,* Yale, CT: Yale University Press.

Pemberton, A. and Locke, R. (1971) 'Towards a Radical Critique of Social Work and Social Welfare Ideology', *Australian Journal of Social Work*, 6(2), pp. 48-60.

Penketh, L. (2000) *Tackling Institutional Racism*, Bristol: The Policy Press.

PERM (Point St. Charles Equal Rights Movement) (1971) Video, Montreal: Parallel Institute.

Pethick, E. (1989) '"Working Girls' Clubs"' in Reason, W. (ed.) *University and Social Settlements*, pp. 35-44, London: Methuen and Co.

Pethick-Lawrence, E. (1938) *My Part in a Changing World,* London: Victor Gollanz.

Philpot, T. (ed.) (1999) *Political Correctness and Social Work*, London: IEA Health and Welfare Unit.

Pincus, A. and Minahan, A. (1973) *Social Work Practice: Model and Method,* Itasca, IL: Peacock.

PNGO (Palestinian NGO Network) (2006) www.pngo.net/pngo.htm

Powell, F. (2001) *The Politics of Social Work*, London: Sage.

Prado Hernández, I. and Palacios, M. (2005) 'Importancia y Vigencia del Moviemiento de Reconceptualización del Trabajo Social en Nicaragua, in Alayón, N. (ed.) (2005), *Trabajo Social Latinoamericano: a 40 Años de la Reconceptualización*, Buenos Aires: Espacio Editorial, pp. 233-44.

Prado Hernández, I. and Wilson, M.G. (1996). 'International Partnerships in Project Management: Lessons from Nicaragua', International Participatory Development Symposium, University of Calgary, February.

Prigmore and Atherton (1979) *Social Welfare Policy*, Lexington MA: D.C. Health.

Psycho-Social Co-ordinating Body, The (2003) 'Mental Health: The Balance between Humans and Their Environment' (unpublished).

Qouta, S. (2003) *Prevalence of PTSD among Palestinian Children,* available online: www.gcmhp.net/

Rees, J. (2006) *Imperialism and Resistance,* London: Routledge.

Reisch, M. and Andrews, J. (2002) *The Road Not Taken: A history of Radical Social Work in the United States,* London: Brunner-Routledge.

Republic of Slovenia, Ministry for Internal Affairs (2004) www.sigov.si/mnz/si/13334.php, accessed 1 August 2005.

Republic of Slovenia, Ministry for Internal Affairs (2005) Ministrstvo za notranje zadeve RS, Novice, O črpanju sredstev iz schengenskega sklada, www.mnz.si/si/194.php?ID=221, accessed 19 April 2005.

Republic of Slovenia, Police (2004) www.policija.si, accessed 3 July 2005.

Republic of South Africa (1966) Coordination of White and Non-White

Welfare Work in National and Local Welfare Organizations, Circular No. 29, Department of Social Welfare & Pensions, Republic of South Africa, Pretoria.

Rosales, C.A. (2006) 'Nicaragua's Woes Threaten Region', *Focal Point: Spotlight on the Americas*, 5(2), pp. 3-4.

Roszak, T. (1970) *The Making of a Counter Culture*, London: Faber.

Ruwhiu, L.A. (2001) 'Bicultural Issues in Aotearoa New Zealand Social Work', in Connolly, M. (ed.) *New Zealand Social Work: Contexts and Practices*, Auckland: Oxford University Press, pp. 54-71.

Save the Children Fund (2004) *Living Behind Barriers: Palestinian Children Speak Out*, London: Save the Children Fund.

Save the Children (UK and Sweden) (2003) *Growing Up Under Curfew: Safeguarding the basic rights of Palestinian Children*, London: Save The Children.

Schütze, F. (1994) 'Ethnographie und sozialwissenschaftliche Methoden der Feldforschung. Eine mögliche methodische Orientierung in der Ausbildung und Praxis der sozialen Arbeit', in Groddeck, N. and Schumann, M. (eds.), *Modernisierung Sozialer Arbeit durch Methodenentwicklung und – Refelxion*, pp. 189-297. Freiburg im Breisgau: Lambertus Verlag.

Schütze, F. (1996) 'Organisationszwänge und hoheitsstaatliche Rahmenbedingungen im Sozialwesen: Ihre Auswirkung auf die Paradoxien des professionellen Handelns', in Combe, A. and Helsper, W. (eds.): *Pädagogische Professionalität*, pp. 183-276, Frankfurt.

Schweppe, C. (1991) *Überleben und Verändern – Volksküchen in Lima: Frauen der Armutsviertel organisieren sich*, Frankfurt: Peter Lang Verlag.

Schweppe, C. (1993) *Organizaciones Populares y Cambio Social en America Latina*, St. Augustin: Richarz Publications.

Scottish Executive (2006) *Changing Lives: Report of the 21st Century Social Work Review*, Edinburgh: Scottish Executive.

Segal, E.A. & Brzuzy, S. (1998) *Social Welfare Policy, Programs and Practice*. Itasca, IL: F.E. Peacock Publishers.

Sewpaul, V. and Lombard, A. (2004) 'Social work education, training and standards in Africa', *Social Work Education*, 23(5) pp. 537-40.

Shepherd, J. (2004) *George Lansbury: At the heart of Old Labour*, Oxford: University Press.

Shragge, E. (1994) 'Anti-poverty movements: Strategies and Approaches', *City Magazine*, 15(2/3), p. 27-9.

Shragge, E. (2003) *Activism and Social Change: Lessons for Community and Local Organizing*, Guelph: Broadway Press.

Simpkin, M. (1983) *Trapped within Welfare* (2nd edition), London: Macmillan.

Smith, L.T. (1999) *Decolonising Methodologies: Research and Indigenous People*, London: Zed Books.

SABSWA (South African Black Social Workers Association) (1996) *Resolution 1/96*, Annual General Meeting Report, Johannesburg: SABSWA.

Specht, H. and Vickery, M. (1977) *Integrating Social Work Methods*, London: Allen and Unwin.

Stedman Jones, G. (1976) *Outcast London: A study in the Relationship between Classes in Victorian Society,* Harmondsworth: Penguin.

Sturzenhecker, B. (2003) 'Aktivierende Jugendarbeit', in Dahme, H.-J. (ed.) *Soziale Arbeit für den aktivierenden Staat*, Opladen, pp. 381-92, Opladen: Leeske and Budrich Verlag.

Tarrow, S. (1998) *Power in Movement* (2nd edition), Cambridge: Cambridge University Press.

Téfel, R.A., López, H.M. and Castillo, J.F. (1985) 'Social Welfare', in Walker, T. (ed.) *Nicaragua: The First Five Years*, p. 365-82, New York: Praeger.

Thiersch, H. (1986) *Die Erfahrung der Wirklichkeit – Perspektiven einer Alltagsorientierten Sozialpädagogik*, München: Weinheim.

Thiersch, H. (1992) *Lebensweltorientierte Soziale Arbeit: Aufgabe der Praxis im Sozialen Wandel*, München: Weinheim.

Thiersch, H. (2000) 'Lebensweltorientierung in der Sozialen Arbeit – als radikalisierte Programm – Eine Skizze', in Müller, S., Sünker, H., Otto, H.-U., Ballert, K. (eds.) *Soziale Arbeit: Gesellschaftliche Bedingungen und Professionelle Perspektiven*, pp. 529-45, Neuwied: Luchterhand Verlag.

Thole, W. and Cloos, P. (2000) 'Soziale Arbeit als professionelle Dienstleistung: Zur "Transformation des beruflichen Handelns" zwischen Ökonomie und eigenständiger Fachkultur', in Müller, S. *et. al* (eds.): *Soziale Arbeit: Gesellschaftliche Bedingungen und professionelle Perspektiven*, pp. 547-68, Neuwied: Luchterhand Verlag.

Thompson, N. (2002) 'Social movements, social justice and social work', *British Journal of Social Work*, 32, pp. 711-22.

Throssell, H. (1975) 'Social Work Overview', in Throssell, H. (ed.) *Social Work: Radical Essays*, pp. 3-25, St Lucia: University of Queensland Press.

Tomlinson, J. (1977) *Is Bandaid Social Work Enough*, Darwin: The Wobbly Press.

Tomlinson, J. (1982) *Betrayed by Bureaucracy*, Darwin: Wobbly Press.

Tomlinson, J. (1985) 'The history of Aboriginal community work', in Thorpe, R. and Petruchenia, J. (eds) *Community Work or Social Change? An Australian Perspective*, London: Routledge and Kegan Paul, pp. 144-64.

Trainor, B. (2003) 'Foucault and the Human Service Professions: A Critical Appraisal', in Trainor, B. and Jeffreys, H. *The Human Service 'Disciplines' and Social Work: The Foucault Effect*, Quebec: World Heritage Press, pp. 3-68.

Tropman, E.J. (1989) *American Values & Social Welfare: Cultural Contradictions in the welfare state*, Englewood Cliff, NJ: Prentice Hall.

Trube, A. and Wohlfahrt, N. (2001)'Der aktivierende Sozialstaat – Sozialpolitik zwischen Individualisierung und einer neuen Ökonomie der inneren Sicherheit', in: *WSI-Mitteilungen*, 1, pp. 27-35.

UK, Home Office (2005), www.homeoffice.gov.uk/rds/pdfs06/asylum405/pdf, accessed 26 April 2006.

UNGAR (United Nations General Assembly Resolution) 194 (III) of 1948.

UNGAR (United Nations General Assembly Resolution) 302 (IV) of 1949.

UN Security Council Resolution 242 of 1967.

UNDP (United Nations Development Programme) (1994) *Human Development Report*, New York: Oxford University Press.

United States Committee for Refugees and Immigrants World Survey 2004, p. 22, www.refugee.org/article.aspx?id=1156

Union of Palestinian Medical Relief Committees, www.upmrc.org

Union of Social Workers, Psychologists and Sociologists (Bethlehem Branch) (2005a) 'The project of developing regulatory law and policies and code of ethics for the professions of social work and psychology', unpublished.

Union of Social Workers, Psychologists and Sociologists (2005b) 'Raising the professional reality for its members and the sociological changes within the Palestinian society', (unpublished).

United for Intercultural Action (2005) 'The Dead List', www.unitedagainstracism.org, accessed 17 June 2006 in 'The Deadly Consequences of "Fortress Eurpoe"', www.united.non-profit.nl/pages/info24.htm, accessed 19 April 2005.

UNRWA (United Nations Relief and Works Agency (2006) www.un.org/unrwa/index.html, last accessed 14 September 2006.

Van Eeden, E.S., Ryke, E.H. & De Mecher, C.M. (2000) "The Welfare Function of the Southern African Government before and after Apartheid", *Social Work: A Professional Journal for the Social Worker*, Vol. 36(1), pp. 5-12.

Vodopivec, P. (2001) 'O Evropi, Balkanu in metageografiji', in Todorova, M., *Imaginarij Balkana*, Ljubljana: Vita Activa, pp. 381-401.

Vrečer, N. (2005) 'Etničnost, integracija in civilna druž ba: Prisilni migranti v Sloveniji', in Komac, M. and Medvešek, M. (eds.), *Percepcije Slovenske Integracijske Politike*. Ljubljana: Inštitut za narodnostna vprasanja, pp. 659-71.

Walker, P. (2002) 'Te Whanau Arohanui – Partnerships in Practice', *Social Work Review*, Spring, pp.18-21.

Walker, T.(ed.) (1985) *Nicaragua: The First Five Years*, New York: Praeger.

Walton, R.G. (1975) *Women in Social Work,* London: RKP.

Webber-Dreardon, E. (1999) 'He Taonga Mo o Matou Tipnuna (A gift handed down by our ancestors): An indigenous approach to social work supervision', *Social Work Review*, December, pp. 7-11.

Wharf, B. (ed.) (1990) *Social Work and Social Change in Canada*, Toronto: McClelland and Stewart.

Wharf, B. (1992) *Communities and Social Policy in Canada*, Toronto: McClelland and Stewart.

Whelan, R. (2001) *Helping the Poor,* London: Civitas.

Wilson, F. and Ramphele, M. (1989) *Uprooting Poverty*. Report of the second Carnegie Inquiry into Poverty and Development in South Africa. New York: Norton.

Wilson, M.G. (1993) 'What Difference Could a Revolution Make? Group Work in the New Nicaragua', in Garland, J.A. (ed.), *Group Work*

Reaching Out: People, Places, and Power, New York: Haworth Press, pp. 301-14.

Wilson, M.G. (2003) 'South-North Development Partnership: Lessons from a Nicaragua-Canada Experience', in Asamoah, Y., Healy, L. and Hokenstad, M.C., *Models of International Collaboration in Social Work Education*, New York: CSWE Press, pp. 111-23.

Wilson, M.G. and Whitmore, E. (2000) *Seeds of Fire: Social Development in an Era of Globalism*, Croton-on-Hudson, NY: Apex Press.

WCLAC (Women's Centre for Legal Aid and Counselling) www.wclac.org/about/about.html, last accessed 14 September 2006.

Yeatman, A. (1990) *Bureaucrats, technocrats, femocrats: Essays in the Contemporary Australian State*, Sydney: Allen and Unwin.

Zadnikar, D. (2004) 'Kronika radostnega uporništva (author of the additional text)', in Holloway, J., *Spreminjamo svet brez boja za oblast: pomen revolucije danes, Študentska založ ba*, Ljubljana: pp. 201-25.

Zakon o azilu Republike Slovenija [Asylum Act of the Republic Slovenia] (ZAzil) Official Gazette No. 61/99, 66/00, 124/00, 67/01, 98/03, 134/03.

Zakon o drž avljanstvu Republike Slovenije [Citizenship of the Republic Slovenia Act] (ZDRS) Official Gazette No. 1/91-I, 30/91-I, 38/92, 61/92, 13/94, 59/99, 96/02.

Zakon o tujcih Republike Slovenije [Aliens Act of the Republic Slovenia] (ZTuj-1) Official Gazette No. 61/99, 96/2002.

Zakon o tujcih Republike Slovenije [Aliens Act of the Republic Slovenia] (ZTuj), Official Gazette No. 1/91, 44/97.

Zakon o začasnem zatočišču [Temporary Protection Act of the Republic Slovenia], Official Gazette No. 20/1997

Zaviršek, D. (2000) *Hendikep kot kulturna travma: Historizacija podob, teles in vsakdanjih praks prizadetih ljudi*, Založ ba: Ljubljana.

Zavratnik Zimic, S. (2003) 'Fortress Europe or Open Europe? Challenges Facing the Countries on the "Schengen Periphery"', in Pajnik, M. and Zavratnik Zimic, S. (eds.), *Migration – Globalization – European Union*, Ljubljana: Peace Institute, pp. 181-211.

Zorn, J. (2003) 'Etnografija vsakdanjega življenja ljudi brez slovenskega drž avljanstva' [Ethnography of People without the Slovene Citizenship], PhD dissertation, University of Ljubljana, Faculty of

Social Sciences, Ljubljana.

Zorn, J. (2005) 'Ethnic Citizenship in the Slovenian State', *Citizenship Studies*, 9(2), Routledge: pp.135-52.

Zorn, Jelka (2006a): Farhat Khan, najslavnejša angleška azilantka, intervju [an interview with Farhat Khan]. Mladina, 13/2/2006, no. 7, p.: 35-39.